THE CASE OF
ALAN TURING

THE CASE OF ALAN TURING

THE EXTRAORDINARY AND TRAGIC STORY OF THE LEGENDARY CODEBREAKER

DRAWINGS BY ÉRIC **LIBERGE**
TEXT BY ARNAUD **DELALANDE**

TRANSLATED BY DAVID **HOMEL**

ARSENAL PULP PRESS
VANCOUVER

THE CASE OF ALAN TURING

First published in French as *Le Cas Alan Turing*, © Éditions des Arènes, Paris, 2015.

ARSENAL PULP PRESS
#202-211 East Georgia Street
Vancouver, BC V6A 1Z6
Canada
arsenalpulp.com

This book has been supported by the French Ministry of Foreign Affairs as part of the translation grant program.
Cet ouvrage est soutenu au titre des programmes d'aide à la publication du Ministère des Affaires étrangères.

Liberté • Égalité • Fraternité
RÉPUBLIQUE FRANÇAISE

The publisher gratefully acknowledges the support of the Government of Canada (through the Canada Book Fund) and the Government of British Columbia (through the Book Publishing Tax Credit) for its publishing activities.

Canada

Editing of translation by Brian Lam
Design and production by Oliver McPartlin
Printed and bound in Canada

CANADIAN CATALOGUING IN PUBLICATION DATA:
Liberge, Eric, 1965-
[Cas de Alan Turing. English]
The case of Alan Turing : the extraordinary and tragic story of the legendary codebreaker / Eric Liberge ; Arnaud Delalande, illustrator.

Translation of: Le cas de Alan Turing.
Issued in print and electronic formats.
ISBN 978-1-55152-650-8 (hardback).--ISBN 978-1-55152-651-5 (html).--
ISBN 978-1-55152-652-2 (epub)

1. Turing, Alan Mathison, 1912-1954--Comic books, strips, etc.
2. Mathematicians--Great Britain--Biography--Comics books, strips, etc.
3. Cryptographers--Great Britain--Biography--Comic books, strips, etc.
4. Gay men--Great Britain--Biography--Comic books, strips, etc.
5. Graphic novels. I. Delalande, Arnaud, illustrator II. Title. III. Title:
Cas de Alan Turing. English.

QA29.T8L5313 2016 510.92 C2016-903229-9
C2016-903230-2

The authors would like to thank Laurent Muller, Laurent Beccaria, and Jean-Baptiste Bourrat for their trust in us during the creation of this book.

Thanks also to Arnaud Delalande and the Éditions des Arènes team for having brought me into this project.

—Éric Liberge

Alan Turing's work is present in many of the things we do in our everyday lives. We hope this book will increase awareness of him and his wonderful contributions to our world.

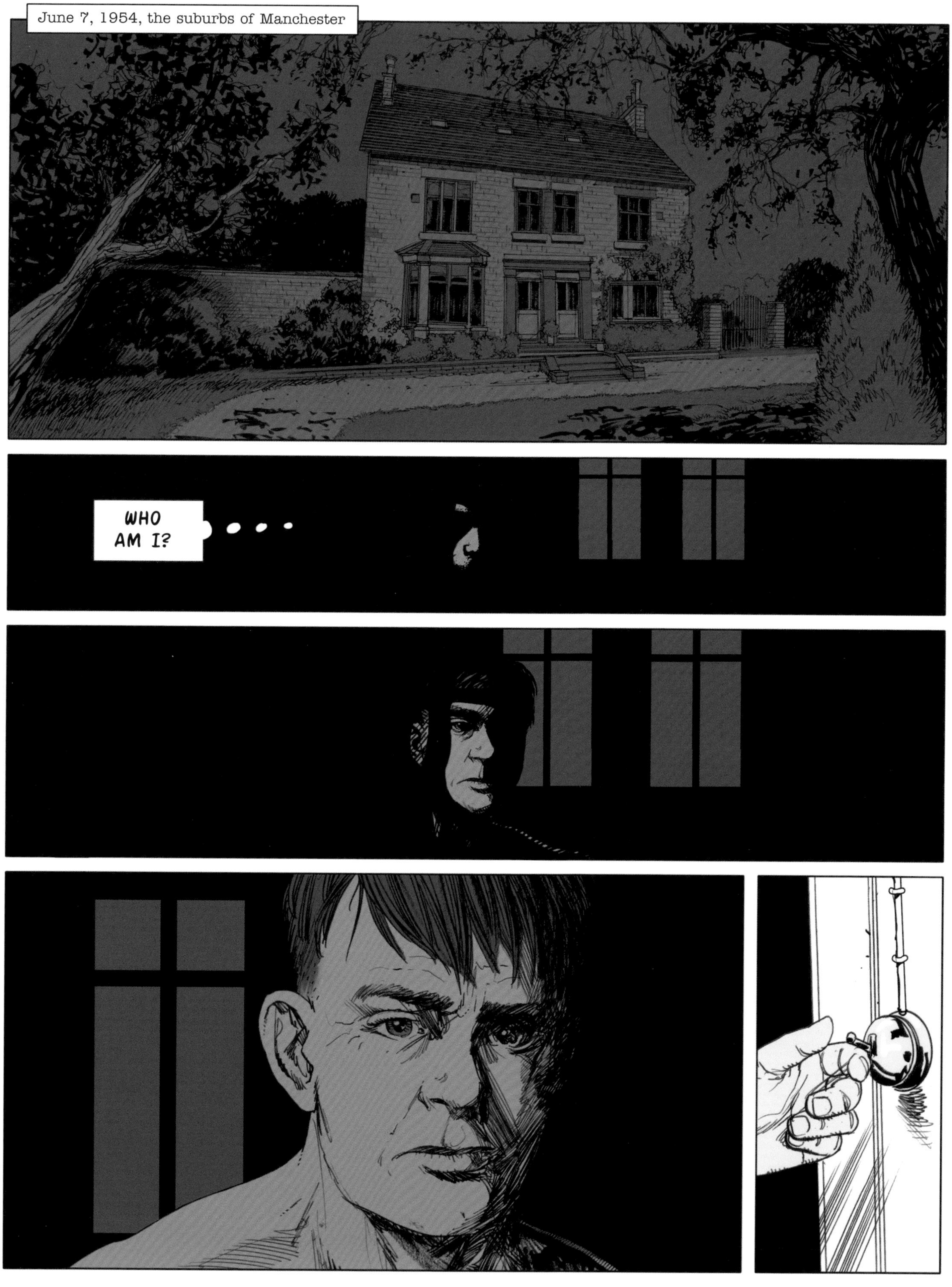
June 7, 1954, the suburbs of Manchester
WHO AM I?

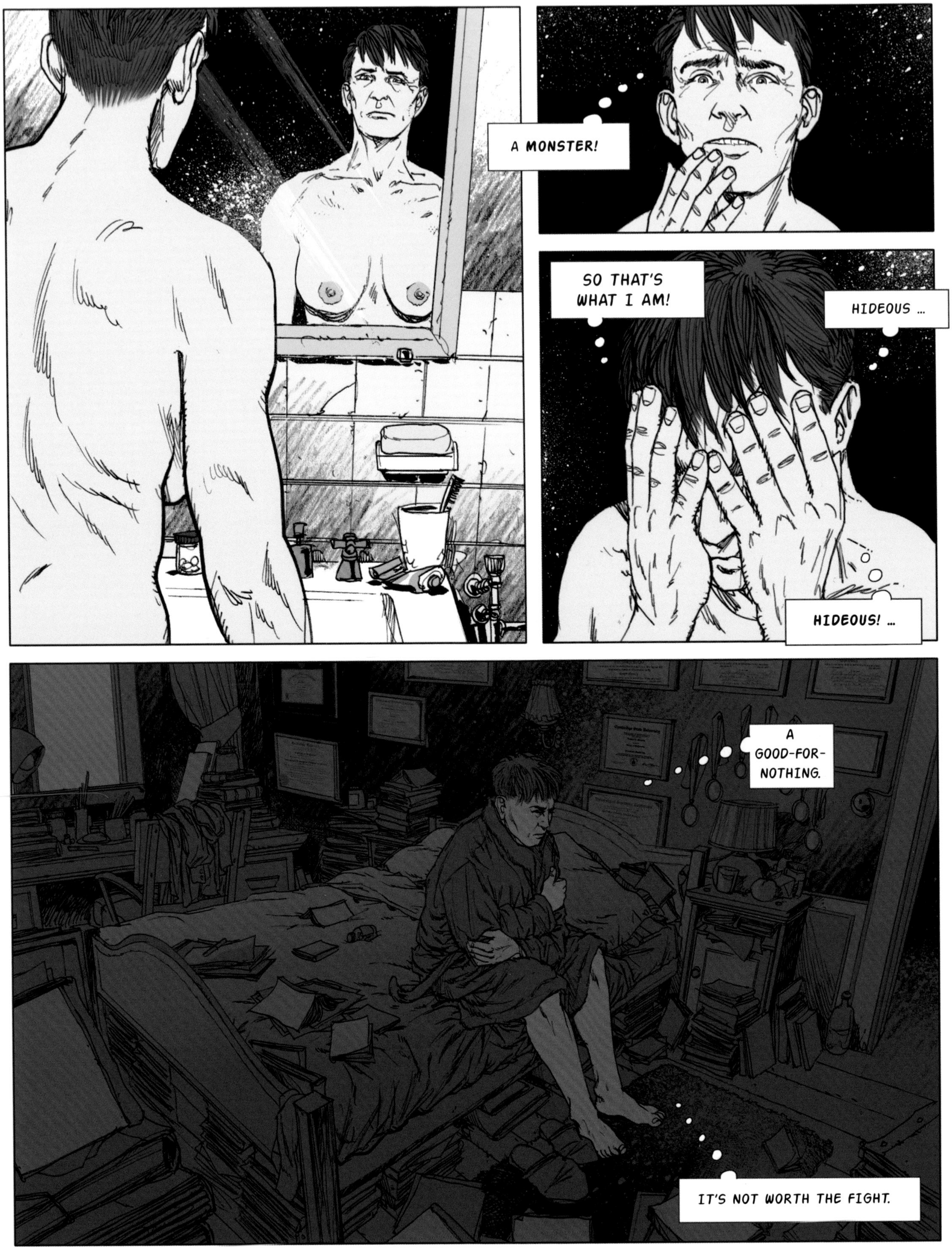
A MONSTER!
SO THAT'S WHAT I AM!
HIDEOUS ...
HIDEOUS! ...
A GOOD-FOR-NOTHING.
IT'S NOT WORTH THE FIGHT.

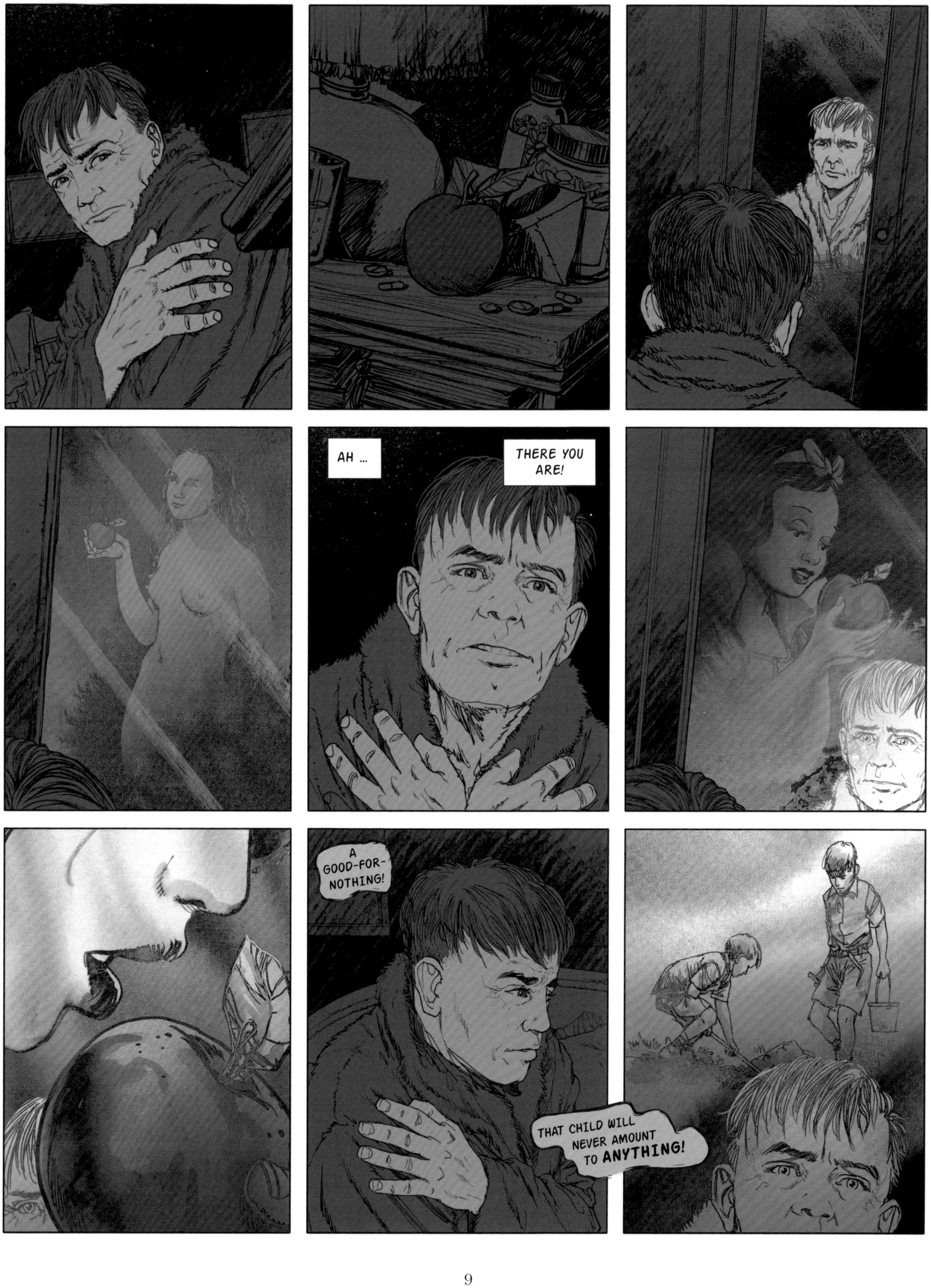
AH ...
THERE YOU ARE!
A GOOD-FOR-NOTHING!
THAT CHILD WILL NEVER AMOUNT TO ANYTHING!

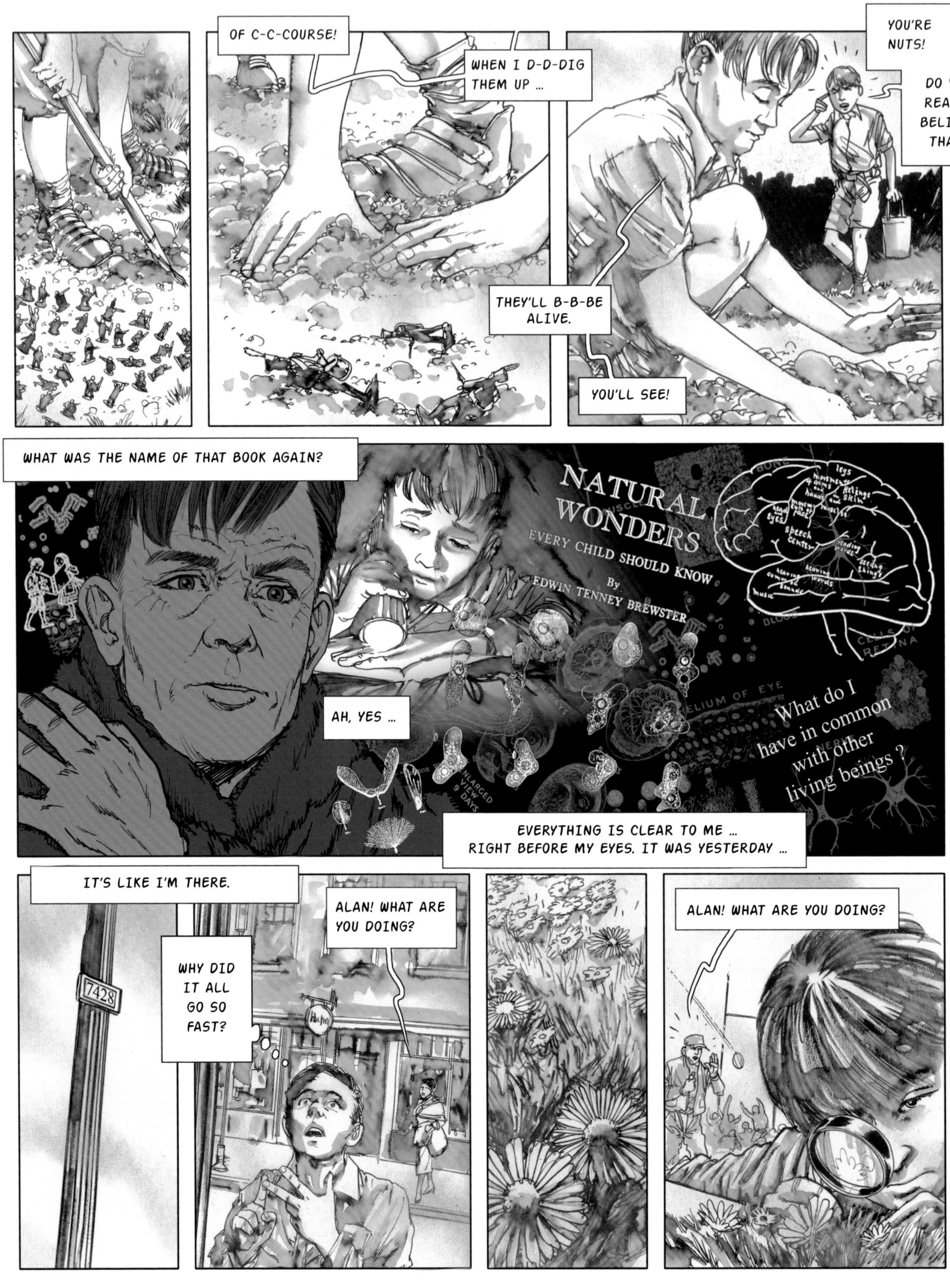
OF C-C-COURSE!
WHEN I D-D-DIG THEM UP ...
THEY'LL B-B-BE ALIVE.
YOU'LL SEE!
YOU'RE NUTS!
DO YOU REALLY BELIEVE THAT?
WHAT WAS THE NAME OF THAT BOOK AGAIN?
NATURAL WONDERS
EVERY CHILD SHOULD KNOW
By
EDWIN TENNEY BREWSTER
AH, YES ...
What do I have in common with other living beings ?
EVERYTHING IS CLEAR TO ME ...
RIGHT BEFORE MY EYES. IT WAS YESTERDAY ...
IT'S LIKE I'M THERE.
7428
WHY DID IT ALL GO SO FAST?
ALAN! WHAT ARE YOU DOING?
ALAN! WHAT ARE YOU DOING?

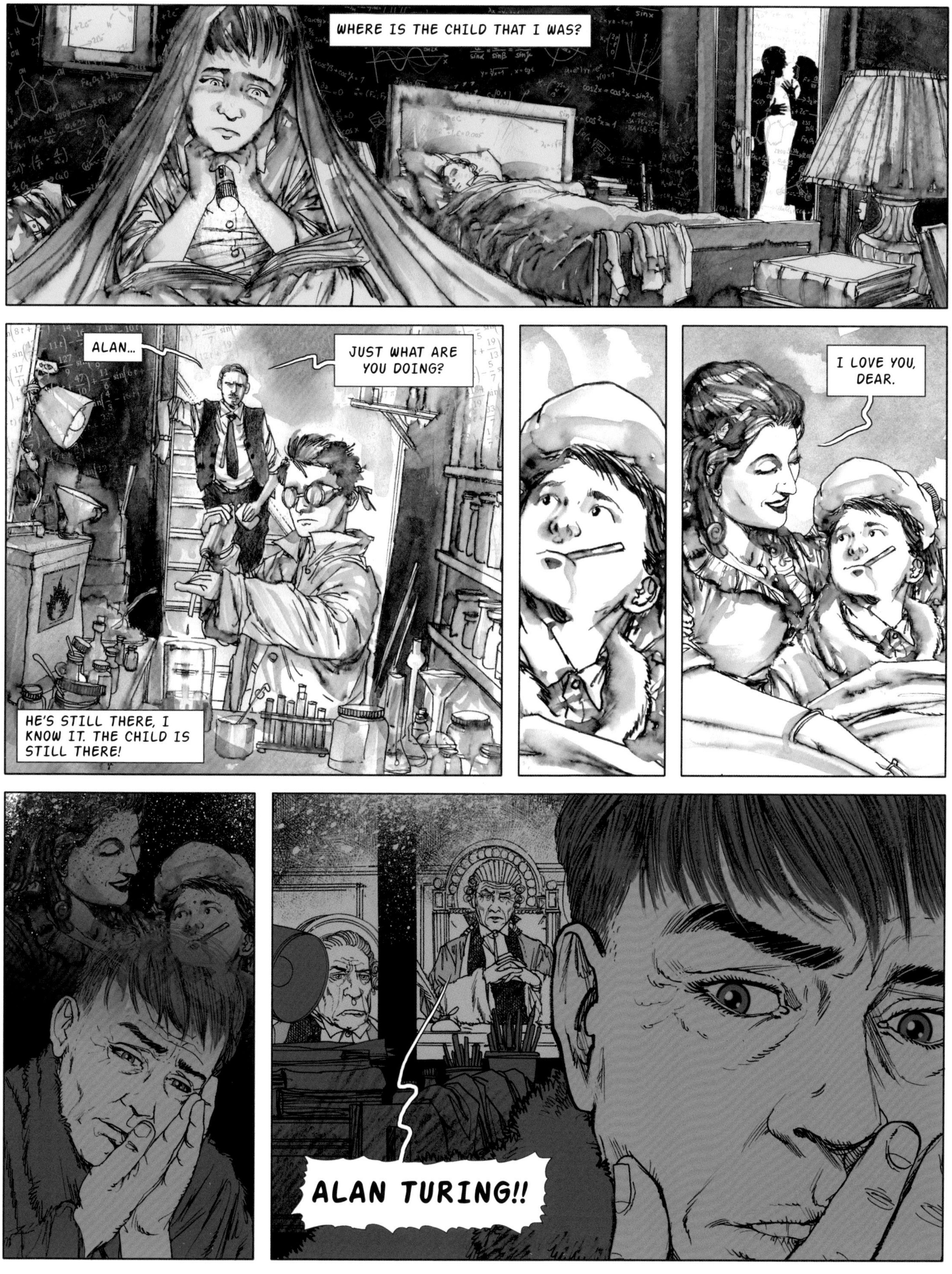
WHERE IS THE CHILD THAT I WAS?
ALAN...
JUST WHAT ARE YOU DOING?
HE'S STILL THERE, I KNOW IT. THE CHILD IS STILL THERE!
I LOVE YOU, DEAR.
ALAN TURING!!

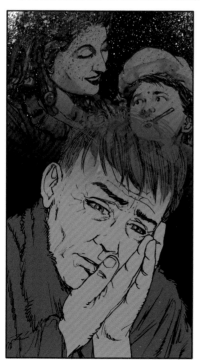

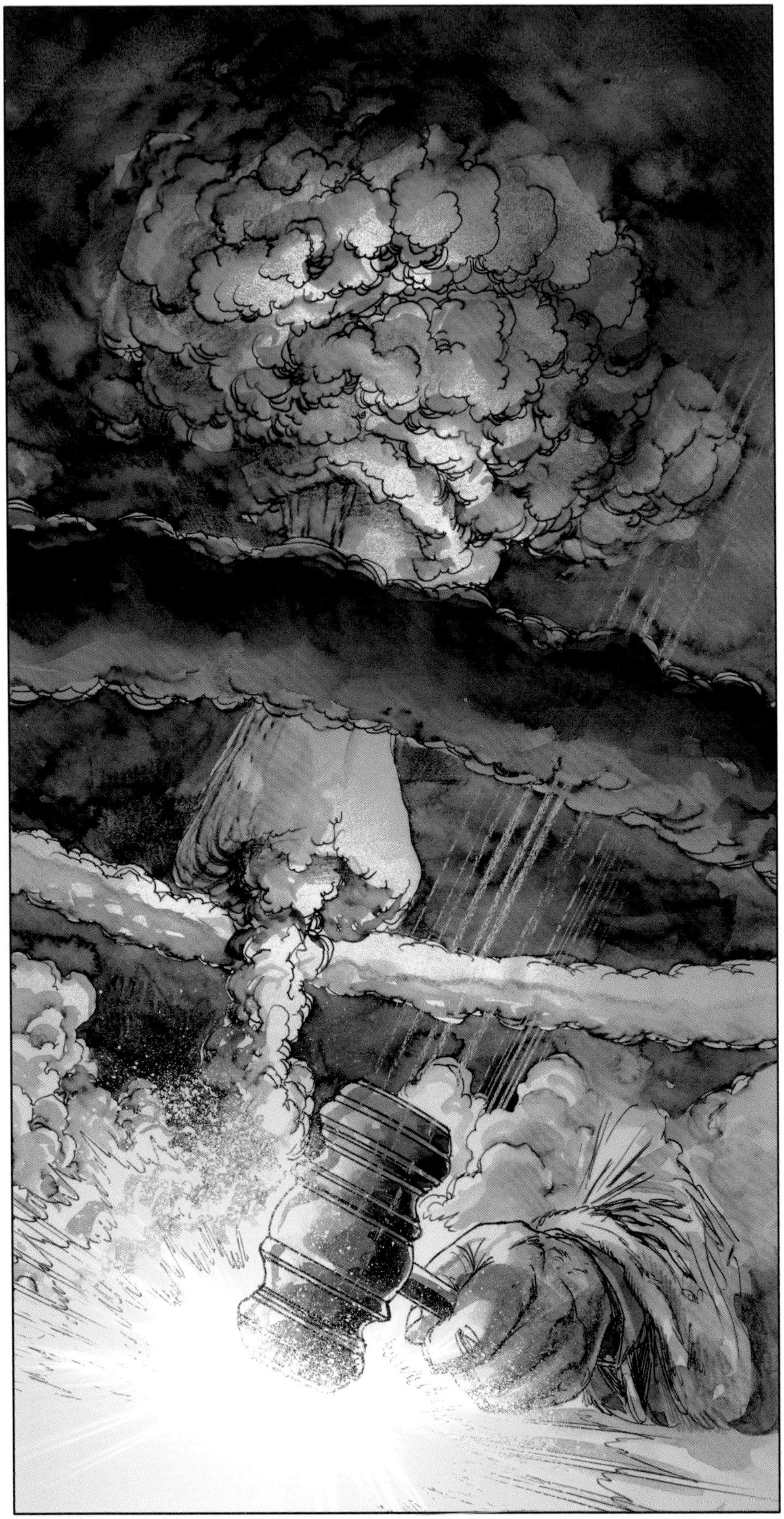

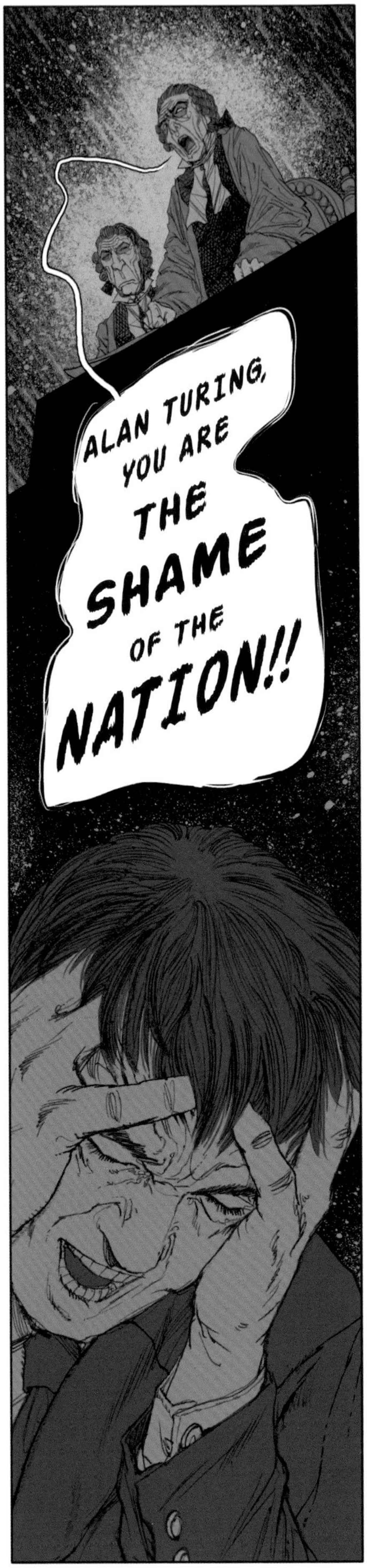
ALAN TURING, YOU ARE THE SHAME OF THE NATION!!

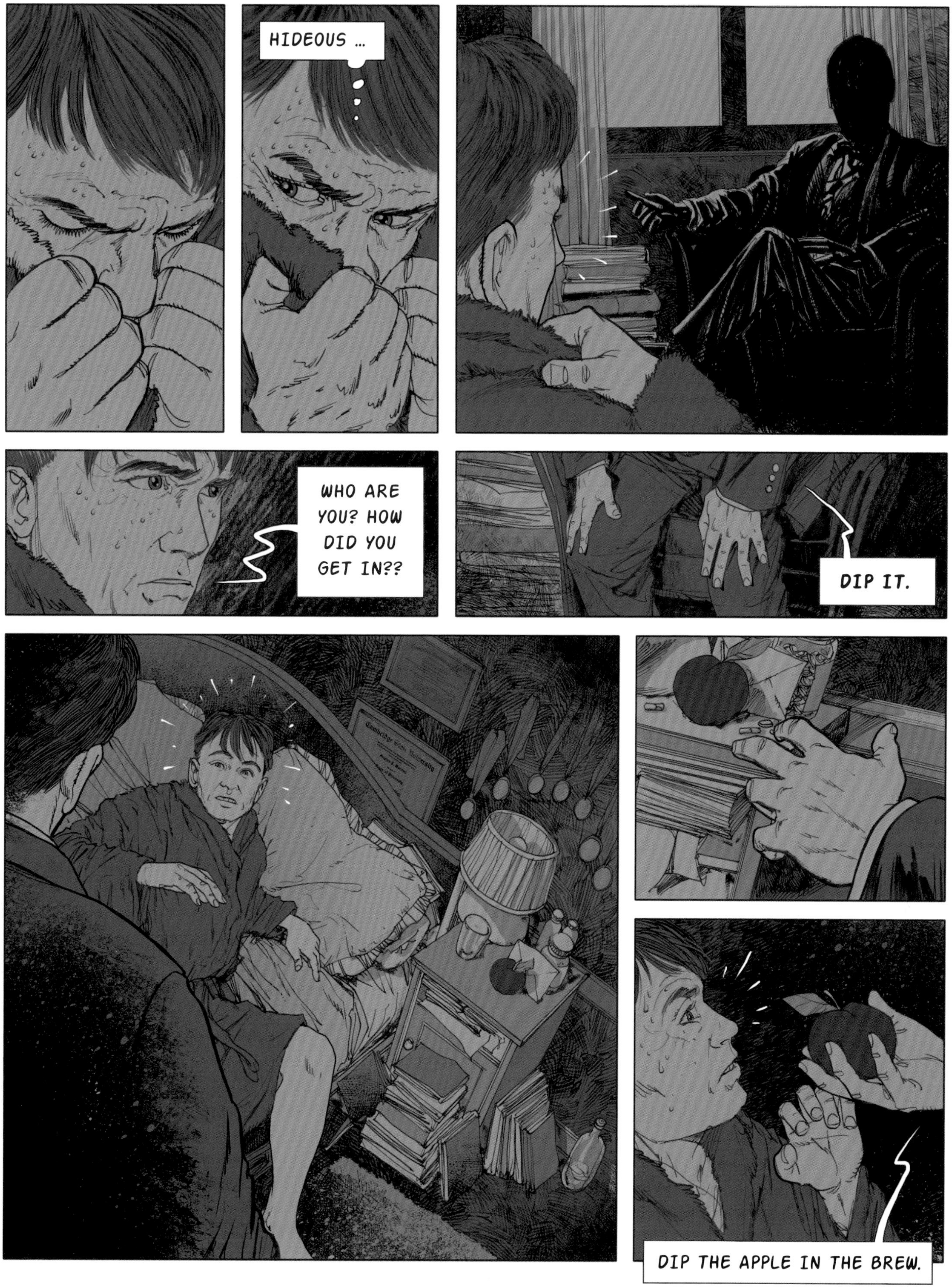
HIDEOUS ...
WHO ARE YOU? HOW DID YOU GET IN??
DIP IT.
DIP THE APPLE IN THE BREW.

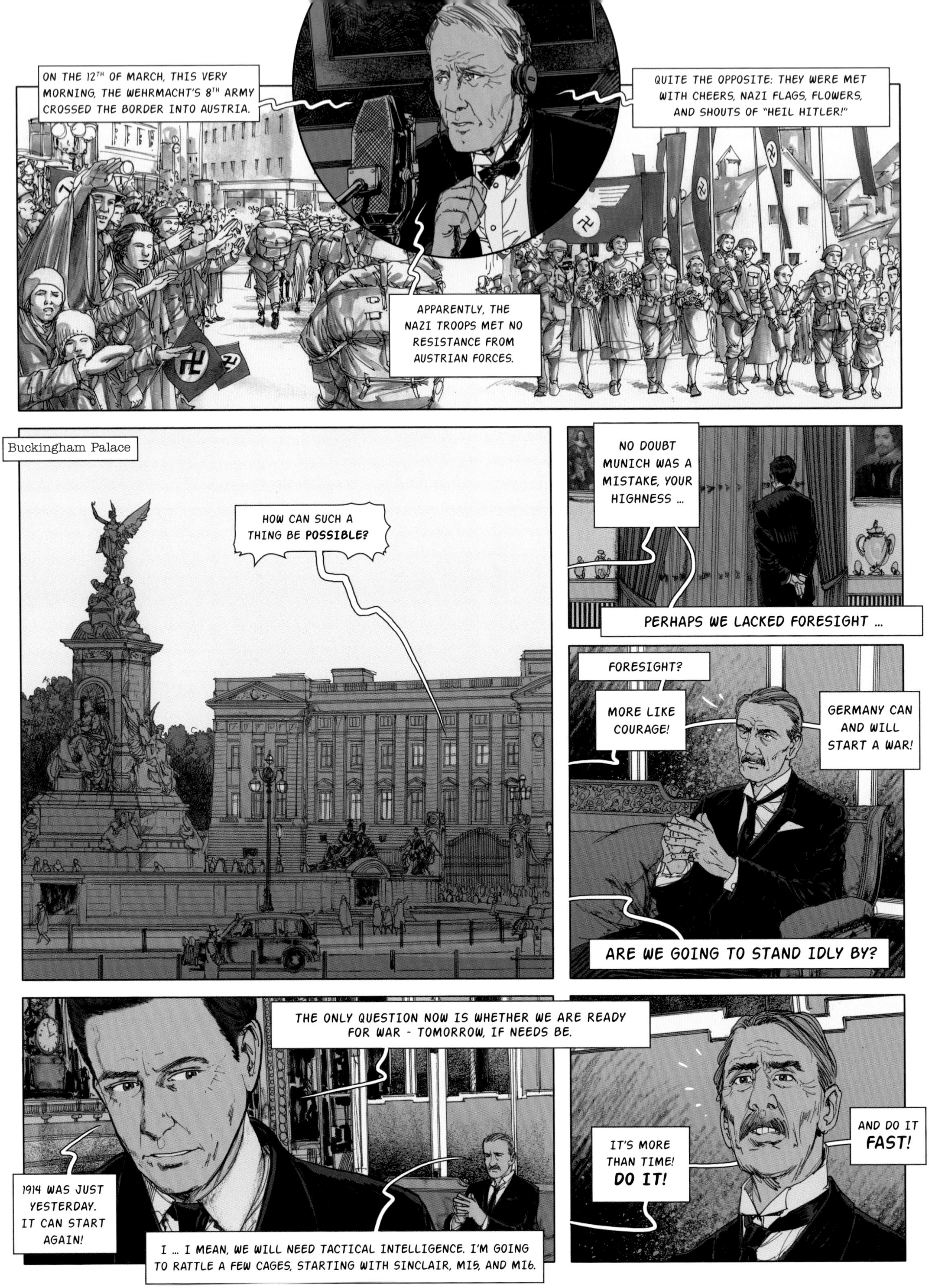

ON THE 12TH OF MARCH, THIS VERY MORNING, THE WEHRMACHT'S 8TH ARMY CROSSED THE BORDER INTO AUSTRIA.
QUITE THE OPPOSITE: THEY WERE MET WITH CHEERS, NAZI FLAGS, FLOWERS, AND SHOUTS OF "HEIL HITLER!"
APPARENTLY, THE NAZI TROOPS MET NO RESISTANCE FROM AUSTRIAN FORCES.
Buckingham Palace
HOW CAN SUCH A THING BE POSSIBLE?
NO DOUBT MUNICH WAS A MISTAKE, YOUR HIGHNESS ...
PERHAPS WE LACKED FORESIGHT ...
FORESIGHT?
MORE LIKE COURAGE!
GERMANY CAN AND WILL START A WAR!
ARE WE GOING TO STAND IDLY BY?
THE ONLY QUESTION NOW IS WHETHER WE ARE READY FOR WAR - TOMORROW, IF NEEDS BE.
1914 WAS JUST YESTERDAY. IT CAN START AGAIN!
I ... I MEAN, WE WILL NEED TACTICAL INTELLIGENCE. I'M GOING TO RATTLE A FEW CAGES, STARTING WITH SINCLAIR, MI5, AND MI6.
IT'S MORE THAN TIME! DO IT!
AND DO IT FAST!

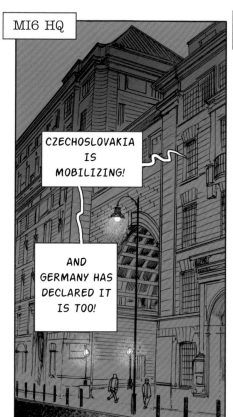

CZECHOSLOVAKIA IS MOBILIZING!

AND GERMANY HAS DECLARED IT IS TOO!

HIS MAJESTY IS CONCERNED. WE MUST PREPARE!

WE HAVE … (COUGH, COUGH) … PUT OUR BEST AGENTS ON INTELLIGENCE ASSIGNMENTS… (COUGH) … IN EASTERN EUROPE …
(COUGH, COUGH!!)

COUGH!! COUGH!!

HITLER IS ADVANCING. HE'S ON A FATAL COLLISION COURSE!

WE MUST ACT!

Admiral Hugh SINCLAIR, Chief of British Intelligence

HAVE ALL THE REPORTS SENT UP TO US!

WHAT DO THE INTELLIGENCE SERVICE AND THE GC&CS SAY?

HQ, Government Code and Cypher School (GC&CS)

DAMN IT… IT'S INCOMPREHENSIBLE!!

NAZI COMMUNICATIONS ARE GOING EVERY WHICH WAY! THEY'RE PREPARING SOMETHING BIG, THERE'S NO DOUBT. BUT, GOOD GOD … IT'S LIKE WE'RE DEAF AND BLIND!!

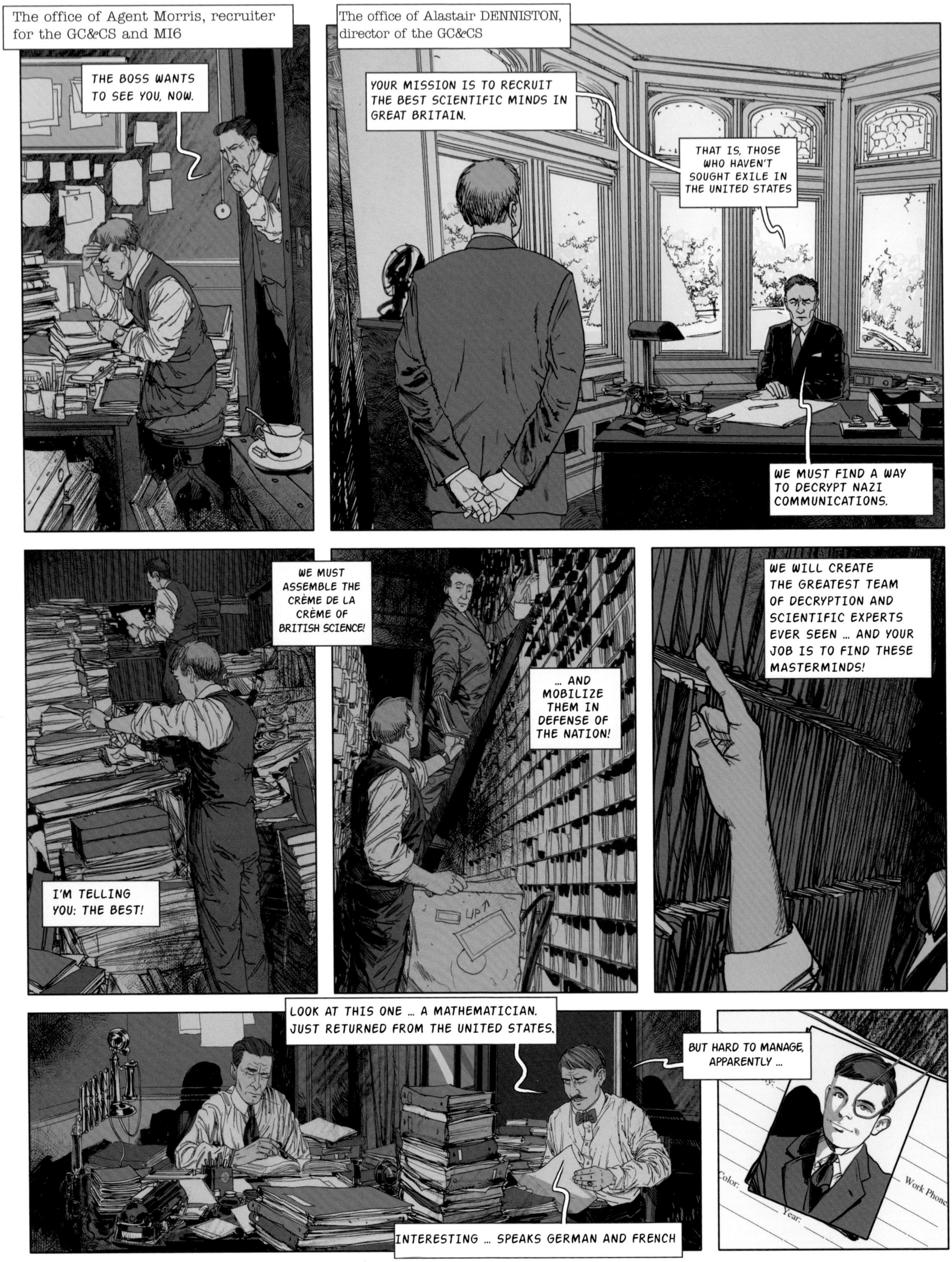
The office of Agent Morris, recruiter for the GC&CS and MI6
THE BOSS WANTS TO SEE YOU, NOW.
The office of Alastair DENNISTON, director of the GC&CS
YOUR MISSION IS TO RECRUIT THE BEST SCIENTIFIC MINDS IN GREAT BRITAIN.
THAT IS, THOSE WHO HAVEN'T SOUGHT EXILE IN THE UNITED STATES
WE MUST FIND A WAY TO DECRYPT NAZI COMMUNICATIONS.
WE MUST ASSEMBLE THE CRÈME DE LA CRÈME OF BRITISH SCIENCE!
I'M TELLING YOU: THE BEST!
... AND MOBILIZE THEM IN DEFENSE OF THE NATION!
WE WILL CREATE THE GREATEST TEAM OF DECRYPTION AND SCIENTIFIC EXPERTS EVER SEEN ... AND YOUR JOB IS TO FIND THESE MASTERMINDS!
LOOK AT THIS ONE ... A MATHEMATICIAN. JUST RETURNED FROM THE UNITED STATES.
INTERESTING ... SPEAKS GERMAN AND FRENCH
BUT HARD TO MANAGE, APPARENTLY ...
Color:
Year:
Work Phone

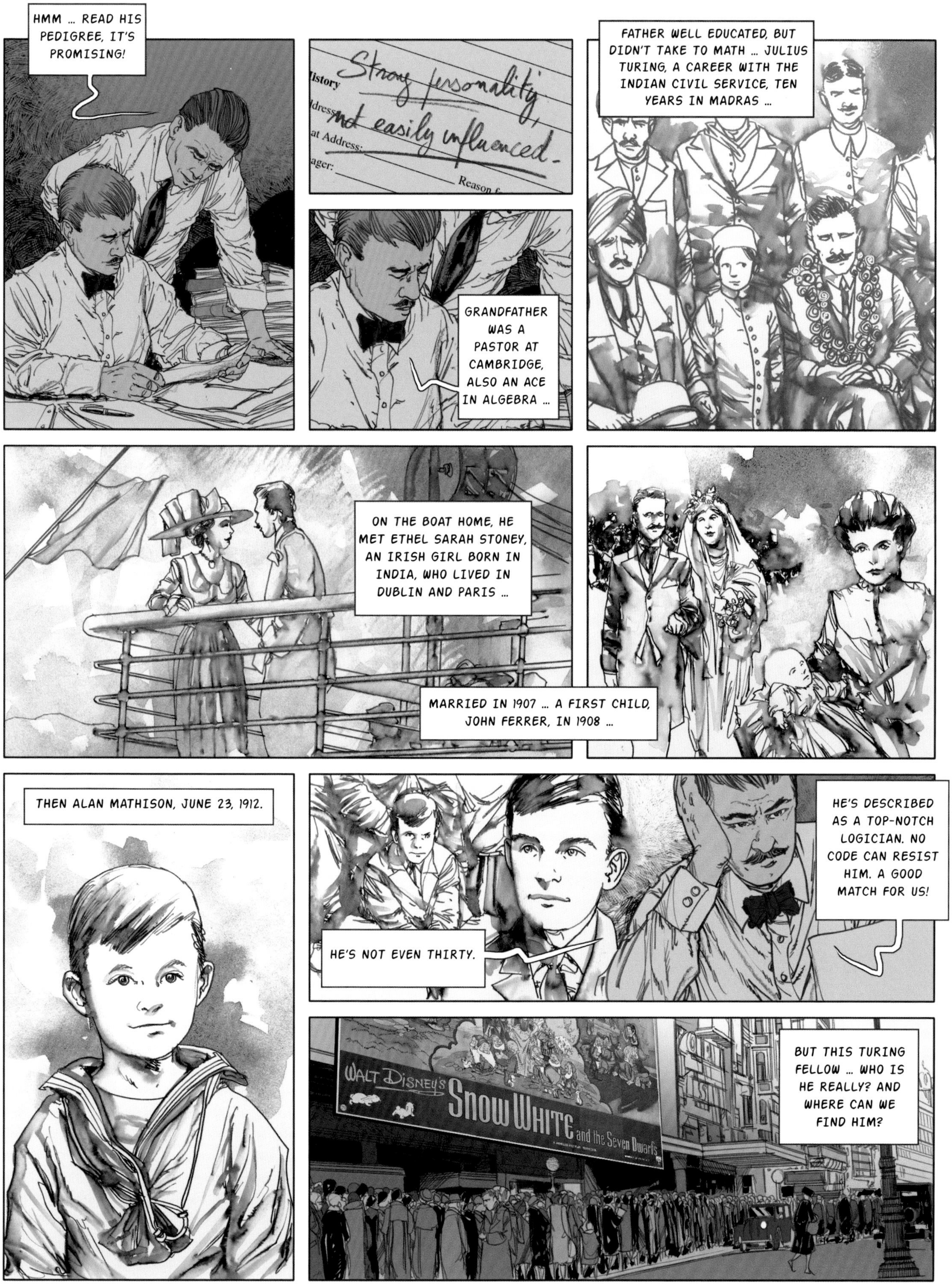
HMM ... READ HIS PEDIGREE, IT'S PROMISING!
History
Strong personality, not easily influenced.
GRANDFATHER WAS A PASTOR AT CAMBRIDGE, ALSO AN ACE IN ALGEBRA ...
FATHER WELL EDUCATED, BUT DIDN'T TAKE TO MATH ... JULIUS TURING, A CAREER WITH THE INDIAN CIVIL SERVICE, TEN YEARS IN MADRAS ...
ON THE BOAT HOME, HE MET ETHEL SARAH STONEY, AN IRISH GIRL BORN IN INDIA, WHO LIVED IN DUBLIN AND PARIS ...
MARRIED IN 1907 ... A FIRST CHILD, JOHN FERRER, IN 1908 ...
THEN ALAN MATHISON, JUNE 23, 1912.
HE'S NOT EVEN THIRTY.
HE'S DESCRIBED AS A TOP-NOTCH LOGICIAN. NO CODE CAN RESIST HIM. A GOOD MATCH FOR US!
WALT DISNEY'S SNOW WHITE and the Seven Dwarfs
BUT THIS TURING FELLOW ... WHO IS HE REALLY? AND WHERE CAN WE FIND HIM?

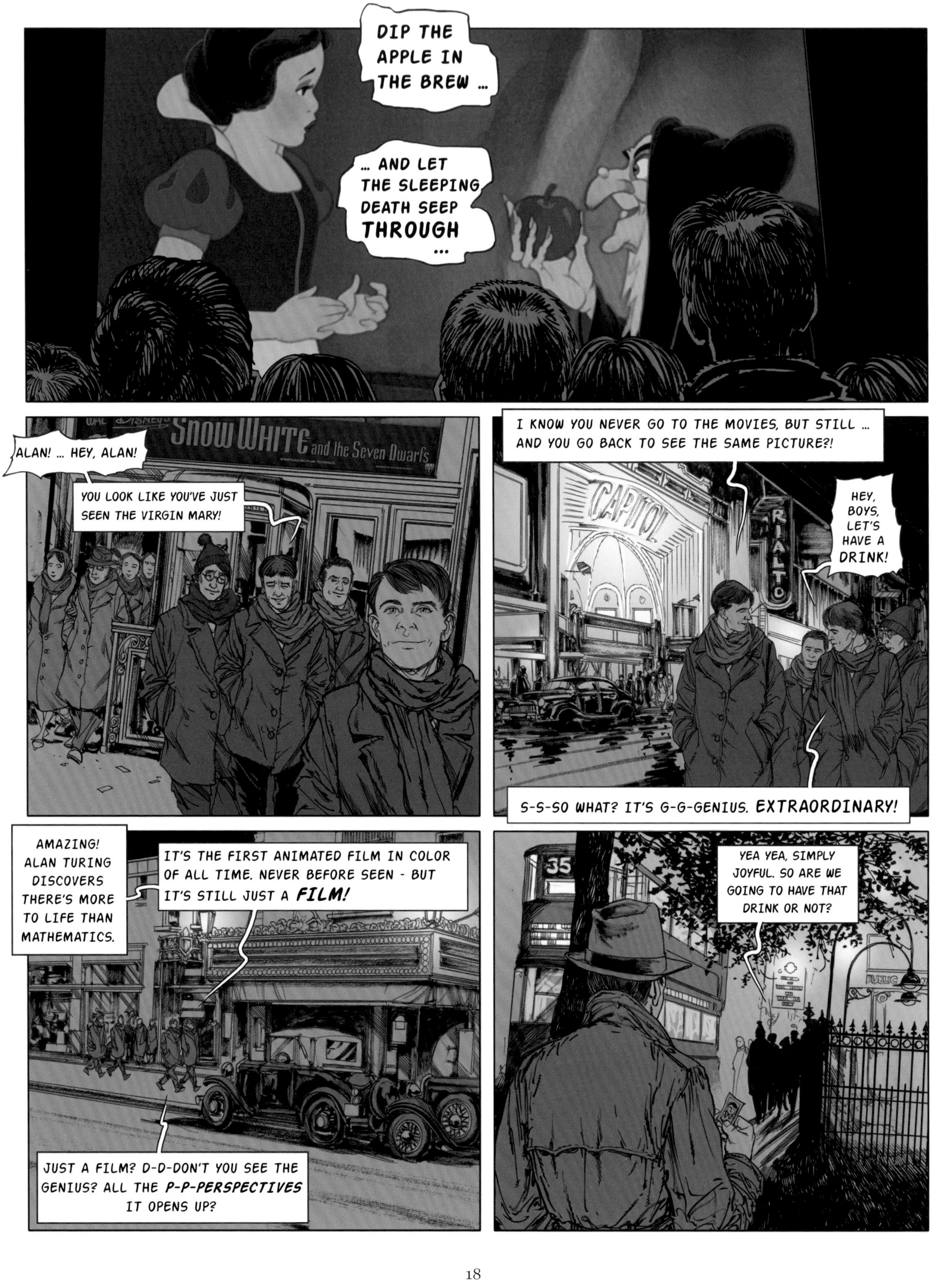
DIP THE APPLE IN THE BREW ...
... AND LET THE SLEEPING DEATH SEEP THROUGH ...
Snow White and the Seven Dwarfs
ALAN! ... HEY, ALAN!
YOU LOOK LIKE YOU'VE JUST SEEN THE VIRGIN MARY!
I KNOW YOU NEVER GO TO THE MOVIES, BUT STILL ... AND YOU GO BACK TO SEE THE SAME PICTURE?!
CAPITOL
RIALTO
HEY, BOYS, LET'S HAVE A DRINK!
S-S-SO WHAT? IT'S G-G-GENIUS. EXTRAORDINARY!
AMAZING! ALAN TURING DISCOVERS THERE'S MORE TO LIFE THAN MATHEMATICS.
IT'S THE FIRST ANIMATED FILM IN COLOR OF ALL TIME. NEVER BEFORE SEEN - BUT IT'S STILL JUST A FILM!
JUST A FILM? D-D-DON'T YOU SEE THE GENIUS? ALL THE P-P-PERSPECTIVES IT OPENS UP?
35
YEA YEA, SIMPLY JOYFUL. SO ARE WE GOING TO HAVE THAT DRINK OR NOT?

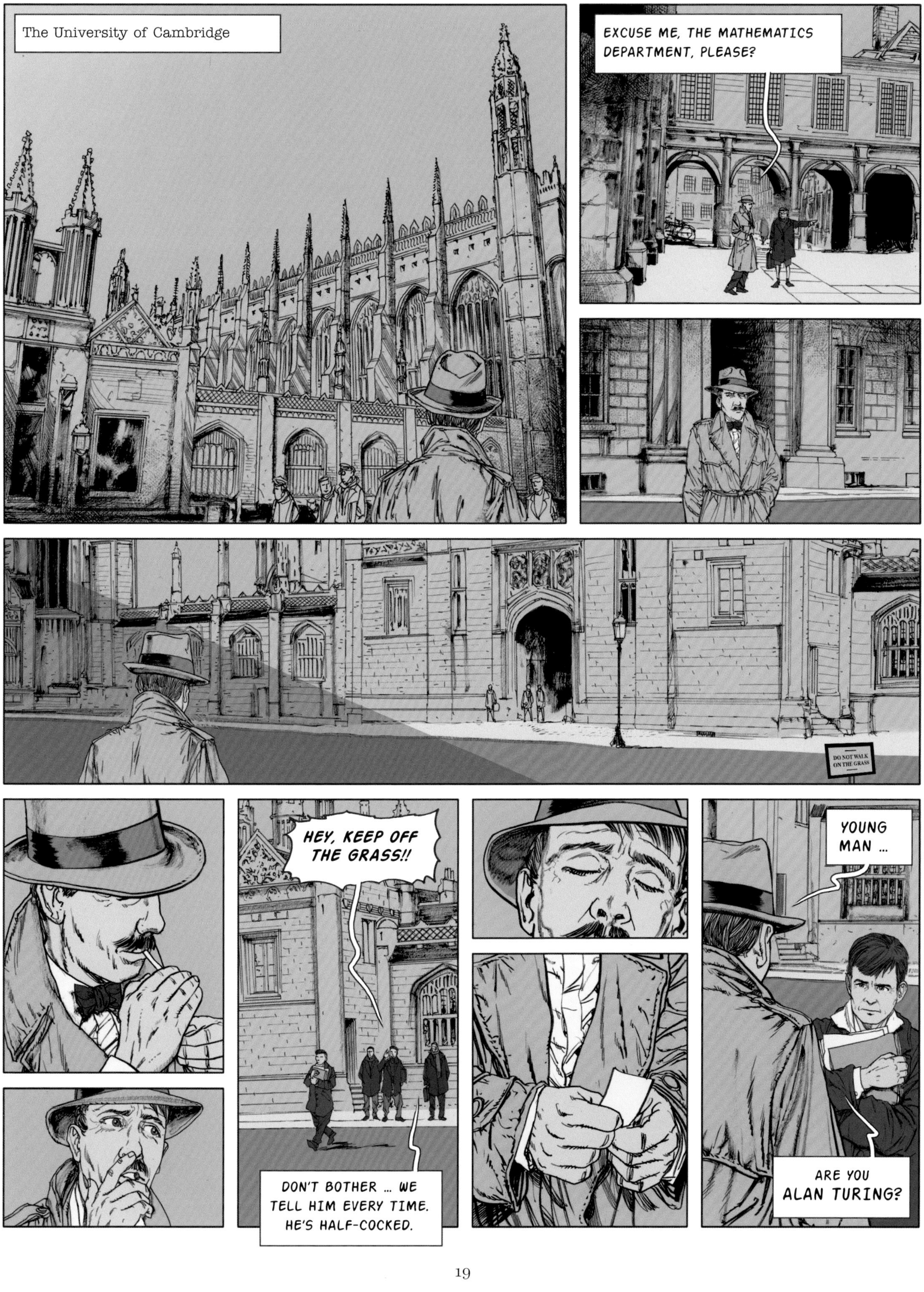

The University of Cambridge
EXCUSE ME, THE MATHEMATICS DEPARTMENT, PLEASE?
DO NOT WALK ON THE GRASS
HEY, KEEP OFF THE GRASS!!
DON'T BOTHER ... WE TELL HIM EVERY TIME. HE'S HALF-COCKED.
YOUNG MAN ...
ARE YOU ALAN TURING?

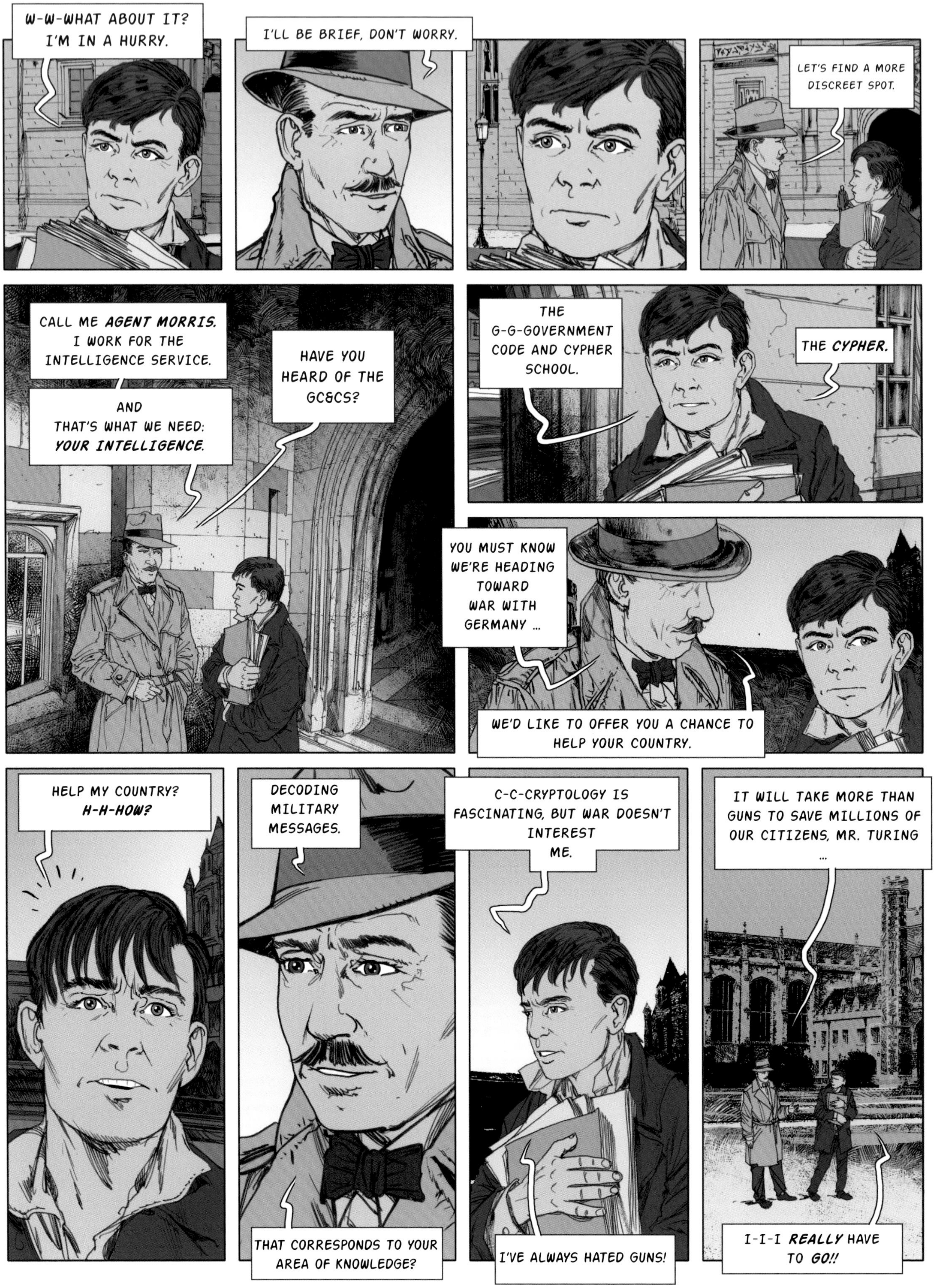
W-W-WHAT ABOUT IT? I'M IN A HURRY.
I'LL BE BRIEF, DON'T WORRY.
LET'S FIND A MORE DISCREET SPOT.
CALL ME AGENT MORRIS. I WORK FOR THE INTELLIGENCE SERVICE.
AND THAT'S WHAT WE NEED: YOUR INTELLIGENCE.
HAVE YOU HEARD OF THE GC&CS?
THE G-G-GOVERNMENT CODE AND CYPHER SCHOOL.
THE CYPHER.
YOU MUST KNOW WE'RE HEADING TOWARD WAR WITH GERMANY ...
WE'D LIKE TO OFFER YOU A CHANCE TO HELP YOUR COUNTRY.
HELP MY COUNTRY? H-H-HOW?
DECODING MILITARY MESSAGES.
THAT CORRESPONDS TO YOUR AREA OF KNOWLEDGE?
C-C-CRYPTOLOGY IS FASCINATING, BUT WAR DOESN'T INTEREST ME.
I'VE ALWAYS HATED GUNS!
IT WILL TAKE MORE THAN GUNS TO SAVE MILLIONS OF OUR CITIZENS, MR. TURING ...
I-I-I REALLY HAVE TO GO!!

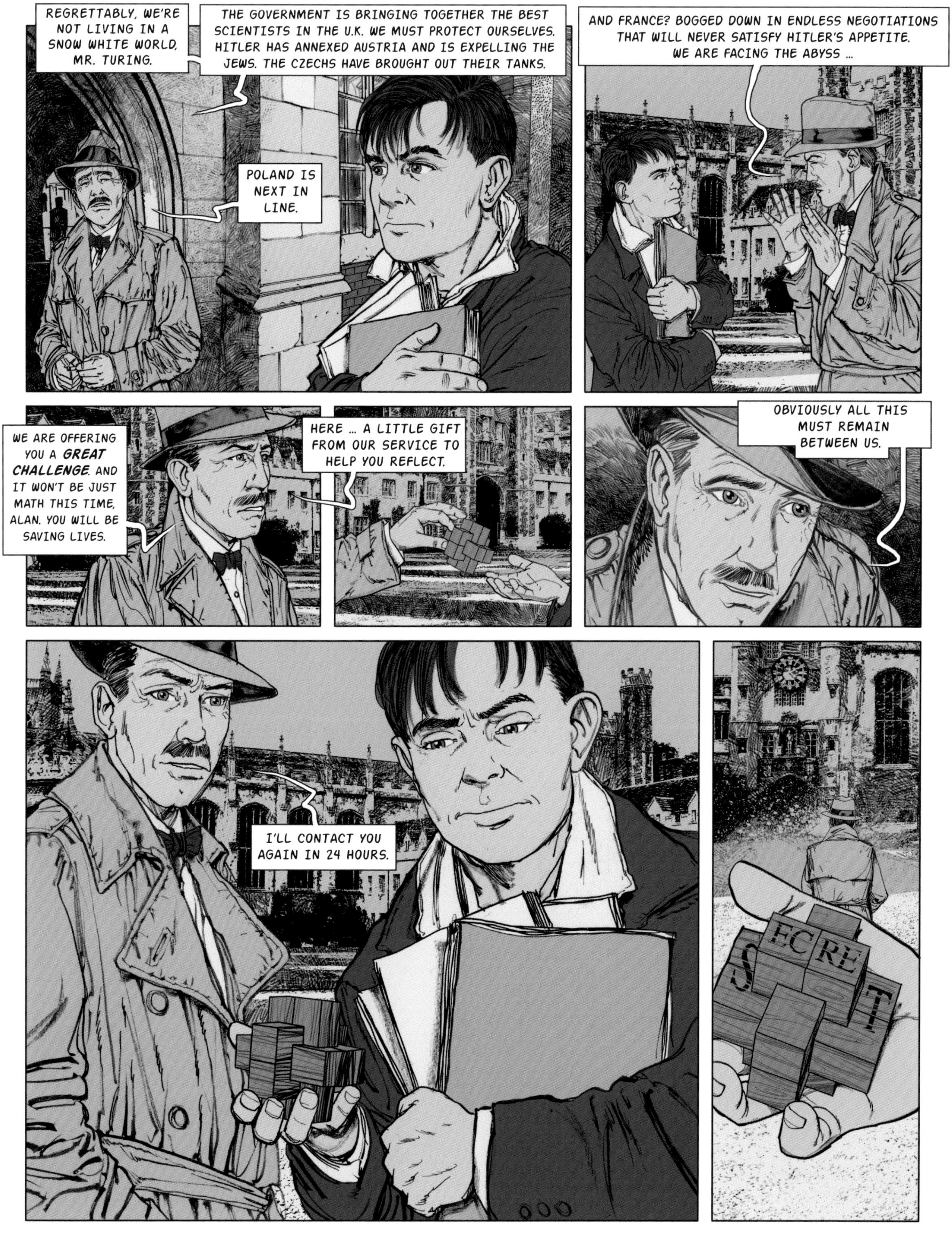
REGRETTABLY, WE'RE NOT LIVING IN A SNOW WHITE WORLD, MR. TURING.
THE GOVERNMENT IS BRINGING TOGETHER THE BEST SCIENTISTS IN THE U.K. WE MUST PROTECT OURSELVES. HITLER HAS ANNEXED AUSTRIA AND IS EXPELLING THE JEWS. THE CZECHS HAVE BROUGHT OUT THEIR TANKS.
POLAND IS NEXT IN LINE.
AND FRANCE? BOGGED DOWN IN ENDLESS NEGOTIATIONS THAT WILL NEVER SATISFY HITLER'S APPETITE. WE ARE FACING THE ABYSS ...
WE ARE OFFERING YOU A GREAT CHALLENGE. AND IT WON'T BE JUST MATH THIS TIME, ALAN. YOU WILL BE SAVING LIVES.
HERE ... A LITTLE GIFT FROM OUR SERVICE TO HELP YOU REFLECT.
OBVIOUSLY ALL THIS MUST REMAIN BETWEEN US.
I'LL CONTACT YOU AGAIN IN 24 HOURS.
SECRET

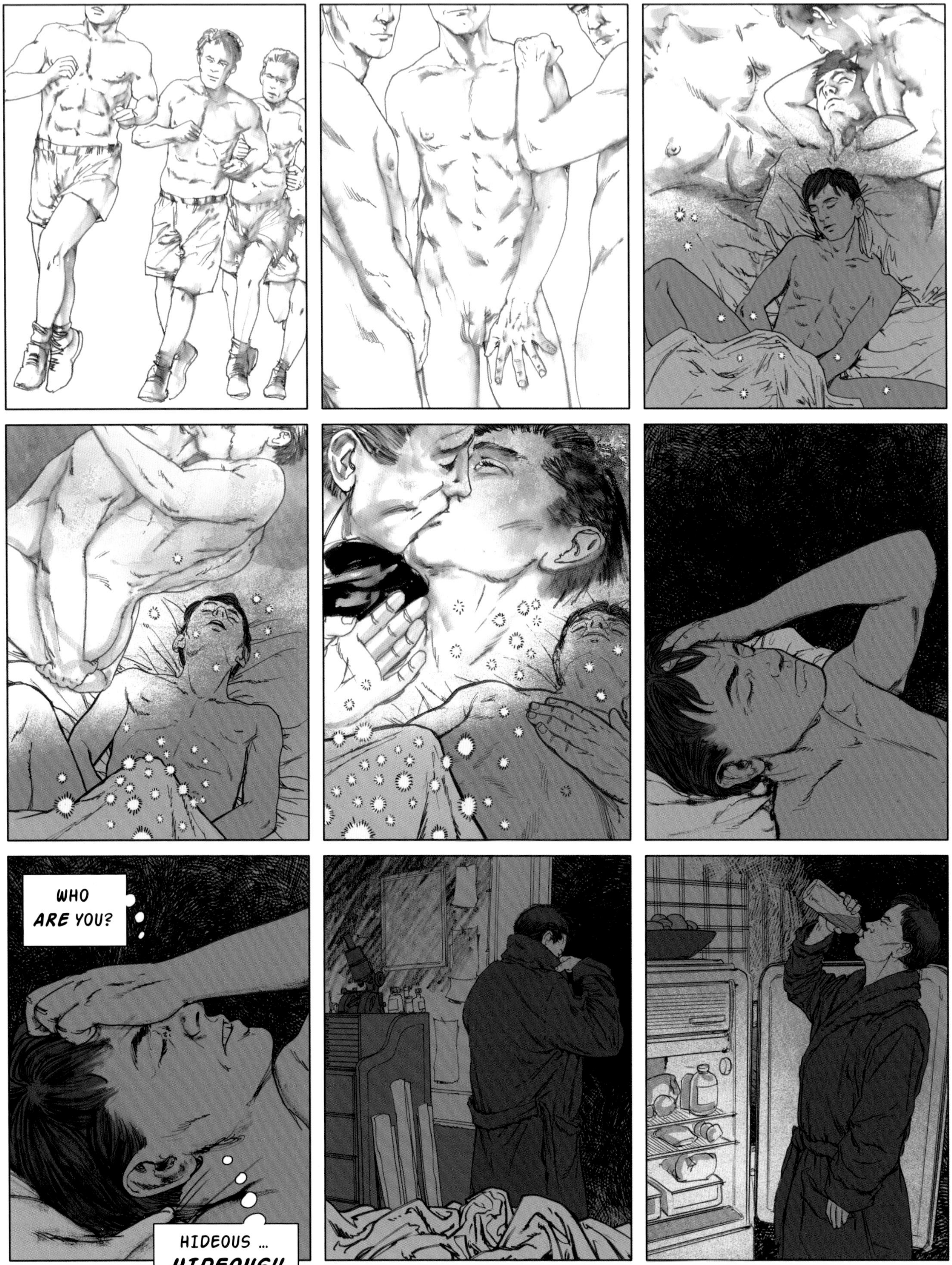
WHO ARE YOU?
HIDEOUS ... HIDEOUS!!

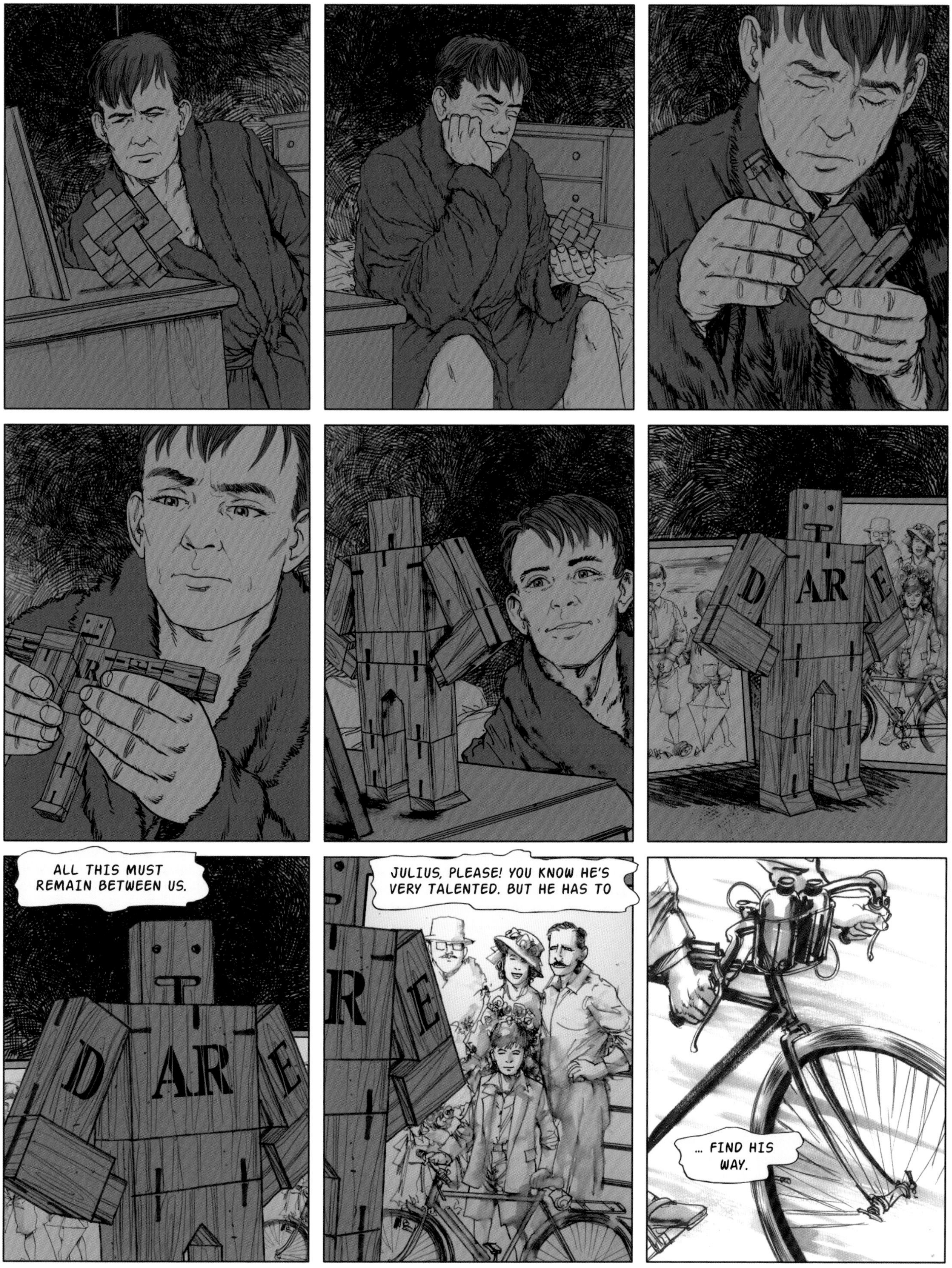
D
AR
E
ALL THIS MUST REMAIN BETWEEN US.
D
AR
E
R
E
JULIUS, PLEASE! YOU KNOW HE'S VERY TALENTED. BUT HE HAS TO
... FIND HIS WAY.

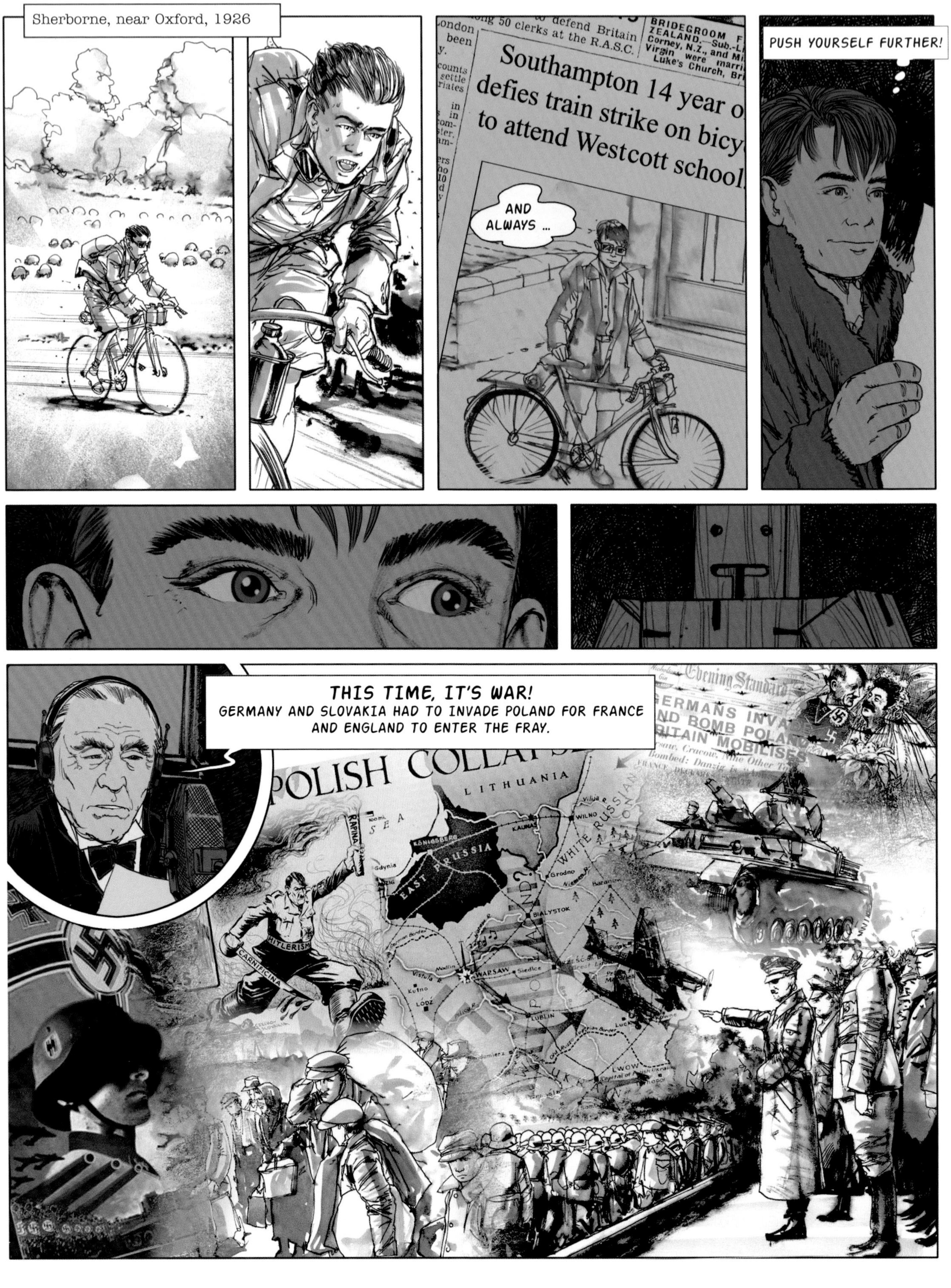
Sherborne, near Oxford, 1926
Southampton 14 year o
defies train strike on bicy
to attend Westcott school
AND ALWAYS ...
PUSH YOURSELF FURTHER!
THIS TIME, IT'S WAR!
GERMANY AND SLOVAKIA HAD TO INVADE POLAND FOR FRANCE AND ENGLAND TO ENTER THE FRAY.
Evening Standard
GERMANS INVA
ND BOMB POLAN
RITAIN MOBILISES
POLISH COLLAPS
LITHUANIA
EAST PRUSSIA
HITLERISM
WARSAW
LUBLIN
LODZ
BIALYSTOK

... YESTERDAY, THE UNITED KINGDOM AND HER EMPIRE AT 11 O'CLOCK, AND FRANCE AND HER EMPIRE AT 2 O'CLOCK, BUT ALSO AUSTRALIA AND NEW ZEALAND AT 9:30 PM OFFICIALLY DECLARED WAR ON GERMANY. FOR NOW, THE BELLIGERENTS SEEM TO BE IN A STAND-OFF REGARDING POLAND ...

Bletchley Park

BLETCHLEY RADIO MANUFACTURING

NO TRESPASSING

WAR

YOU ARE
TO PROCE
THIS

SORRY TO BOTHER YOU, MORRIS ... CAN YOU COME? THERE SEEMS TO BE A PROBLEM.

INDEED, NOT, S-S-SIR! I-I-I DON'T SEE W-W-WHY I WOULD **SIGN!**

THE R-R-RULE STIPULATES THAT N-N-NO-THING MUST BE WRITTEN ON OFFICIAL D-D-DOCUMENTS. IT'S S-S-STATED THERE. SO I WILL NOT SIGN THIS P-P-PASS!

IT'S A L-L-LOGICAL CONTRADICTION, UNDERSTAND?

HELLO, TURING!

AH, MR. MORRIS! YOU C-C-CAN EXPLAIN TO HIM!

THERE'S A G-G-GROSS **CONTRADICTION** IN YOUR R-R-R ...

TURING! YOUR ARGUMENTATIVE SIDE IS A GREAT EXAMPLE OF YOUR RELATION TO AUTHORITY, BUT IT HAS NO PLACE INSIDE THESE WALLS! AND IT'S NOT THE ONLY BLEMISH ON YOUR FILE ...

B-B-BUT I JUST WANTED ...

AT EASE, SERGEANT. I'LL SEE TO IT.

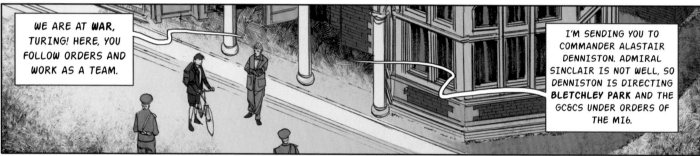

WE ARE AT **WAR**, TURING! HERE, YOU FOLLOW ORDERS AND WORK AS A TEAM.

I'M SENDING YOU TO COMMANDER ALASTAIR DENNISTON. ADMIRAL SINCLAIR IS NOT WELL, SO DENNISTON IS DIRECTING **BLETCHLEY PARK** AND THE GC&CS UNDER ORDERS OF THE MI6.

DENNISTON IS ONE OF THE MOST STRATEGIC FIGURES IN THE UNITED KINGDOM. FOR HEAVEN'S SAKE, DON'T PUT ON A SHOW FOR HIM.

HIS OFFICE IS FACING YOU, IN THE MAIN BUILDING.

DON'T MAKE ME SORRY I CHOSE YOU!

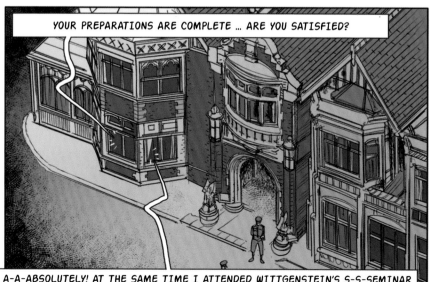

YOUR PREPARATIONS ARE COMPLETE ... ARE YOU SATISFIED?

IT WAS F-F-FASCINATING, YOU SEE ...

EVEN IF I D-D-DON'T ALWAYS AGREE WITH HIM ON SOME P-P-P ...

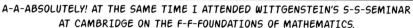

A-A-ABSOLUTELY! AT THE SAME TIME I ATTENDED WITTGENSTEIN'S S-S-SEMINAR AT CAMBRIDGE ON THE F-F-FOUNDATIONS OF MATHEMATICS.

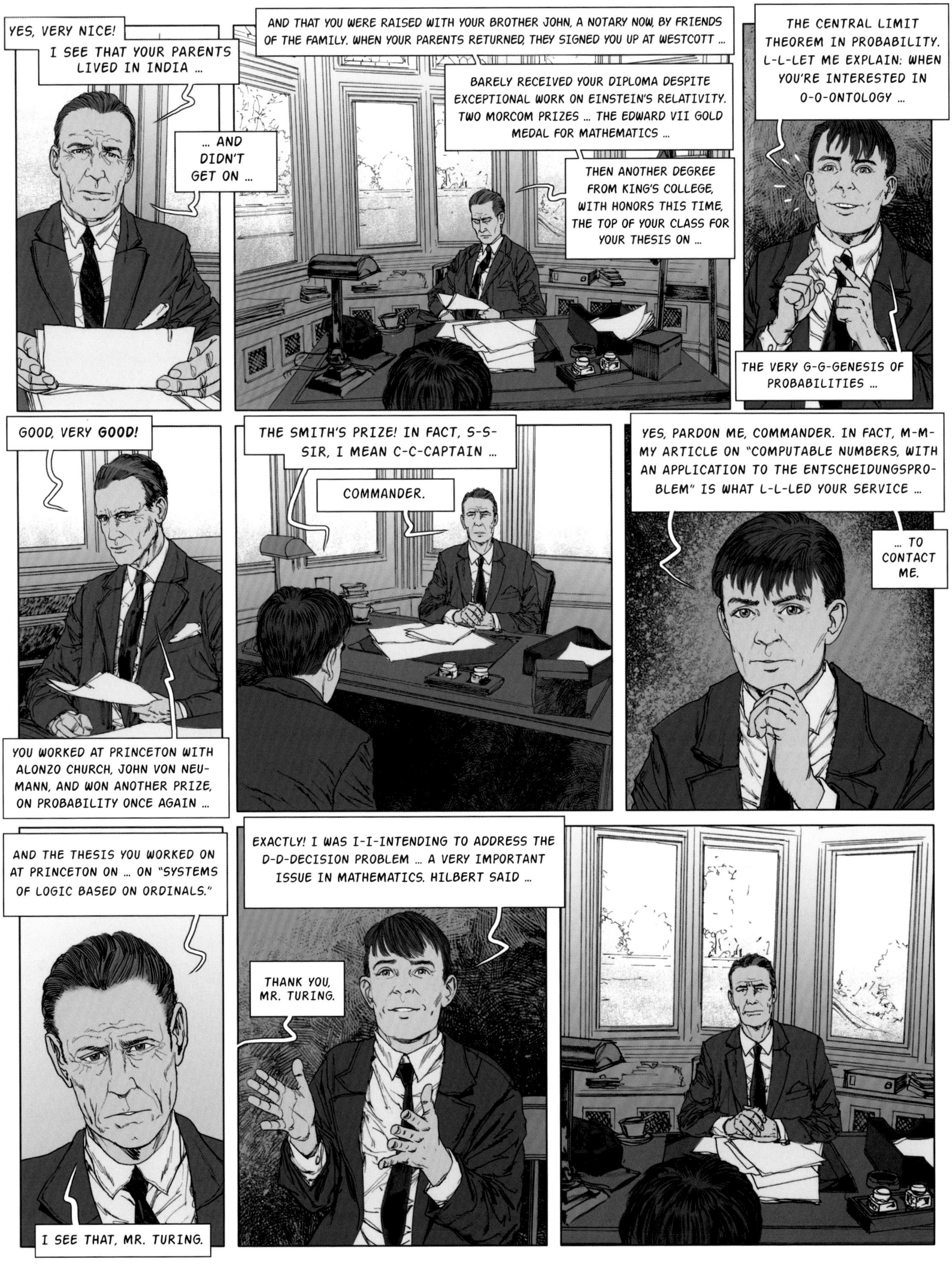
YES, VERY NICE!
I SEE THAT YOUR PARENTS LIVED IN INDIA ...
... AND DIDN'T GET ON ...
AND THAT YOU WERE RAISED WITH YOUR BROTHER JOHN, A NOTARY NOW, BY FRIENDS OF THE FAMILY. WHEN YOUR PARENTS RETURNED, THEY SIGNED YOU UP AT WESTCOTT ...
BARELY RECEIVED YOUR DIPLOMA DESPITE EXCEPTIONAL WORK ON EINSTEIN'S RELATIVITY. TWO MORCOM PRIZES ... THE EDWARD VII GOLD MEDAL FOR MATHEMATICS ...
THEN ANOTHER DEGREE FROM KING'S COLLEGE, WITH HONORS THIS TIME, THE TOP OF YOUR CLASS FOR YOUR THESIS ON ...
THE CENTRAL LIMIT THEOREM IN PROBABILITY. L-L-LET ME EXPLAIN: WHEN YOU'RE INTERESTED IN O-O-ONTOLOGY ...
THE VERY G-G-GENESIS OF PROBABILITIES ...
GOOD, VERY **GOOD!**
YOU WORKED AT PRINCETON WITH ALONZO CHURCH, JOHN VON NEU-MANN, AND WON ANOTHER PRIZE, ON PROBABILITY ONCE AGAIN ...
THE SMITH'S PRIZE! IN FACT, S-S-SIR, I MEAN C-C-CAPTAIN ...
COMMANDER.
YES, PARDON ME, COMMANDER. IN FACT, M-M-MY ARTICLE ON "COMPUTABLE NUMBERS, WITH AN APPLICATION TO THE ENTSCHEIDUNGSPRO-BLEM" IS WHAT L-L-LED YOUR SERVICE ...
... TO CONTACT ME.
AND THE THESIS YOU WORKED ON AT PRINCETON ON ... ON "SYSTEMS OF LOGIC BASED ON ORDINALS."
I SEE THAT, MR. TURING.
EXACTLY! I WAS I-I-INTENDING TO ADDRESS THE D-D-DECISION PROBLEM ... A VERY IMPORTANT ISSUE IN MATHEMATICS. HILBERT SAID ...
THANK YOU, MR. TURING.

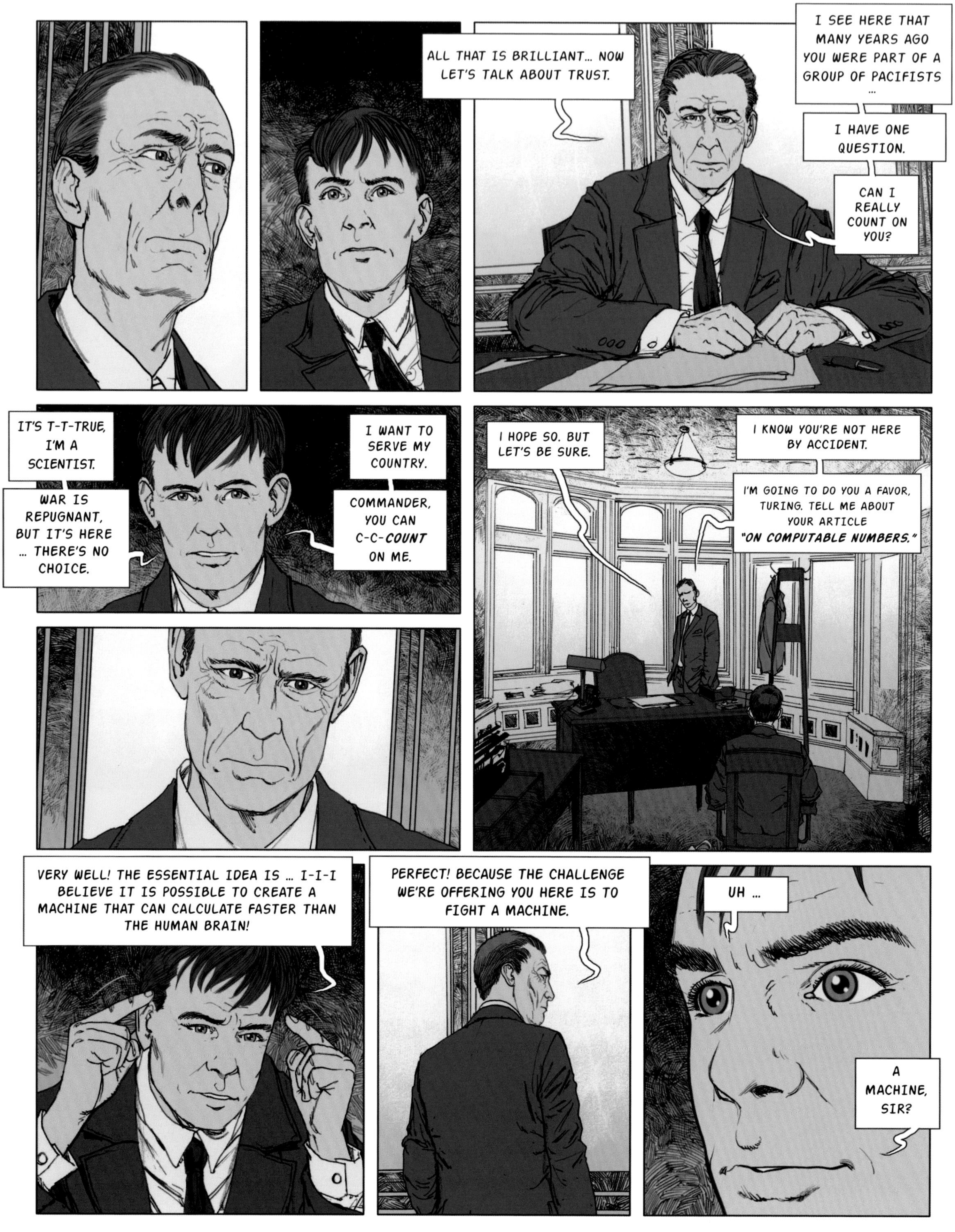
ALL THAT IS BRILLIANT... NOW LET'S TALK ABOUT TRUST.
I SEE HERE THAT MANY YEARS AGO YOU WERE PART OF A GROUP OF PACIFISTS ...
I HAVE ONE QUESTION.
CAN I REALLY COUNT ON YOU?
IT'S T-T-TRUE, I'M A SCIENTIST.
WAR IS REPUGNANT, BUT IT'S HERE ... THERE'S NO CHOICE.
I WANT TO SERVE MY COUNTRY.
COMMANDER, YOU CAN C-C-COUNT ON ME.
I HOPE SO. BUT LET'S BE SURE.
I KNOW YOU'RE NOT HERE BY ACCIDENT.
I'M GOING TO DO YOU A FAVOR, TURING. TELL ME ABOUT YOUR ARTICLE "ON COMPUTABLE NUMBERS."
VERY WELL! THE ESSENTIAL IDEA IS ... I-I-I BELIEVE IT IS POSSIBLE TO CREATE A MACHINE THAT CAN CALCULATE FASTER THAN THE HUMAN BRAIN!
PERFECT! BECAUSE THE CHALLENGE WE'RE OFFERING YOU HERE IS TO FIGHT A MACHINE.
UH ...
A MACHINE, SIR?

YOU'LL BE WORKING AT THE HIGHEST LEVEL OF SECRECY, TURING.

THE NAZIS HAVE DEVELOPED A MACHINE CALLED ENIGMA THAT ALLOWS THEM TO TRANSMIT THE FÜHRER'S MILITARY STRATEGY TO THE GERMAN FORCES.

YOUR OBJECTIVE IS TO BREAK THE ENIGMA CODE BY THE MATHEMATICAL MEANS YOU HAVE AT YOUR DISPOSAL. NEEDLESS TO SAY, THE STAKES ARE STAGGERING!

I HOPE YOU'RE NOT HIDING ANYTHING, TURING, AND THAT YOU'RE WORTHY OF OUR TRUST.

BECAUSE YOU SHARE THAT SECRET WITH US, GOD, AND THE KING.

WHICH MEANS, FROM NOW ON, YOU ARE THE PROPERTY OF GREAT BRITAIN!

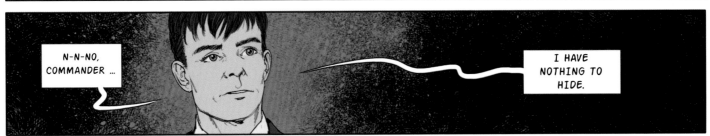

N-N-NO, COMMANDER ...

I HAVE NOTHING TO HIDE.

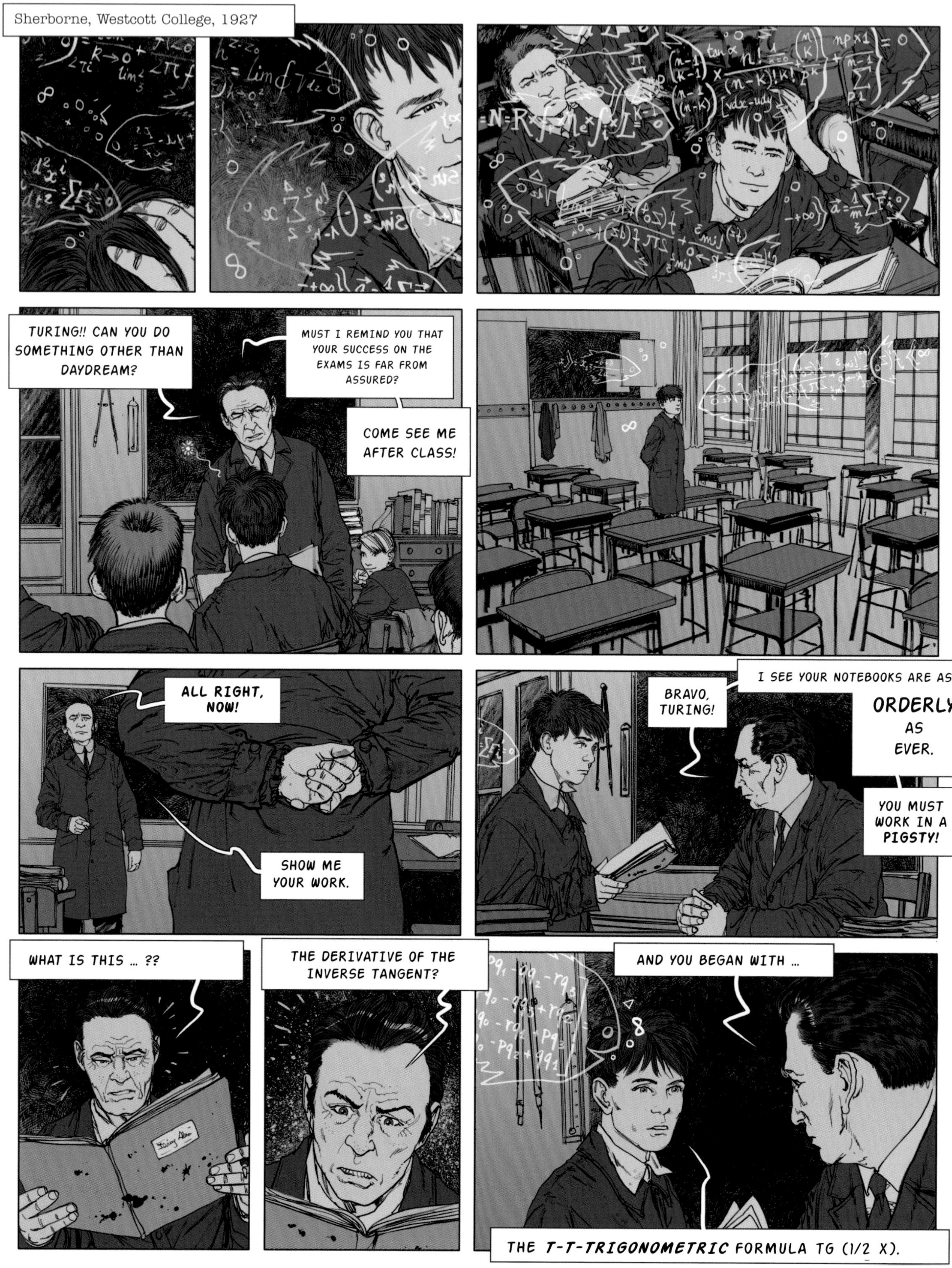
Sherborne, Westcott College, 1927
TURING!! CAN YOU DO SOMETHING OTHER THAN DAYDREAM?
MUST I REMIND YOU THAT YOUR SUCCESS ON THE EXAMS IS FAR FROM ASSURED?
COME SEE ME AFTER CLASS!
ALL RIGHT, NOW!
SHOW ME YOUR WORK.
BRAVO, TURING!
I SEE YOUR NOTEBOOKS ARE AS ORDERLY AS EVER.
YOU MUST WORK IN A PIGSTY!
WHAT IS THIS ... ??
THE DERIVATIVE OF THE INVERSE TANGENT?
AND YOU BEGAN WITH ...
THE T-T-TRIGONOMETRIC FORMULA TG (1/2 X).

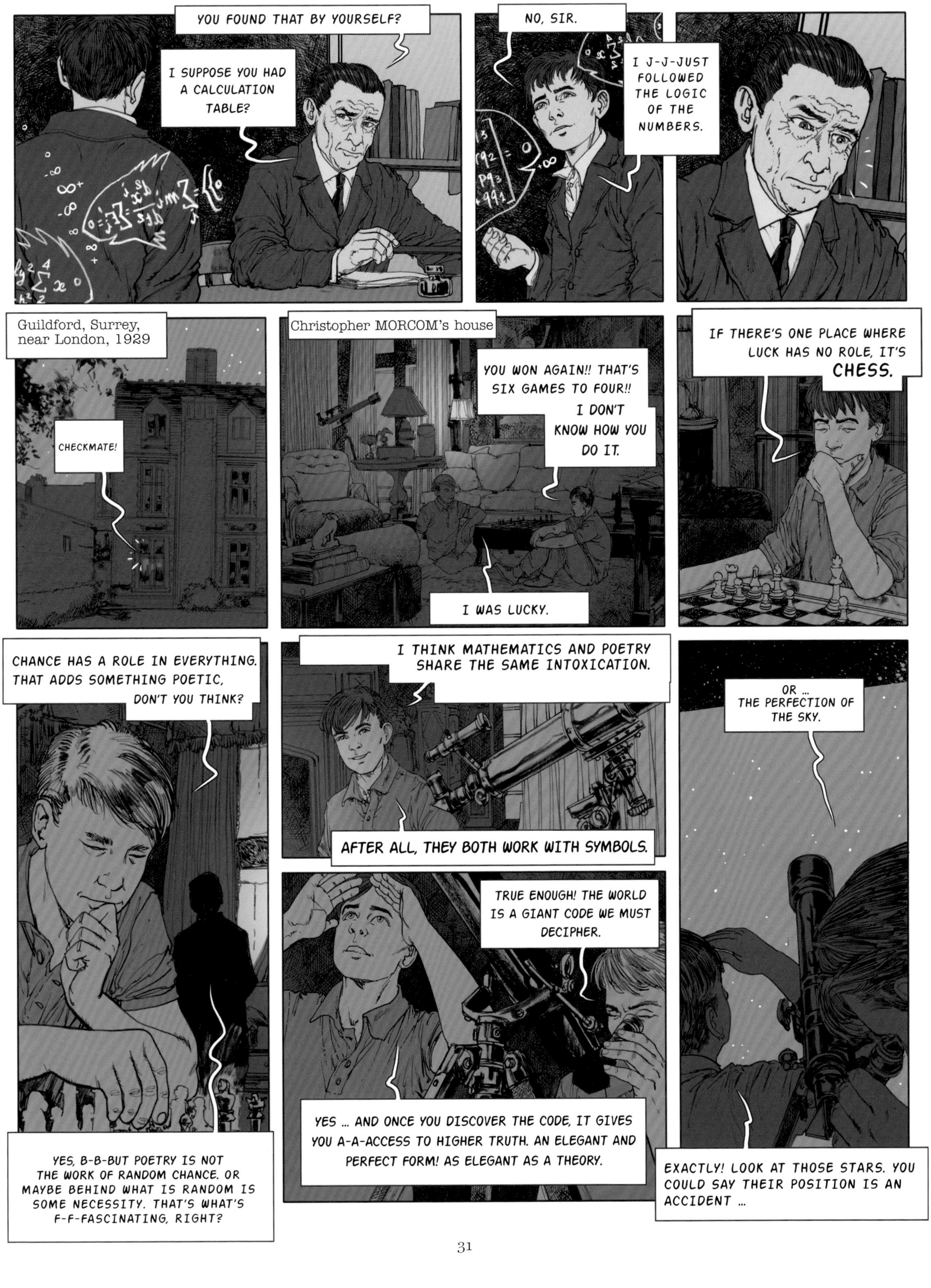
YOU FOUND THAT BY YOURSELF?
I SUPPOSE YOU HAD A CALCULATION TABLE?
NO, SIR.
I J-J-JUST FOLLOWED THE LOGIC OF THE NUMBERS.
Guildford, Surrey, near London, 1929
CHECKMATE!
Christopher MORCOM's house
YOU WON AGAIN!! THAT'S SIX GAMES TO FOUR!!
I DON'T KNOW HOW YOU DO IT.
I WAS LUCKY.
IF THERE'S ONE PLACE WHERE LUCK HAS NO ROLE, IT'S CHESS.
CHANCE HAS A ROLE IN EVERYTHING. THAT ADDS SOMETHING POETIC, DON'T YOU THINK?
YES, B-B-BUT POETRY IS NOT THE WORK OF RANDOM CHANCE. OR MAYBE BEHIND WHAT IS RANDOM IS SOME NECESSITY. THAT'S WHAT'S F-F-FASCINATING, RIGHT?
I THINK MATHEMATICS AND POETRY SHARE THE SAME INTOXICATION.
AFTER ALL, THEY BOTH WORK WITH SYMBOLS.
TRUE ENOUGH! THE WORLD IS A GIANT CODE WE MUST DECIPHER.
YES ... AND ONCE YOU DISCOVER THE CODE, IT GIVES YOU A-A-ACCESS TO HIGHER TRUTH. AN ELEGANT AND PERFECT FORM! AS ELEGANT AS A THEORY.
OR ... THE PERFECTION OF THE SKY.
EXACTLY! LOOK AT THOSE STARS. YOU COULD SAY THEIR POSITION IS AN ACCIDENT ...

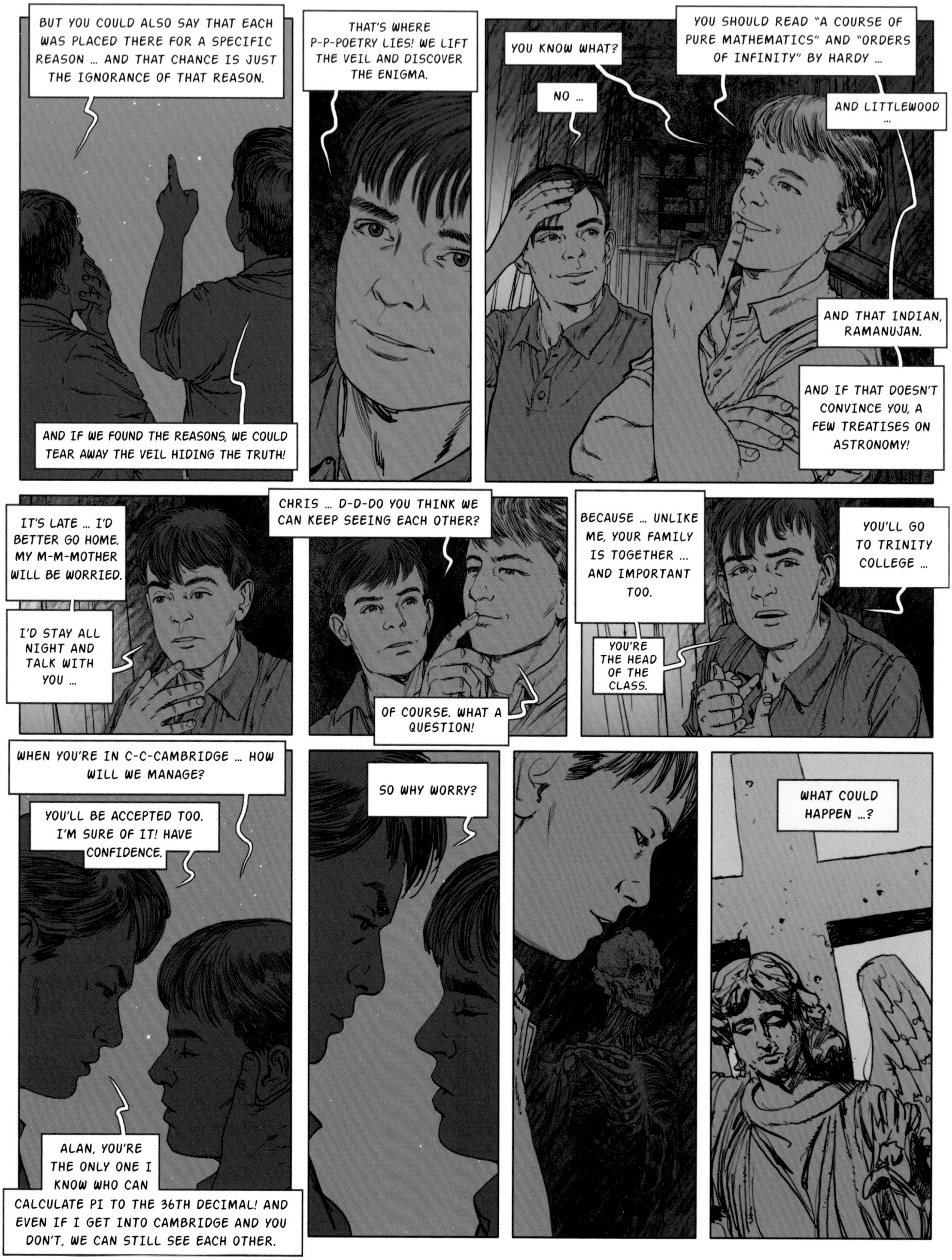
BUT YOU COULD ALSO SAY THAT EACH WAS PLACED THERE FOR A SPECIFIC REASON ... AND THAT CHANCE IS JUST THE IGNORANCE OF THAT REASON.
AND IF WE FOUND THE REASONS, WE COULD TEAR AWAY THE VEIL HIDING THE TRUTH!
THAT'S WHERE P-P-POETRY LIES! WE LIFT THE VEIL AND DISCOVER THE ENIGMA.
YOU KNOW WHAT?
NO ...
YOU SHOULD READ "A COURSE OF PURE MATHEMATICS" AND "ORDERS OF INFINITY" BY HARDY ...
AND LITTLEWOOD ...
AND THAT INDIAN, RAMANUJAN.
AND IF THAT DOESN'T CONVINCE YOU, A FEW TREATISES ON ASTRONOMY!
IT'S LATE ... I'D BETTER GO HOME. MY M-M-MOTHER WILL BE WORRIED.
I'D STAY ALL NIGHT AND TALK WITH YOU ...
CHRIS ... D-D-DO YOU THINK WE CAN KEEP SEEING EACH OTHER?
OF COURSE. WHAT A QUESTION!
BECAUSE ... UNLIKE ME, YOUR FAMILY IS TOGETHER ... AND IMPORTANT TOO.
YOU'RE THE HEAD OF THE CLASS.
YOU'LL GO TO TRINITY COLLEGE ...
WHEN YOU'RE IN C-C-CAMBRIDGE ... HOW WILL WE MANAGE?
YOU'LL BE ACCEPTED TOO. I'M SURE OF IT! HAVE CONFIDENCE.
ALAN, YOU'RE THE ONLY ONE I KNOW WHO CAN
CALCULATE PI TO THE 36TH DECIMAL! AND EVEN IF I GET INTO CAMBRIDGE AND YOU DON'T, WE CAN STILL SEE EACH OTHER.
SO WHY WORRY?
WHAT COULD HAPPEN ...?

SIX DAYS OF SUFFERING...

... FOR DRINKING A FEW SIPS OF CONTAMINATED MILK ... AND CONTRACTING BOVINE TUBERCULOSIS.

HE DIED FROM DRINKING MILK.

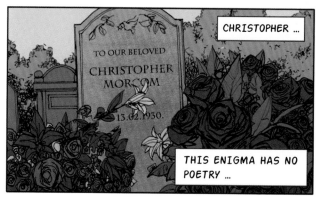

TO OUR BELOVED
CHRISTOPHER
MORCOM

13.02.1930.

CHRISTOPHER ...

THIS ENIGMA HAS NO POETRY ...

IT'S INDECIPHERABLE ...

I WISH I COULD DIE.

BECAUSE I LOVED YOU.

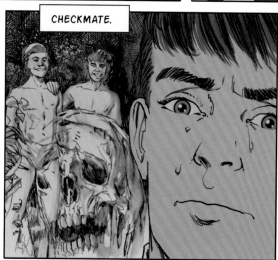

CHECKMATE.

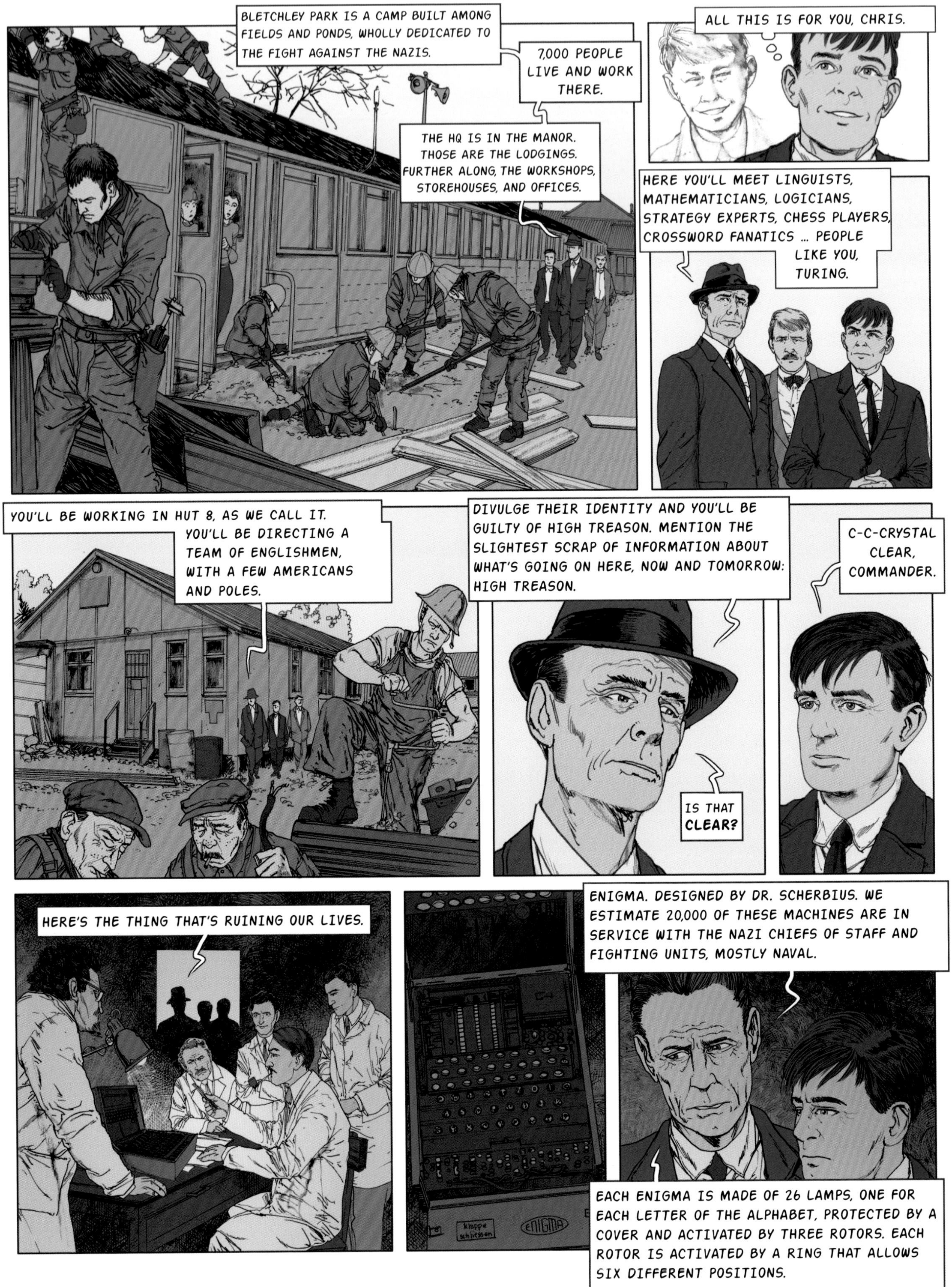
BLETCHLEY PARK IS A CAMP BUILT AMONG FIELDS AND PONDS, WHOLLY DEDICATED TO THE FIGHT AGAINST THE NAZIS.
7,000 PEOPLE LIVE AND WORK THERE.
THE HQ IS IN THE MANOR. THOSE ARE THE LODGINGS. FURTHER ALONG, THE WORKSHOPS, STOREHOUSES, AND OFFICES.
ALL THIS IS FOR YOU, CHRIS.
HERE YOU'LL MEET LINGUISTS, MATHEMATICIANS, LOGICIANS, STRATEGY EXPERTS, CHESS PLAYERS, CROSSWORD FANATICS ... PEOPLE
LIKE YOU, TURING.
YOU'LL BE WORKING IN HUT 8, AS WE CALL IT.
YOU'LL BE DIRECTING A TEAM OF ENGLISHMEN, WITH A FEW AMERICANS AND POLES.
DIVULGE THEIR IDENTITY AND YOU'LL BE GUILTY OF HIGH TREASON. MENTION THE SLIGHTEST SCRAP OF INFORMATION ABOUT WHAT'S GOING ON HERE, NOW AND TOMORROW: HIGH TREASON.
IS THAT **CLEAR?**
C-C-CRYSTAL CLEAR, COMMANDER.
HERE'S THE THING THAT'S RUINING OUR LIVES.
klappe schliessen
ENIGMA
ENIGMA. DESIGNED BY DR. SCHERBIUS. WE ESTIMATE 20,000 OF THESE MACHINES ARE IN SERVICE WITH THE NAZI CHIEFS OF STAFF AND FIGHTING UNITS, MOSTLY NAVAL.
EACH ENIGMA IS MADE OF 26 LAMPS, ONE FOR EACH LETTER OF THE ALPHABET, PROTECTED BY A COVER AND ACTIVATED BY THREE ROTORS. EACH ROTOR IS ACTIVATED BY A RING THAT ALLOWS SIX DIFFERENT POSITIONS.

THE PRINCIPLE OF ENCRYPTION IS SIMPLE: THE SENDER CREATES PERMUTATIONS OF LETTERS OF THE ALPHABET, AND THE RECEIVER DECRYPTS THEM WITH A SECRET CODE.

Hugh ALEXANDER, cryptanalyst and chess player

THE CURRENT RUNS FROM THE KEYBOARD TO THE ROTORS THAT CARRY OUT THE SUCCESSIVE PERMUTATIONS OF THE LETTERS, CHANGING THEM EACH TIME. EVERY DAY, THE GERMANS CHANGE THE LETTER KEYS AND THE ORDER OF RINGS AND ROTORS.

A SINGLE LETTER CAN HAVE MORE THAN 17,000 DIFFERENT COMBINATIONS. THE NUMBER OF POSSIBLE KEYS IS 10 MILLION BILLIONS, AND WE HAVE TO START OVER **EVERY DAY.**

THAT FACT MAKES ENIGMA **INDECIPHERABLE!**

William Gordon WELCHMAN, cryptographer and mathematician

F-F-FASCINATING ...

a chess game! a puzzle as big as the world!

IT'S A HERCULEAN TASK! AN IMPOSSIBLE MATHEMATICAL PUZZLE!

Stuart MILNER-BARRY, cryptanalyst and chess player

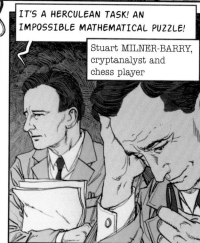

YET NOT ONLY MUST WE FIND THE WAY TO DEFEAT ENIGMA, WE HAVE TO DO IT QUICKLY!

IT'S MORE THAN WORTH OUR WHILE. BREAKING ENIGMA IS TANTAMOUNT TO READING HITLER'S MIND. IT WILL MEAN SAVING THOUSANDS OF LIVES, NOT TO MENTION GOODS AND MERCHANDISE.

GOOD LUCK!

TURING, YOU WILL BE WORKING ON THE MADDEST DECRYPTION PROJECT IN HUMAN **HISTORY**

NO MORE, NO LESS.

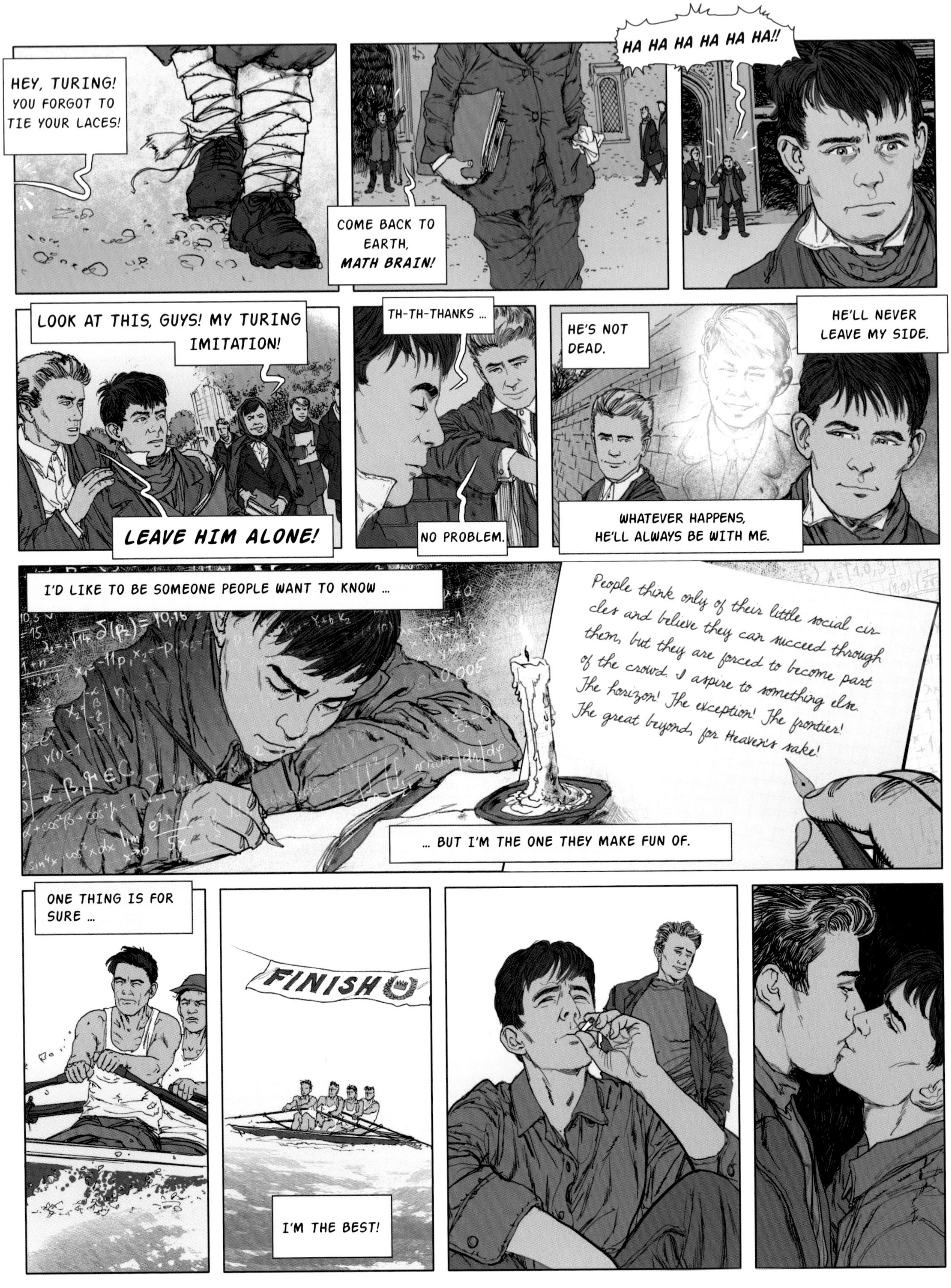
HEY, TURING! YOU FORGOT TO TIE YOUR LACES!
COME BACK TO EARTH, *MATH BRAIN!*
HA HA HA HA HA HA!!
LOOK AT THIS, GUYS! MY TURING IMITATION!
LEAVE HIM ALONE!
TH-TH-THANKS ...
NO PROBLEM.
HE'S NOT DEAD.
HE'LL NEVER LEAVE MY SIDE.
WHATEVER HAPPENS, HE'LL ALWAYS BE WITH ME.
I'D LIKE TO BE SOMEONE PEOPLE WANT TO KNOW ...
People think only of their little social circles and believe they can succeed through them, but they are forced to become part of the crowd. I aspire to something else. The horizon! The exception! The frontier! The great beyond, for Heaven's sake!
... BUT I'M THE ONE THEY MAKE FUN OF.
ONE THING IS FOR SURE ...
FINISH
I'M THE BEST!

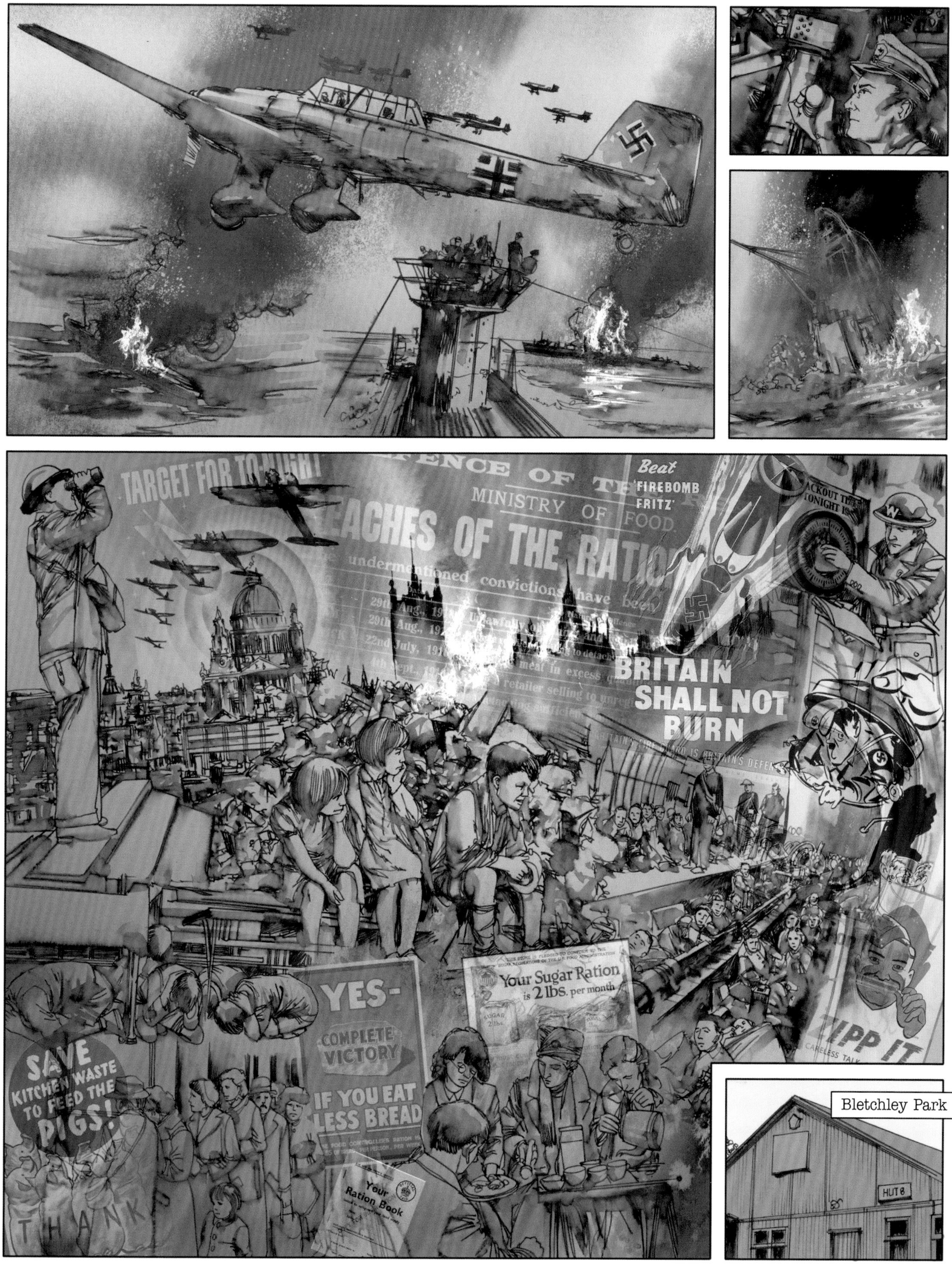
TARGET FOR TO-NIGHT
MINISTRY OF FOOD
Beat 'FIREBOMB FRITZ'
BRITAIN SHALL NOT BURN
YES-
COMPLETE VICTORY
IF YOU EAT LESS BREAD
Your Sugar Ration is 2 lbs. per month
SAVE KITCHEN WASTE TO FEED THE PIGS!
Your Ration Book
THANK
Bletchley Park
HUT 8

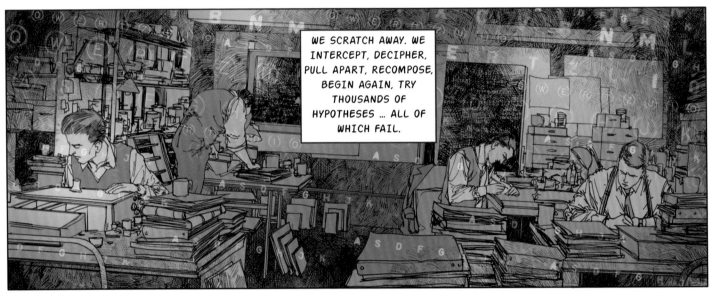

WE SCRATCH AWAY. WE INTERCEPT, DECIPHER, PULL APART, RECOMPOSE, BEGIN AGAIN, TRY THOUSANDS OF HYPOTHESES ... ALL OF WHICH FAIL.

IMPOSSIBLE TO TEST SO MANY COMBINATIONS WITH THE KEY THAT CHANGES EVERY DAY.

EVERY EVENING AT MIDNIGHT, OUR WORK GOES IN THE GARBAGE.

ENIGMA IS TOO STRONG. IT GOES TOO FAST!

WE'LL NEVER SUCCEED THIS WAY.

THE GOLDFISH SMOKE IN THE MAYONNAISE OF THE MORNING ...

INTERESTING.

TRY THIS ONE: THE TOP OF THE BLOO MOUNTAIN EATS SOME ... SOME ... XLPTZV.

QUITE THE RESULTS! ARE YOU SURE TURING IS THE RIGHT HORSE? AND ALL THESE CRYPTANALYSTS ... GOOD GOD, DO YOU UNDERSTAND WHAT WE'RE FACING?

Stewart Graham MENZIES, head of MI6, successor to Admiral Sinclair

LET HIM KEEP WORKING ... DO WE REALLY HAVE A CHOICE, COMMANDER?

HMM ... I AGREE, MENZIES. FOR NOW.

WHAT'S HE DOING WITH A GAS MASK?

HE SAYS IT PROTECTS HIM FROM HAY FEVER ...

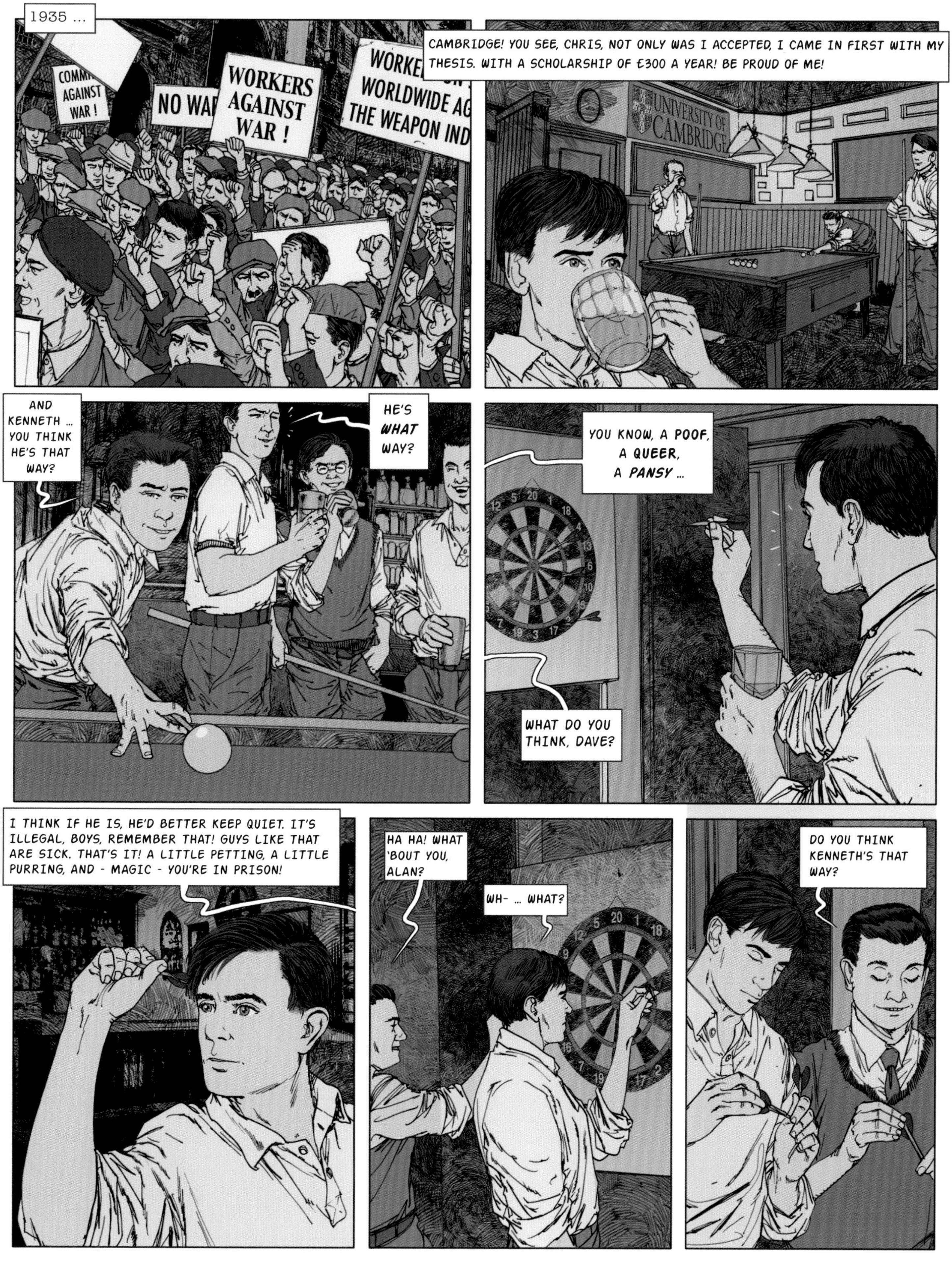
1935 ...
WORKERS AGAINST WAR !
CAMBRIDGE! YOU SEE, CHRIS, NOT ONLY WAS I ACCEPTED, I CAME IN FIRST WITH MY THESIS. WITH A SCHOLARSHIP OF £300 A YEAR! BE PROUD OF ME!
UNIVERSITY OF CAMBRIDGE
AND KENNETH ... YOU THINK HE'S THAT WAY?
HE'S WHAT WAY?
YOU KNOW, A POOF, A QUEER, A PANSY ...
WHAT DO YOU THINK, DAVE?
I THINK IF HE IS, HE'D BETTER KEEP QUIET. IT'S ILLEGAL, BOYS, REMEMBER THAT! GUYS LIKE THAT ARE SICK. THAT'S IT! A LITTLE PETTING, A LITTLE PURRING, AND - MAGIC - YOU'RE IN PRISON!
HA HA! WHAT 'BOUT YOU, ALAN?
WH- ... WHAT?
DO YOU THINK KENNETH'S THAT WAY?

UH ...

I DON'T KNOW. NO IDEA ...

AH, FORGET HIM! SINCE MR. GENIUS CAME IN FIRST, HE'S STOPPED SPEAKING TO US.

N-N-NO! NOT IT AT ALL!!

MAKE FUN IF YOU WANT! BUT IN TEN YEARS, OR TWENTY YEARS, I'LL WIN THE NOBEL, LIKE DIRAC OR SCHRÖDINGER ...

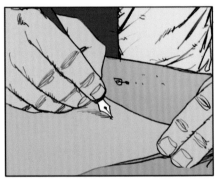

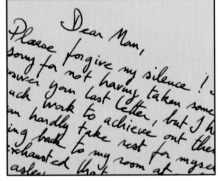

Dear Mom,

Please forgive my silence ! Sorry for not having taken some answer your last letter, but I have such work to achieve out there can hardly take rest for myself ing back to my room at exhausted that asle...

My work in mathematics is taking more and more of my time every day. Don't worry, all is well.

Let me explain.

We can summarily define computable numbers as real values whose decimal expression is computable with finite means ...

Klpftzv...

40

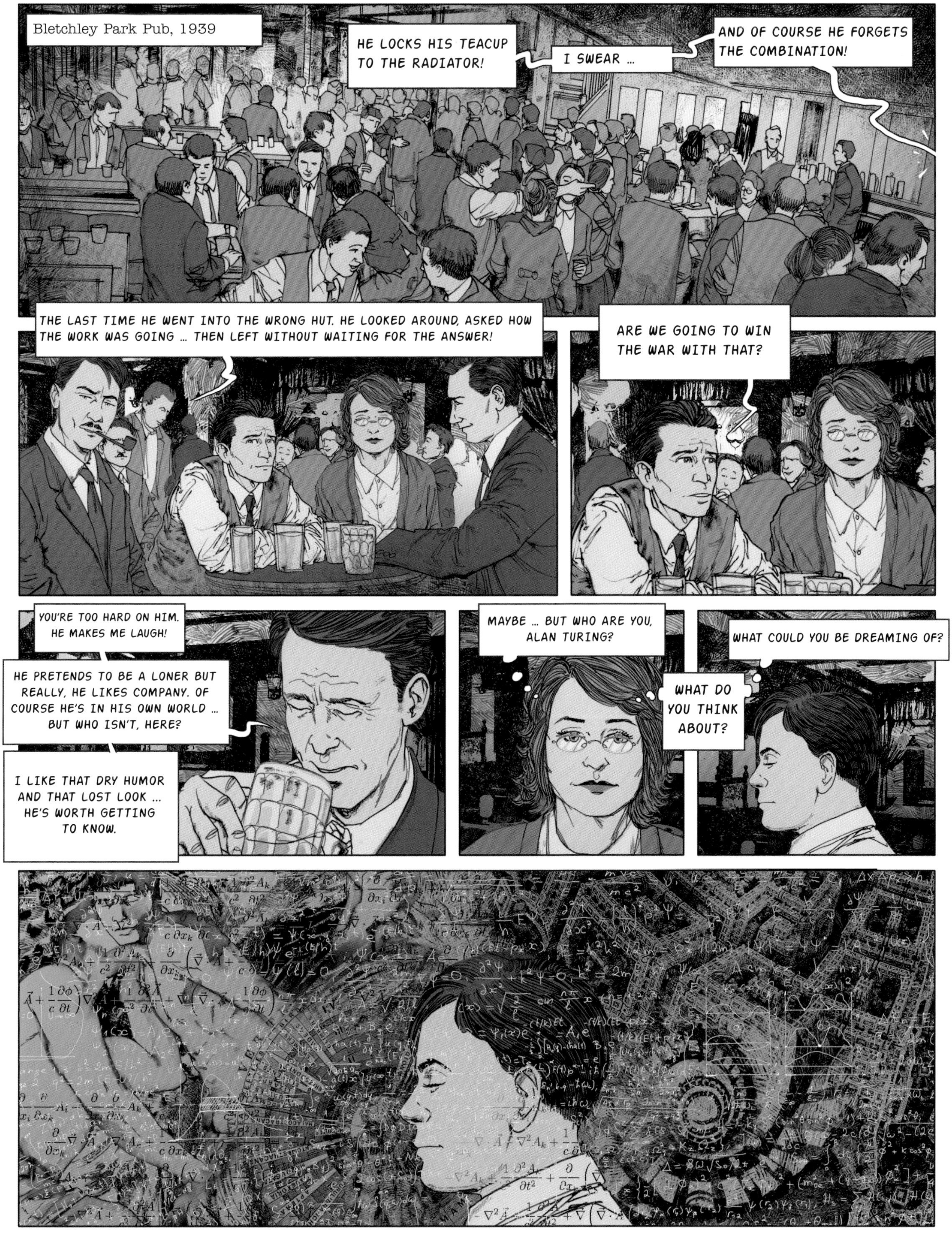
Bletchley Park Pub, 1939
HE LOCKS HIS TEACUP TO THE RADIATOR!
I SWEAR ...
AND OF COURSE HE FORGETS THE COMBINATION!
THE LAST TIME HE WENT INTO THE WRONG HUT, HE LOOKED AROUND, ASKED HOW THE WORK WAS GOING ... THEN LEFT WITHOUT WAITING FOR THE ANSWER!
ARE WE GOING TO WIN THE WAR WITH THAT?
YOU'RE TOO HARD ON HIM. HE MAKES ME LAUGH!
HE PRETENDS TO BE A LONER BUT REALLY, HE LIKES COMPANY. OF COURSE HE'S IN HIS OWN WORLD ... BUT WHO ISN'T, HERE?
I LIKE THAT DRY HUMOR AND THAT LOST LOOK ... HE'S WORTH GETTING TO KNOW.
MAYBE ... BUT WHO ARE YOU, ALAN TURING?
WHAT DO YOU THINK ABOUT?
WHAT COULD YOU BE DREAMING OF?

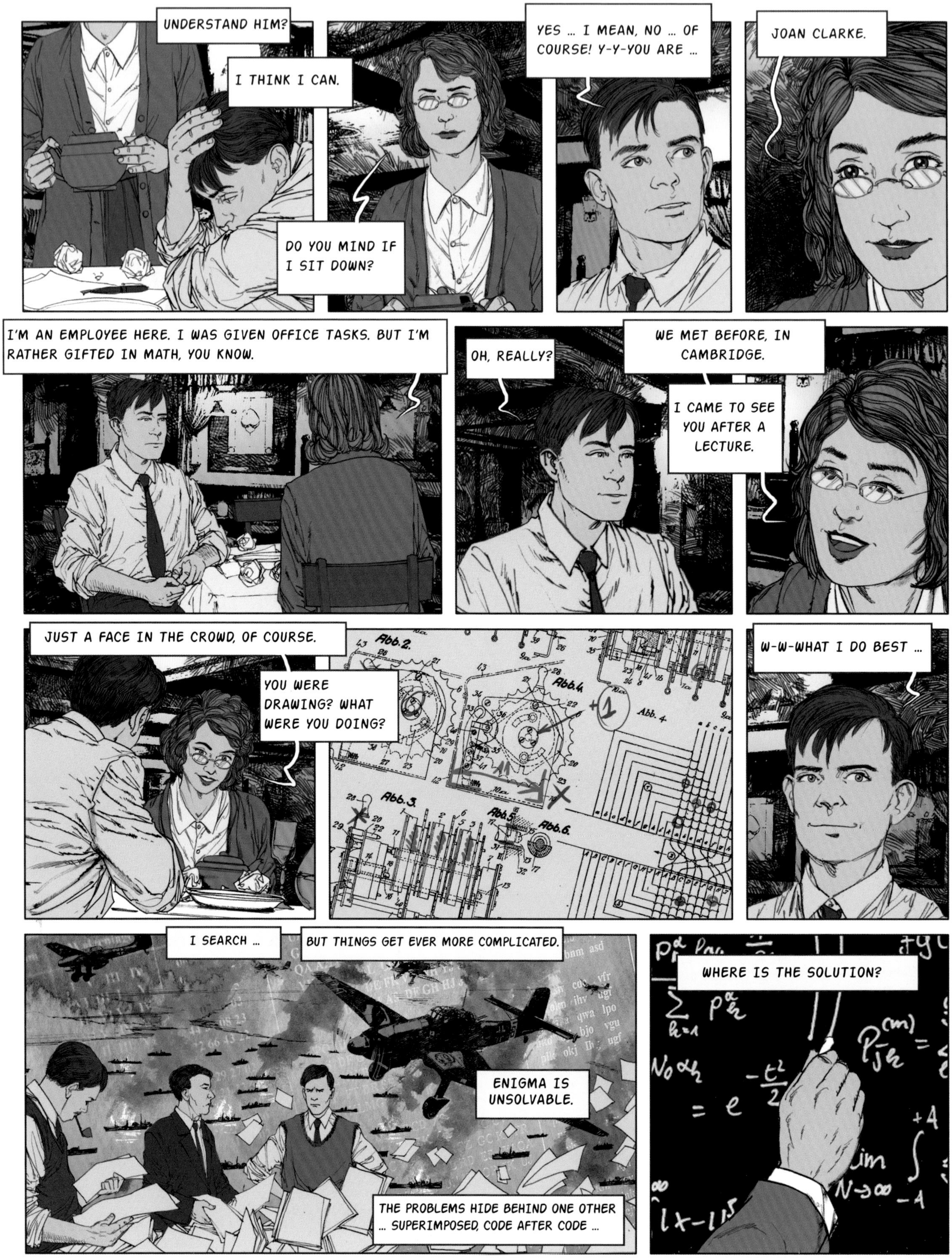
UNDERSTAND HIM?
I THINK I CAN.
DO YOU MIND IF I SIT DOWN?
YES ... I MEAN, NO ... OF COURSE! Y-Y-YOU ARE ...
JOAN CLARKE.
I'M AN EMPLOYEE HERE. I WAS GIVEN OFFICE TASKS. BUT I'M RATHER GIFTED IN MATH, YOU KNOW.
OH, REALLY?
WE MET BEFORE, IN CAMBRIDGE.
I CAME TO SEE YOU AFTER A LECTURE.
JUST A FACE IN THE CROWD, OF COURSE.
YOU WERE DRAWING? WHAT WERE YOU DOING?
W-W-WHAT I DO BEST ...
I SEARCH ...
BUT THINGS GET EVER MORE COMPLICATED.
ENIGMA IS UNSOLVABLE.
THE PROBLEMS HIDE BEHIND ONE OTHER ... SUPERIMPOSED, CODE AFTER CODE ...
WHERE IS THE SOLUTION?

1935, Cambridge. A seminar by John von Neumann, specialist in the logic of mathematics, the fundamentals of quantum mechanics and game theory...

DAVID HILBERT FACED THE UNSOLVABLE. IN AUGUST 1900, HE SET DOWN 23 UNSOLVABLE PROBLEMS, A CHALLENGE TO MATHEMATICIANS.

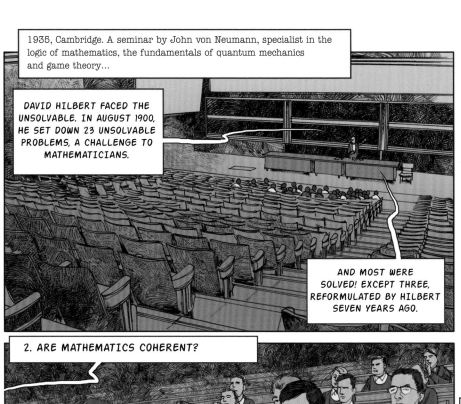

AND MOST WERE SOLVED! EXCEPT THREE, REFORMULATED BY HILBERT SEVEN YEARS AGO.

1. ARE MATHEMATICS COMPLETE? IN OTHER WORDS, CAN EVERY ASSERTION IN MATHEMATICS BE PROVED OR REFUTED?

2. ARE MATHEMATICS COHERENT?

IN OTHER WORDS, HOW CAN WE BE SURE THAT CORRECT REASONING WON'T LEAD TO CONTRADICTIONS OR ABSURDITIES?

3. ARE MATHEMATICS DECIDABLE?

IN OTHER WORDS, IS THERE AN ALGORITHM THAT WILL LET US DETERMINE WHETHER ANY GIVEN ASSERTION IN MATHEMATICS IS TRUE OR FALSE?

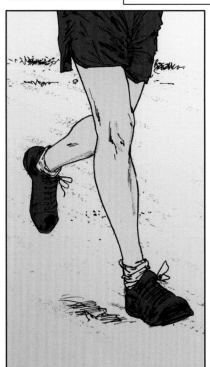

FOUR YEARS AGO, OUR FRIEND KURT GÖDEL ANSWERED THE FIRST QUESTIONS. HE PROVED THAT ANY FORMAL SYSTEM WORTHY OF THE NAME WAS EITHER COHERENT, OR INCOMPLETE.

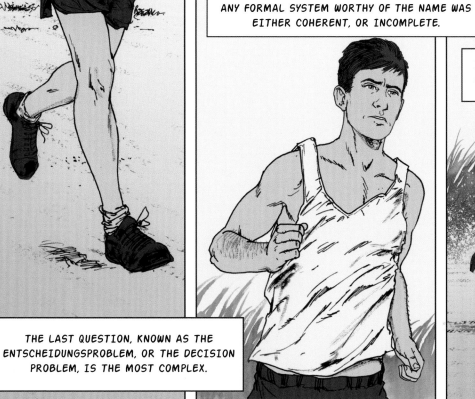

THE LAST QUESTION, KNOWN AS THE ENTSCHEIDUNGSPROBLEM, OR THE DECISION PROBLEM, IS THE MOST COMPLEX.

HOW THE CLOCK FUNCTIONS.

I HAVE TO UNDERSTAND ...

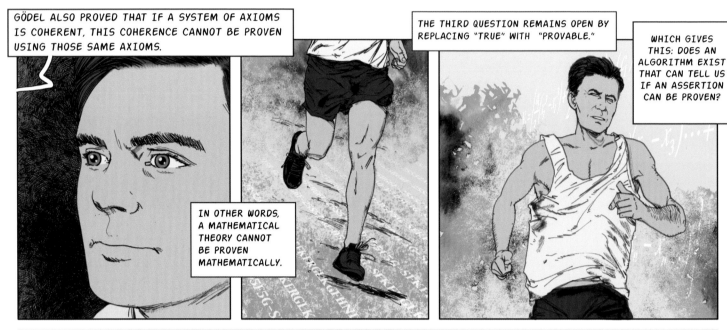

GÖDEL ALSO PROVED THAT IF A SYSTEM OF AXIOMS IS COHERENT, THIS COHERENCE CANNOT BE PROVEN USING THOSE SAME AXIOMS.

IN OTHER WORDS, A MATHEMATICAL THEORY CANNOT BE PROVEN MATHEMATICALLY.

THE THIRD QUESTION REMAINS OPEN BY REPLACING "TRUE" WITH "PROVABLE."

WHICH GIVES THIS: DOES AN ALGORITHM EXIST THAT CAN TELL US IF AN ASSERTION CAN BE PROVEN?

TO ILLUSTRATE THIS, THINK OF THE PARADOX OF THE LIAR. IF I SAY, "I AM A LIAR," AND I AM TELLING THE TRUTH, THEN MY ASSERTION IS FALSE.

IF I LIE, THEN I CAN'T SAY I'M A LIAR. I WOULD SAY, "I'M TELLING THE TRUTH." AND I'D BE LYING.

HOW TO RESOLVE A PROBLEM UNSOLVABLE FOR ANY NORMAL HUMAN BRAIN?

HOW?

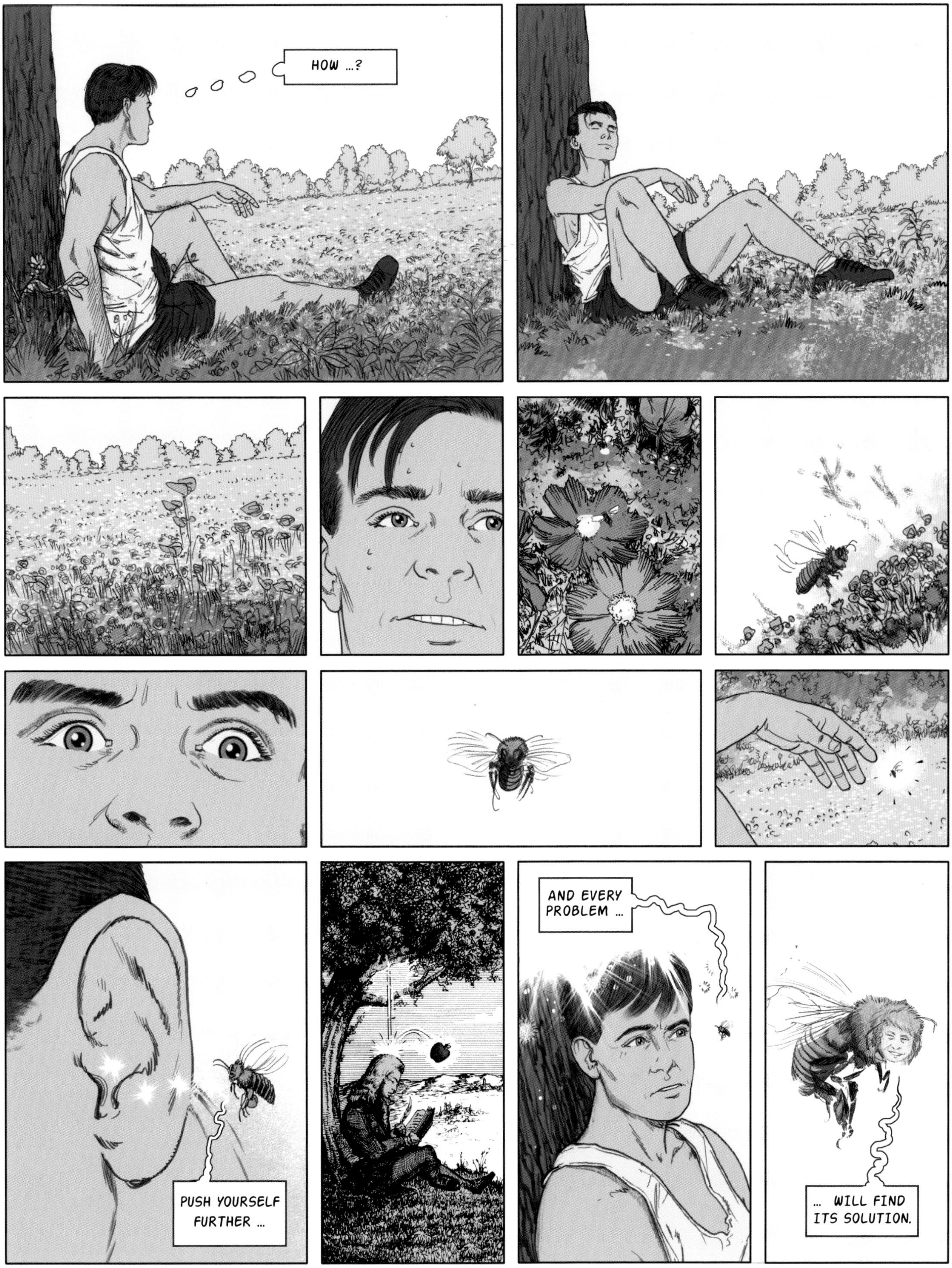
HOW ...?
PUSH YOURSELF FURTHER ...
AND EVERY PROBLEM ...
... WILL FIND ITS SOLUTION.

HOW TO RESOLVE A PROBLEM UNSOLVABLE BY ANY NORMAL HUMAN BRAIN?

ON COMPUTABLE NUMBERS, WITH AN APPLICATION TO THE ENTSCHEIDUNGSPROBLEM

By A. M. TURING.

[Received 28 May, 1936.—Read 12 November, 1936.]

The "computable" numbers may be described briefly as the real numbers whose expressions as a decimal are calculable by finite means. Although the subject of this paper is ostensibly the computable numbers, it is almost equally easy to define and investigate computable functions of an integral variable or a real or computable variable, computable predicates, and so forth. The fundamental problems involved are, however, the same in each case, and I have chosen the computable numbers for explicit treatment as involving the least cumbrous technique. I hope shortly to give an account of the relations of the computable numbers, ... one another. ... another. This will include a development ... in terms of com-

TOO MANY CALCULATIONS, FACTORS, COMBINATIONS, HYPOTHESES ... THE HUMAN BRAIN CANNOT SOLVE DECISION PROBLEMS ...

BUT ... A MACHINE?

A THINKING MACHINE. INTELLIGENT. ABLE TO CALCULATE FASTER THAN THE HUMAN MIND.

WITH NO MISTAKES.

A ROBOT. WITH A FINITE TASK. LIKE THE ONE I WAS CONSIDERING IN MY ARTICLE. A UNIVERSAL TOOL, ABLE TO DECIDE, FOR ANY PROPOSITION, WHETHER IT IS PROVABLE OR NOT ...

A TOOL THAT CAN BEAT ENIGMA BY TESTING ITS COMBINATIONS FOR US.

THE TIME HAS COME TO CREATE IT. MY FIRST INTUITION WAS RIGHT. IT WAS ALWAYS RIGHT! LIKE AT PRINCETON. TO FIGHT A MACHINE, YOU NEED ...

ANOTHER MACHINE!

GOOD GOD, TURING! WHAT ARE YOU DOING HERE ...?

I HAVE A PLAN!

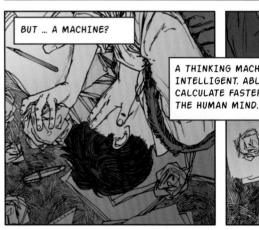

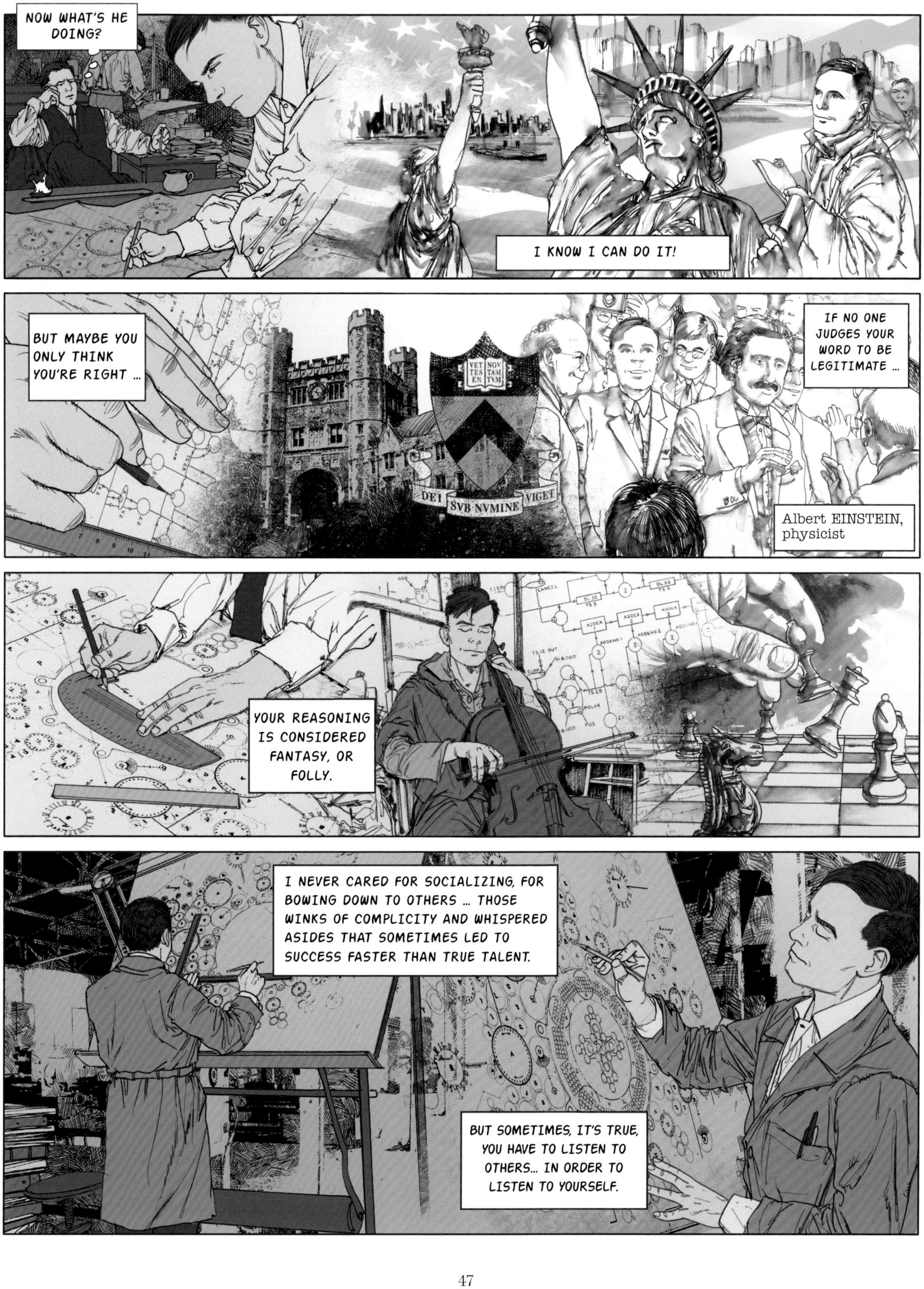
NOW WHAT'S HE DOING?
I KNOW I CAN DO IT!
BUT MAYBE YOU ONLY THINK YOU'RE RIGHT ...
DEI SVB NVMINE VIGET
IF NO ONE JUDGES YOUR WORD TO BE LEGITIMATE ...
Albert EINSTEIN, physicist
YOUR REASONING IS CONSIDERED FANTASY, OR FOLLY.
I NEVER CARED FOR SOCIALIZING, FOR BOWING DOWN TO OTHERS ... THOSE WINKS OF COMPLICITY AND WHISPERED ASIDES THAT SOMETIMES LED TO SUCCESS FASTER THAN TRUE TALENT.
BUT SOMETIMES, IT'S TRUE, YOU HAVE TO LISTEN TO OTHERS... IN ORDER TO LISTEN TO YOURSELF.

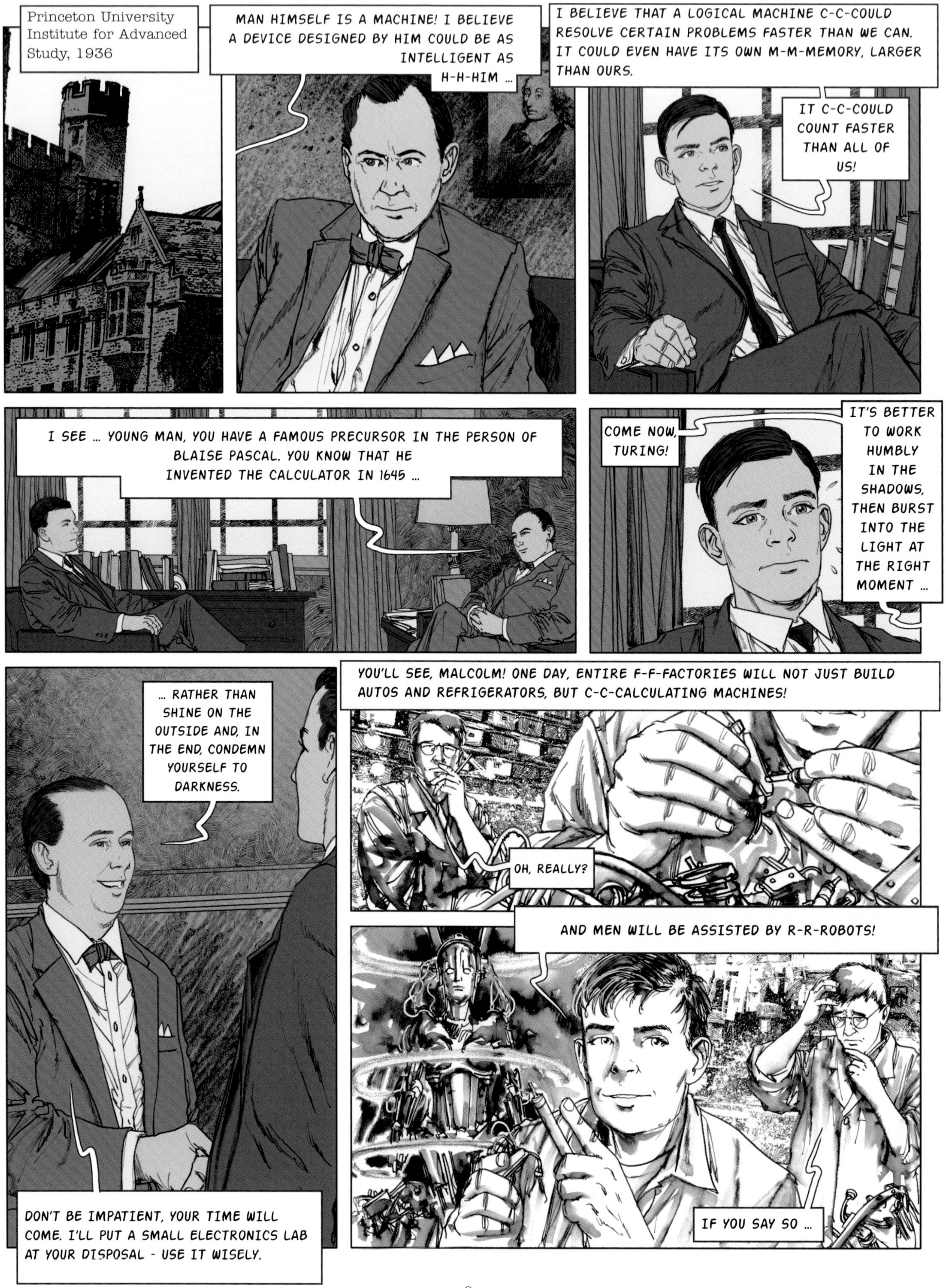

Princeton University Institute for Advanced Study, 1936
MAN HIMSELF IS A MACHINE! I BELIEVE A DEVICE DESIGNED BY HIM COULD BE AS INTELLIGENT AS H-H-HIM ...
I BELIEVE THAT A LOGICAL MACHINE C-C-COULD RESOLVE CERTAIN PROBLEMS FASTER THAN WE CAN. IT COULD EVEN HAVE ITS OWN M-M-MEMORY, LARGER THAN OURS.
IT C-C-COULD COUNT FASTER THAN ALL OF US!
I SEE ... YOUNG MAN, YOU HAVE A FAMOUS PRECURSOR IN THE PERSON OF BLAISE PASCAL. YOU KNOW THAT HE INVENTED THE CALCULATOR IN 1645 ...
COME NOW, TURING!
IT'S BETTER TO WORK HUMBLY IN THE SHADOWS, THEN BURST INTO THE LIGHT AT THE RIGHT MOMENT ...
... RATHER THAN SHINE ON THE OUTSIDE AND, IN THE END, CONDEMN YOURSELF TO DARKNESS.
DON'T BE IMPATIENT, YOUR TIME WILL COME. I'LL PUT A SMALL ELECTRONICS LAB AT YOUR DISPOSAL - USE IT WISELY.
YOU'LL SEE, MALCOLM! ONE DAY, ENTIRE F-F-FACTORIES WILL NOT JUST BUILD AUTOS AND REFRIGERATORS, BUT C-C-CALCULATING MACHINES!
OH, REALLY?
AND MEN WILL BE ASSISTED BY R-R-ROBOTS!
IF YOU SAY SO ...

MY FIRST MACHINE! LOOK! A PERFORATED STRIP RUNS THROUGH IT, LIKE THE SHEET MUSIC OF A PLAYER PIANO. DIVIDED INTO SQUARES ON WHICH NUMBERS AND SYMBOLS ARE WRITTEN.

ONE SQUARE PER OPERATION!

S-S-SOMETIMES IT STOPS, THEN STARTS UP AGAIN LIKE SOMEONE TRYING TO MEMORIZE INFORMATION. IT TESTS C-C-COMBINATIONS. IT'S LEARNING!

IT'S LEARNING.

REALLY?

I REMEMBERED MY FIRST ATTEMPTS AT PRINCETON. WITH A SYSTEM OF BINARY NOTATION USING BOOLEAN ALGEBRA, IT COULD DO EVEN MORE COMPLEX CALCULATIONS.

A SUPER-MACHINE ... A "SUPER-BOMBE" LIKE THE POLES BUILT.

BUT M-M-MUCH BETTER, COMMANDER! AN ELECTROMECHANICAL BOMBE, A CRYPTOLOGICAL BOMBE. B-B-BUT I NEED MORE TIME - AND MONEY!

WE HAVE NO TIME!! AND FINANCING DEPENDS ON RESULTS, TURING. RESULTS!

LISTEN TO HIM, COMMANDER ...

I P-P-PROMISE YOU! WE'RE WORKING FULL-TIME. WE'VE STARTED IMPROVING ON THE "BOMBES" DEVISED BY REJEWSKI AND THE POLES. IT'S COMPLICATED, BUT ...

Edward Wilfrid Harry TRAVIS, cryptanalyst, intelligence officer, and assistant to Alastair DENNISTON

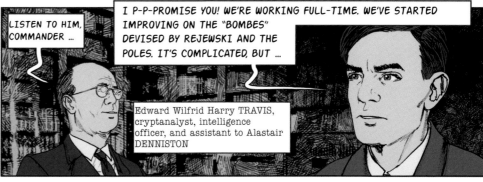

REJEWSKI DIVIDED THE SEARCH FOR THE POSITIONS OF THE SCRAMBLER FROM THE CONNECTIONS OF THE PLUGBOARD. PROBLEMS TREATED SEPARATELY ARE EASIER TO R-R-RESOLVE!

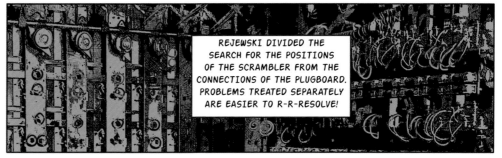

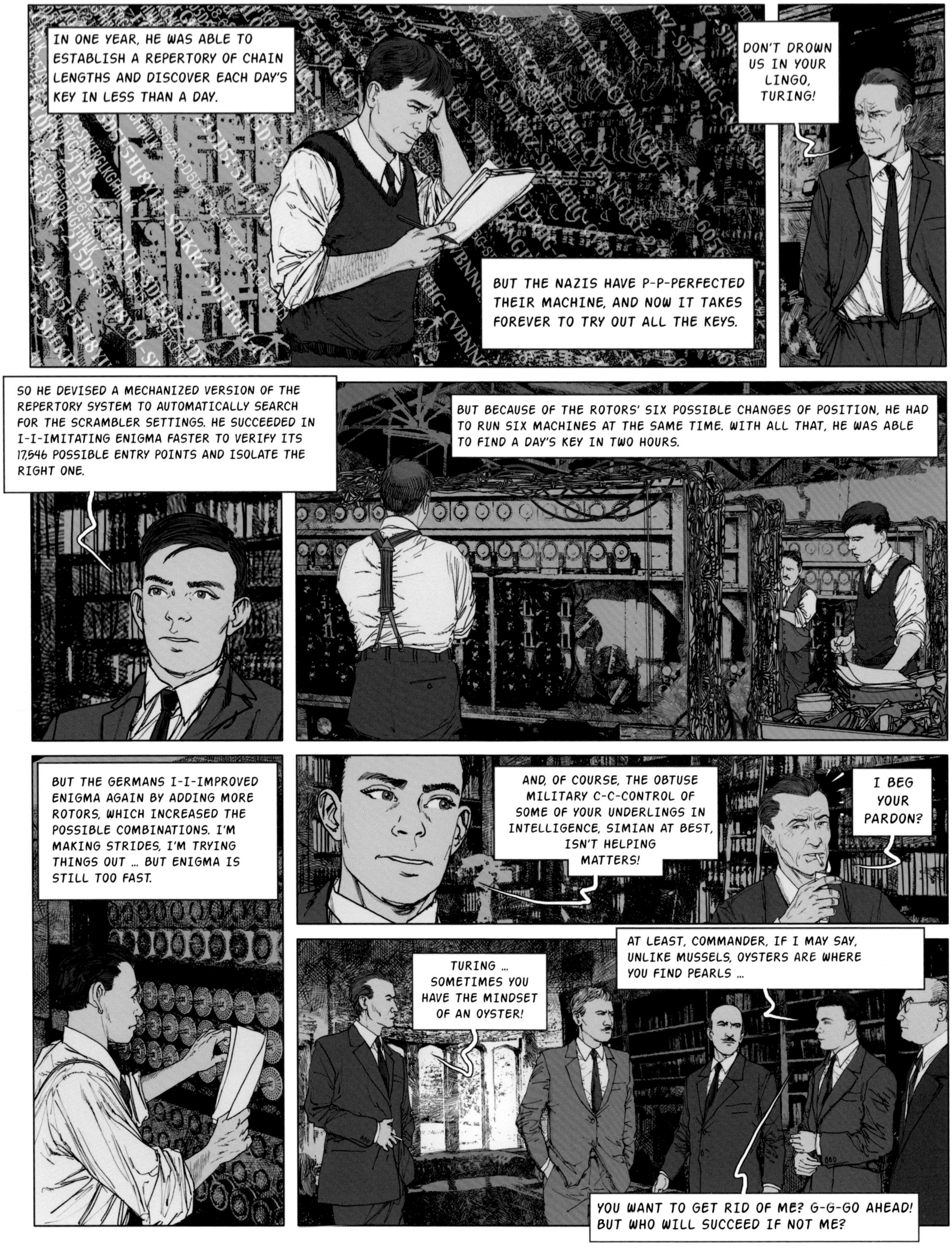
IN ONE YEAR, HE WAS ABLE TO ESTABLISH A REPERTORY OF CHAIN LENGTHS AND DISCOVER EACH DAY'S KEY IN LESS THAN A DAY.
BUT THE NAZIS HAVE P-P-PERFECTED THEIR MACHINE, AND NOW IT TAKES FOREVER TO TRY OUT ALL THE KEYS.
DON'T DROWN US IN YOUR LINGO, TURING!
SO HE DEVISED A MECHANIZED VERSION OF THE REPERTORY SYSTEM TO AUTOMATICALLY SEARCH FOR THE SCRAMBLER SETTINGS. HE SUCCEEDED IN I-I-IMITATING ENIGMA FASTER TO VERIFY ITS 17,576 POSSIBLE ENTRY POINTS AND ISOLATE THE RIGHT ONE.
BUT BECAUSE OF THE ROTORS' SIX POSSIBLE CHANGES OF POSITION, HE HAD TO RUN SIX MACHINES AT THE SAME TIME. WITH ALL THAT, HE WAS ABLE TO FIND A DAY'S KEY IN TWO HOURS.
BUT THE GERMANS I-I-IMPROVED ENIGMA AGAIN BY ADDING MORE ROTORS, WHICH INCREASED THE POSSIBLE COMBINATIONS. I'M MAKING STRIDES, I'M TRYING THINGS OUT ... BUT ENIGMA IS STILL TOO FAST.
AND, OF COURSE, THE OBTUSE MILITARY C-C-CONTROL OF SOME OF YOUR UNDERLINGS IN INTELLIGENCE, SIMIAN AT BEST, ISN'T HELPING MATTERS!
I BEG YOUR PARDON?
TURING ... SOMETIMES YOU HAVE THE MINDSET OF AN OYSTER!
AT LEAST, COMMANDER, IF I MAY SAY, UNLIKE MUSSELS, OYSTERS ARE WHERE YOU FIND PEARLS ...
YOU WANT TO GET RID OF ME? G-G-GO AHEAD! BUT WHO WILL SUCCEED IF NOT ME?

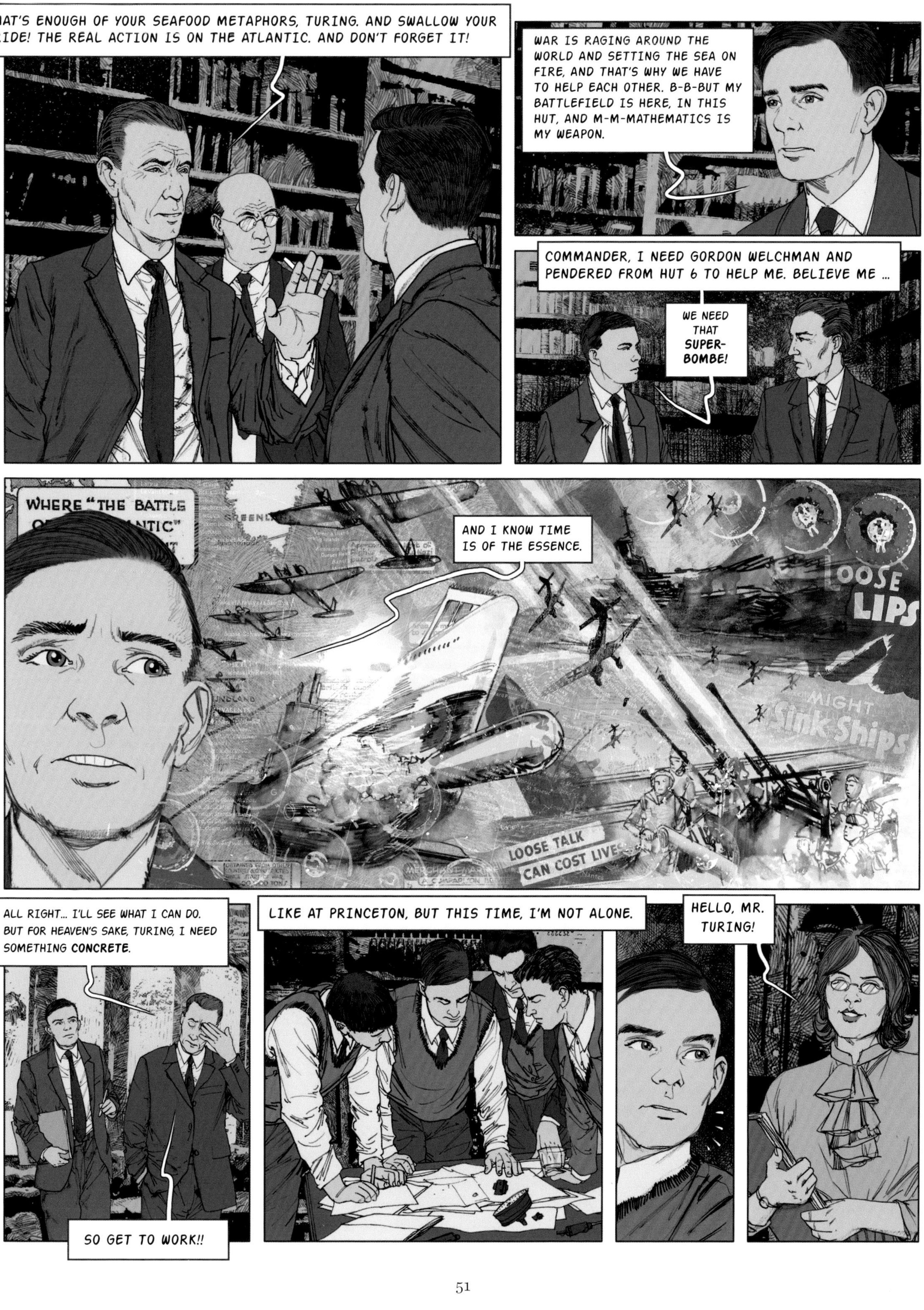
THAT'S ENOUGH OF YOUR SEAFOOD METAPHORS, TURING. AND SWALLOW YOUR PRIDE! THE REAL ACTION IS ON THE ATLANTIC. AND DON'T FORGET IT!
WAR IS RAGING AROUND THE WORLD AND SETTING THE SEA ON FIRE, AND THAT'S WHY WE HAVE TO HELP EACH OTHER. B-B-BUT MY BATTLEFIELD IS HERE, IN THIS HUT, AND M-M-MATHEMATICS IS MY WEAPON.
COMMANDER, I NEED GORDON WELCHMAN AND PENDERED FROM HUT 6 TO HELP ME. BELIEVE ME ...
WE NEED THAT **SUPER-BOMBE!**
AND I KNOW TIME IS OF THE ESSENCE.
LIPS
MIGHT
Sink Ships
LOOSE TALK
ALL RIGHT... I'LL SEE WHAT I CAN DO. BUT FOR HEAVEN'S SAKE, TURING, I NEED SOMETHING **CONCRETE**.
SO GET TO WORK!!
LIKE AT PRINCETON, BUT THIS TIME, I'M NOT ALONE.
HELLO, MR. TURING!

MR. WELCHMAN OFFERED ME A SPOT. I TOLD YOU I HAVE A GIFT FOR MATH ...

AN INTELLECTUAL, AT LAST! THAT WILL MAKE A NICE CHANGE. LET'S GET TO WORK!

THERE'S SOMETHING ELSE. I CAN MAKE ADVANCEMENTS IN CRYPTOGRAPHY. IT'S EASY TO TRANSFORM LETTERS INTO NUMBERS. BUT HOW DO I FIND THE INITIAL KEY?

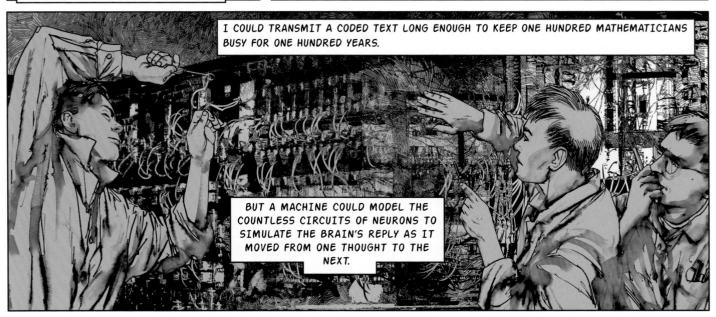

I COULD TRANSMIT A CODED TEXT LONG ENOUGH TO KEEP ONE HUNDRED MATHEMATICIANS BUSY FOR ONE HUNDRED YEARS.

BUT A MACHINE COULD MODEL THE COUNTLESS CIRCUITS OF NEURONS TO SIMULATE THE BRAIN'S REPLY AS IT MOVED FROM ONE THOUGHT TO THE NEXT.

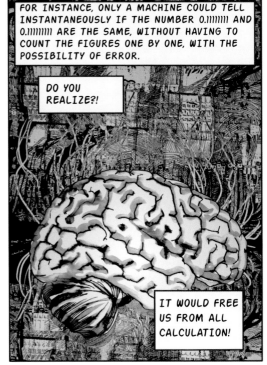

FOR INSTANCE, ONLY A MACHINE COULD TELL INSTANTANEOUSLY IF THE NUMBER 0.111111111 AND 0.111111111 ARE THE SAME, WITHOUT HAVING TO COUNT THE FIGURES ONE BY ONE, WITH THE POSSIBILITY OF ERROR.

DO YOU REALIZE?!

IT WOULD FREE US FROM ALL CALCULATION!

Dear Mother, I could send my work to His Majesty's government in exchange for a handsome sum, but I doubt that would be moral. What do you think?

For you, Christopher ... to beat Enigma, I will create my machine.

Our machine!

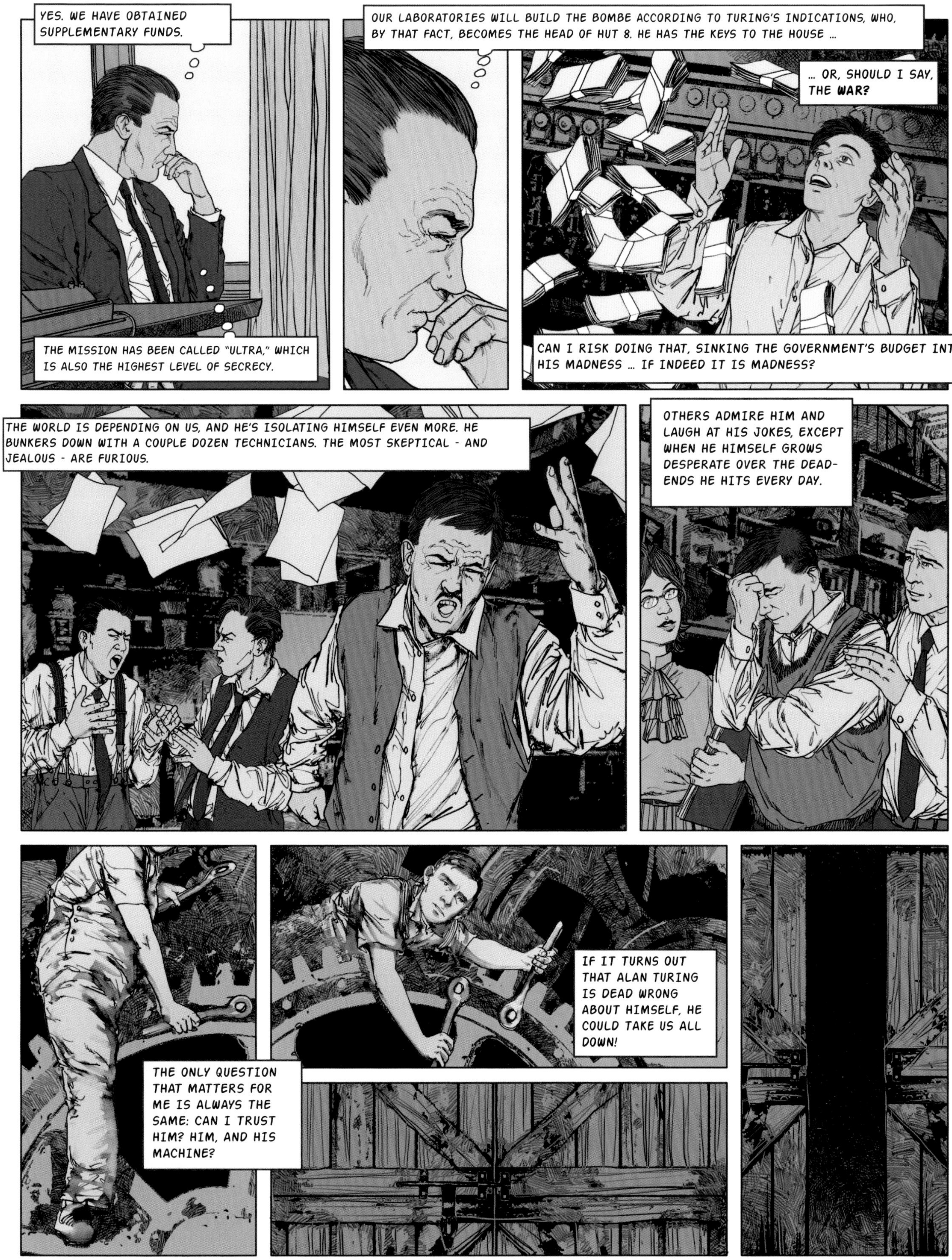
YES. WE HAVE OBTAINED SUPPLEMENTARY FUNDS.
THE MISSION HAS BEEN CALLED "ULTRA," WHICH IS ALSO THE HIGHEST LEVEL OF SECRECY.
OUR LABORATORIES WILL BUILD THE BOMBE ACCORDING TO TURING'S INDICATIONS, WHO, BY THAT FACT, BECOMES THE HEAD OF HUT 8. HE HAS THE KEYS TO THE HOUSE ...
... OR, SHOULD I SAY, THE WAR?
CAN I RISK DOING THAT, SINKING THE GOVERNMENT'S BUDGET INTO HIS MADNESS ... IF INDEED IT IS MADNESS?
THE WORLD IS DEPENDING ON US, AND HE'S ISOLATING HIMSELF EVEN MORE. HE BUNKERS DOWN WITH A COUPLE DOZEN TECHNICIANS. THE MOST SKEPTICAL - AND JEALOUS - ARE FURIOUS.
OTHERS ADMIRE HIM AND LAUGH AT HIS JOKES, EXCEPT WHEN HE HIMSELF GROWS DESPERATE OVER THE DEAD-ENDS HE HITS EVERY DAY.
THE ONLY QUESTION THAT MATTERS FOR ME IS ALWAYS THE SAME: CAN I TRUST HIM? HIM, AND HIS MACHINE?
IF IT TURNS OUT THAT ALAN TURING IS DEAD WRONG ABOUT HIMSELF, HE COULD TAKE US ALL DOWN!

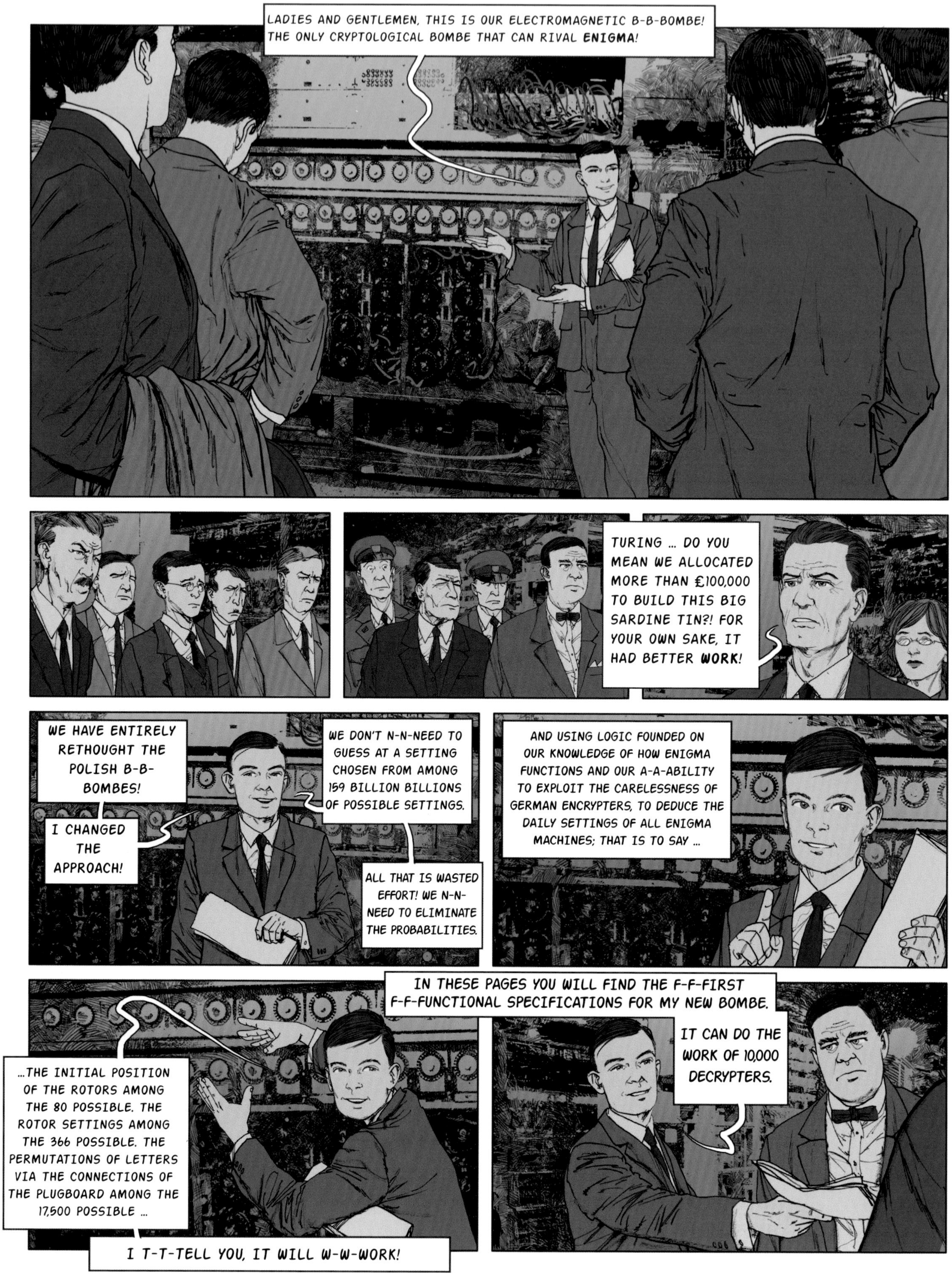
LADIES AND GENTLEMEN, THIS IS OUR ELECTROMAGNETIC B-B-BOMBE! THE ONLY CRYPTOLOGICAL BOMBE THAT CAN RIVAL **ENIGMA**!
TURING ... DO YOU MEAN WE ALLOCATED MORE THAN £100,000 TO BUILD THIS BIG SARDINE TIN?! FOR YOUR OWN SAKE, IT HAD BETTER **WORK**!
WE HAVE ENTIRELY RETHOUGHT THE POLISH B-B-BOMBES!
I CHANGED THE APPROACH!
WE DON'T N-N-NEED TO GUESS AT A SETTING CHOSEN FROM AMONG 159 BILLION BILLIONS OF POSSIBLE SETTINGS.
ALL THAT IS WASTED EFFORT! WE N-N-NEED TO ELIMINATE THE PROBABILITIES.
AND USING LOGIC FOUNDED ON OUR KNOWLEDGE OF HOW ENIGMA FUNCTIONS AND OUR A-A-ABILITY TO EXPLOIT THE CARELESSNESS OF GERMAN ENCRYPTERS, TO DEDUCE THE DAILY SETTINGS OF ALL ENIGMA MACHINES; THAT IS TO SAY ...
...THE INITIAL POSITION OF THE ROTORS AMONG THE 80 POSSIBLE. THE ROTOR SETTINGS AMONG THE 366 POSSIBLE. THE PERMUTATIONS OF LETTERS VIA THE CONNECTIONS OF THE PLUGBOARD AMONG THE 17,500 POSSIBLE ...
I T-T-TELL YOU, IT WILL W-W-WORK!
IN THESE PAGES YOU WILL FIND THE F-F-FIRST F-F-FUNCTIONAL SPECIFICATIONS FOR MY NEW BOMBE.
IT CAN DO THE WORK OF 10,000 DECRYPTERS.

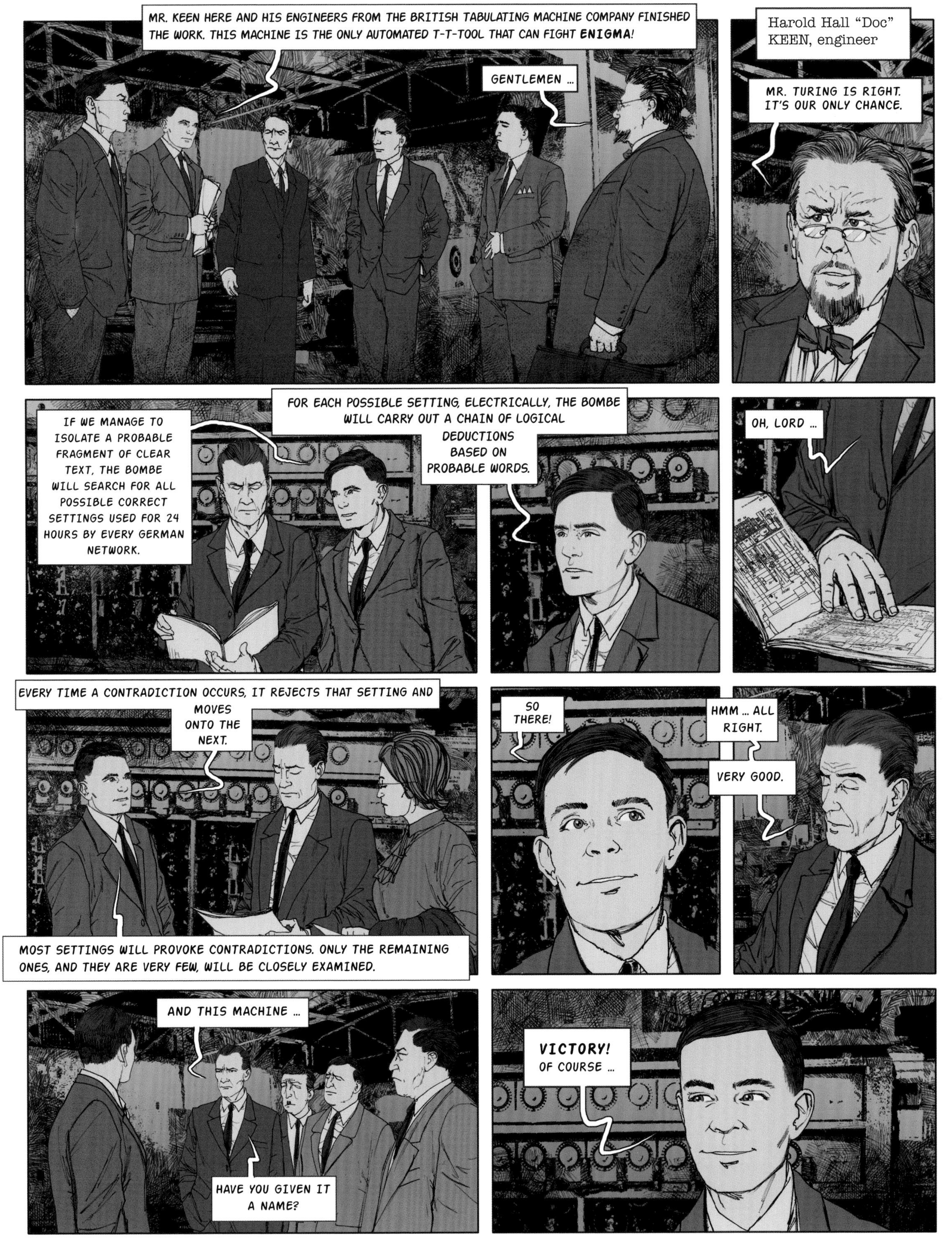
MR. KEEN HERE AND HIS ENGINEERS FROM THE BRITISH TABULATING MACHINE COMPANY FINISHED THE WORK. THIS MACHINE IS THE ONLY AUTOMATED T-T-TOOL THAT CAN FIGHT **ENIGMA**!
GENTLEMEN ...
Harold Hall "Doc" KEEN, engineer
MR. TURING IS RIGHT. IT'S OUR ONLY CHANCE.
IF WE MANAGE TO ISOLATE A PROBABLE FRAGMENT OF CLEAR TEXT, THE BOMBE WILL SEARCH FOR ALL POSSIBLE CORRECT SETTINGS USED FOR 24 HOURS BY EVERY GERMAN NETWORK.
FOR EACH POSSIBLE SETTING, ELECTRICALLY, THE BOMBE WILL CARRY OUT A CHAIN OF LOGICAL DEDUCTIONS BASED ON PROBABLE WORDS.
OH, LORD ...
EVERY TIME A CONTRADICTION OCCURS, IT REJECTS THAT SETTING AND MOVES ONTO THE NEXT.
MOST SETTINGS WILL PROVOKE CONTRADICTIONS. ONLY THE REMAINING ONES, AND THEY ARE VERY FEW, WILL BE CLOSELY EXAMINED.
SO THERE!
HMM ... ALL RIGHT.
VERY GOOD.
AND THIS MACHINE ...
HAVE YOU GIVEN IT A NAME?
VICTORY! OF COURSE ...

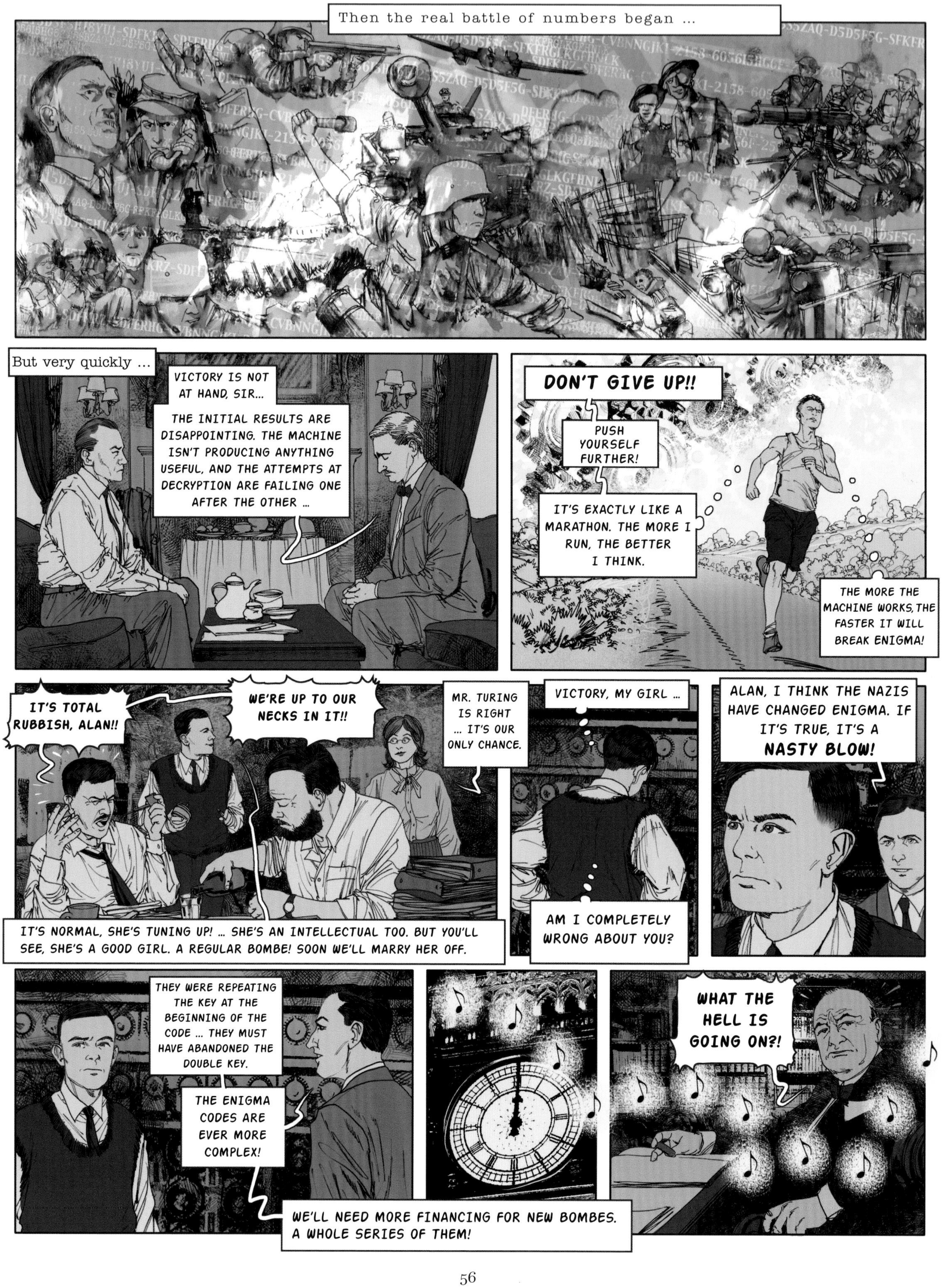
Then the real battle of numbers began ...
But very quickly ...
VICTORY IS NOT AT HAND, SIR...
THE INITIAL RESULTS ARE DISAPPOINTING. THE MACHINE ISN'T PRODUCING ANYTHING USEFUL, AND THE ATTEMPTS AT DECRYPTION ARE FAILING ONE AFTER THE OTHER ...
DON'T GIVE UP!!
PUSH YOURSELF FURTHER!
IT'S EXACTLY LIKE A MARATHON. THE MORE I RUN, THE BETTER I THINK.
THE MORE THE MACHINE WORKS, THE FASTER IT WILL BREAK ENIGMA!
IT'S TOTAL RUBBISH, ALAN!!
WE'RE UP TO OUR NECKS IN IT!!
MR. TURING IS RIGHT ... IT'S OUR ONLY CHANCE.
IT'S NORMAL, SHE'S TUNING UP! ... SHE'S AN INTELLECTUAL TOO. BUT YOU'LL SEE, SHE'S A GOOD GIRL. A REGULAR BOMBE! SOON WE'LL MARRY HER OFF.
VICTORY, MY GIRL ...
AM I COMPLETELY WRONG ABOUT YOU?
ALAN, I THINK THE NAZIS HAVE CHANGED ENIGMA. IF IT'S TRUE, IT'S A NASTY BLOW!
THEY WERE REPEATING THE KEY AT THE BEGINNING OF THE CODE ... THEY MUST HAVE ABANDONED THE DOUBLE KEY.
THE ENIGMA CODES ARE EVER MORE COMPLEX!
WE'LL NEED MORE FINANCING FOR NEW BOMBES. A WHOLE SERIES OF THEM!
WHAT THE HELL IS GOING ON?!

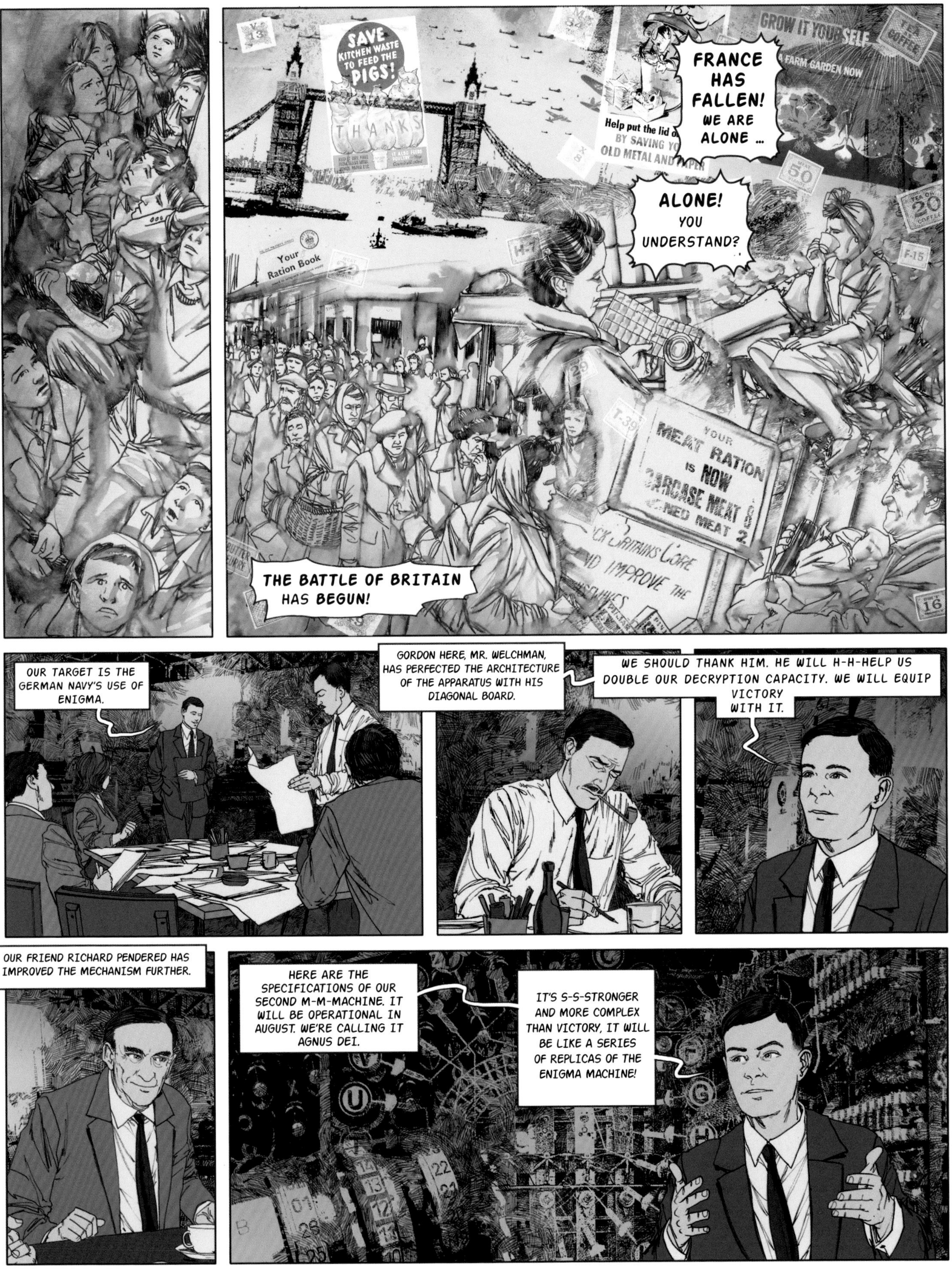
SAVE KITCHEN WASTE TO FEED THE PIGS!
THANKS
GROW IT YOURSELF
A FARM GARDEN NOW
FRANCE HAS FALLEN! WE ARE ALONE ...
ALONE! YOU UNDERSTAND?
Your Ration Book
YOUR MEAT RATION IS NOW
THE BATTLE OF BRITAIN HAS BEGUN!
OUR TARGET IS THE GERMAN NAVY'S USE OF ENIGMA.
GORDON HERE, MR. WELCHMAN, HAS PERFECTED THE ARCHITECTURE OF THE APPARATUS WITH HIS DIAGONAL BOARD.
WE SHOULD THANK HIM. HE WILL H-H-HELP US DOUBLE OUR DECRYPTION CAPACITY. WE WILL EQUIP VICTORY WITH IT.
OUR FRIEND RICHARD PENDERED HAS IMPROVED THE MECHANISM FURTHER.
HERE ARE THE SPECIFICATIONS OF OUR SECOND M-M-MACHINE. IT WILL BE OPERATIONAL IN AUGUST. WE'RE CALLING IT AGNUS DEI.
IT'S S-S-STRONGER AND MORE COMPLEX THAN VICTORY, IT WILL BE LIKE A SERIES OF REPLICAS OF THE ENIGMA MACHINE!

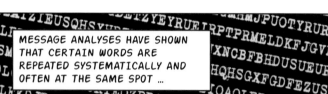

MESSAGE ANALYSES HAVE SHOWN THAT CERTAIN WORDS ARE REPEATED SYSTEMATICALLY AND OFTEN AT THE SAME SPOT ...
RECURRENCES IN THE MESSAGES ARE THE REAL KEY! OUR WORK IS TO TRY ALL COMBINATIONS, AND FIND THOSE THAT TRANSFORM THOSE WORDS INTO LINES OF CHARACTERS WE CAN LOCATE. THAT'S HOW THE POLES WERE WORKING.
A "CRIB," A PLAUSIBLE CORRESPONDENCE BETWEEN PLAINTEXT AND CIPHERTEXT, IS SIMULATED BY THE MACHINE THAT TRIES A KEY. IF MORE THAN ONE SOLUTION IS PRODUCED, THE KEY IS WRONG.
IF ALL CONNECTIONS CORRESPOND AND RESULT IN ONLY ONE ANSWER, THE BOMBE STOPS AND THE PLAUSIBLE KEY IS HAND-TESTED.
IF ENIGMA WAS USED CORRECTLY, WE WOULD HAVE TOO MANY COMBINATIONS TO TEST.
FORTUNATELY, NAZI ENCRYPTERS MAKE MISTAKES THAT REDUCE THE NUMBER OF PLAUSIBLE KEYS.
WE MUST SEARCH FOR CYCLES OF LETTERS. FROM ONE CYCLE, WE CAN DEDUCE THE CHARACTERISTIC FEATURES OF THE ROTORS: WE TRY ALL THE POSSIBILITIES TO FIND THE ONE THAT PRODUCES THE FEATURE WE WOULD EXPECT.
abcdefghijklmnopq
JYCQRPNYDEMCJMRSR
SPRUCHNUMMERXEINS
OUR BOMBES THAT REPRODUCE THE ENIGMA ROTORS WILL ALLOW US TO TRY, IN PARALLEL FASHION ...
UP TO 20,000 CONFIGURATIONS A SECOND.
ONCE WE DETERMINE THE POSITION OF THE ROTORS, IT'S POSSIBLE TO DECRYPT PART OF THE MESSAGE AND DEDUCE THE TRANSPOSITIONS.
I TOLD YOU, IT WILL WORK.
IT'S MATHEMATICS!

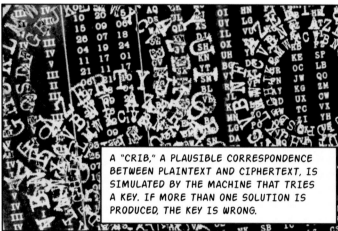

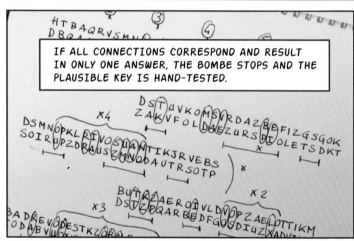

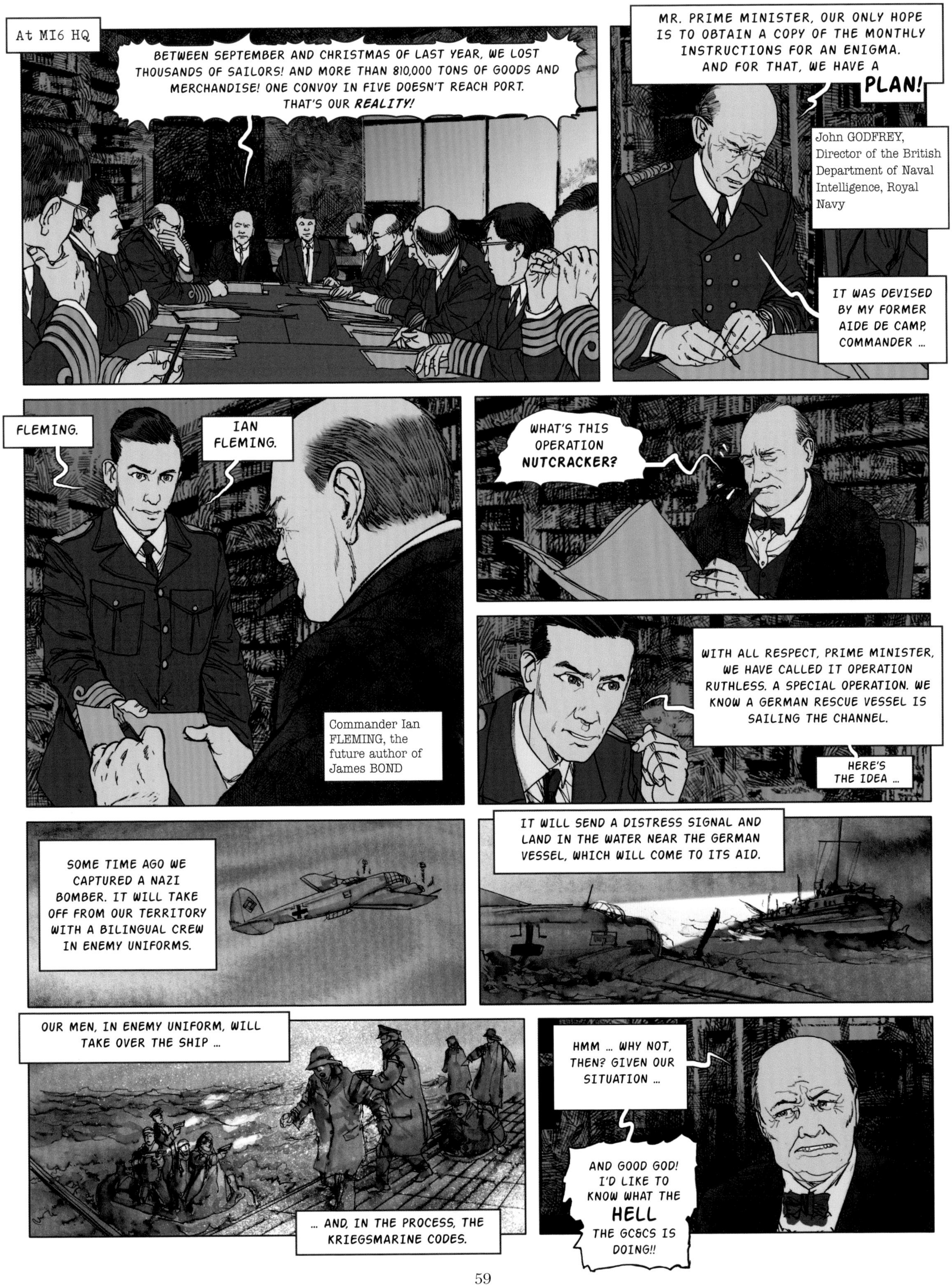
At MI6 HQ
BETWEEN SEPTEMBER AND CHRISTMAS OF LAST YEAR, WE LOST THOUSANDS OF SAILORS! AND MORE THAN 810,000 TONS OF GOODS AND MERCHANDISE! ONE CONVOY IN FIVE DOESN'T REACH PORT. THAT'S OUR REALITY!
MR. PRIME MINISTER, OUR ONLY HOPE IS TO OBTAIN A COPY OF THE MONTHLY INSTRUCTIONS FOR AN ENIGMA. AND FOR THAT, WE HAVE A PLAN!
John GODFREY, Director of the British Department of Naval Intelligence, Royal Navy
IT WAS DEVISED BY MY FORMER AIDE DE CAMP, COMMANDER ...
FLEMING.
IAN FLEMING.
Commander Ian FLEMING, the future author of James BOND
WHAT'S THIS OPERATION NUTCRACKER?
WITH ALL RESPECT, PRIME MINISTER, WE HAVE CALLED IT OPERATION RUTHLESS. A SPECIAL OPERATION. WE KNOW A GERMAN RESCUE VESSEL IS SAILING THE CHANNEL.
HERE'S THE IDEA ...
SOME TIME AGO WE CAPTURED A NAZI BOMBER. IT WILL TAKE OFF FROM OUR TERRITORY WITH A BILINGUAL CREW IN ENEMY UNIFORMS.
IT WILL SEND A DISTRESS SIGNAL AND LAND IN THE WATER NEAR THE GERMAN VESSEL, WHICH WILL COME TO ITS AID.
OUR MEN, IN ENEMY UNIFORM, WILL TAKE OVER THE SHIP ...
... AND, IN THE PROCESS, THE KRIEGSMARINE CODES.
HMM ... WHY NOT, THEN? GIVEN OUR SITUATION ...
AND GOOD GOD! I'D LIKE TO KNOW WHAT THE HELL THE GC&CS IS DOING!!

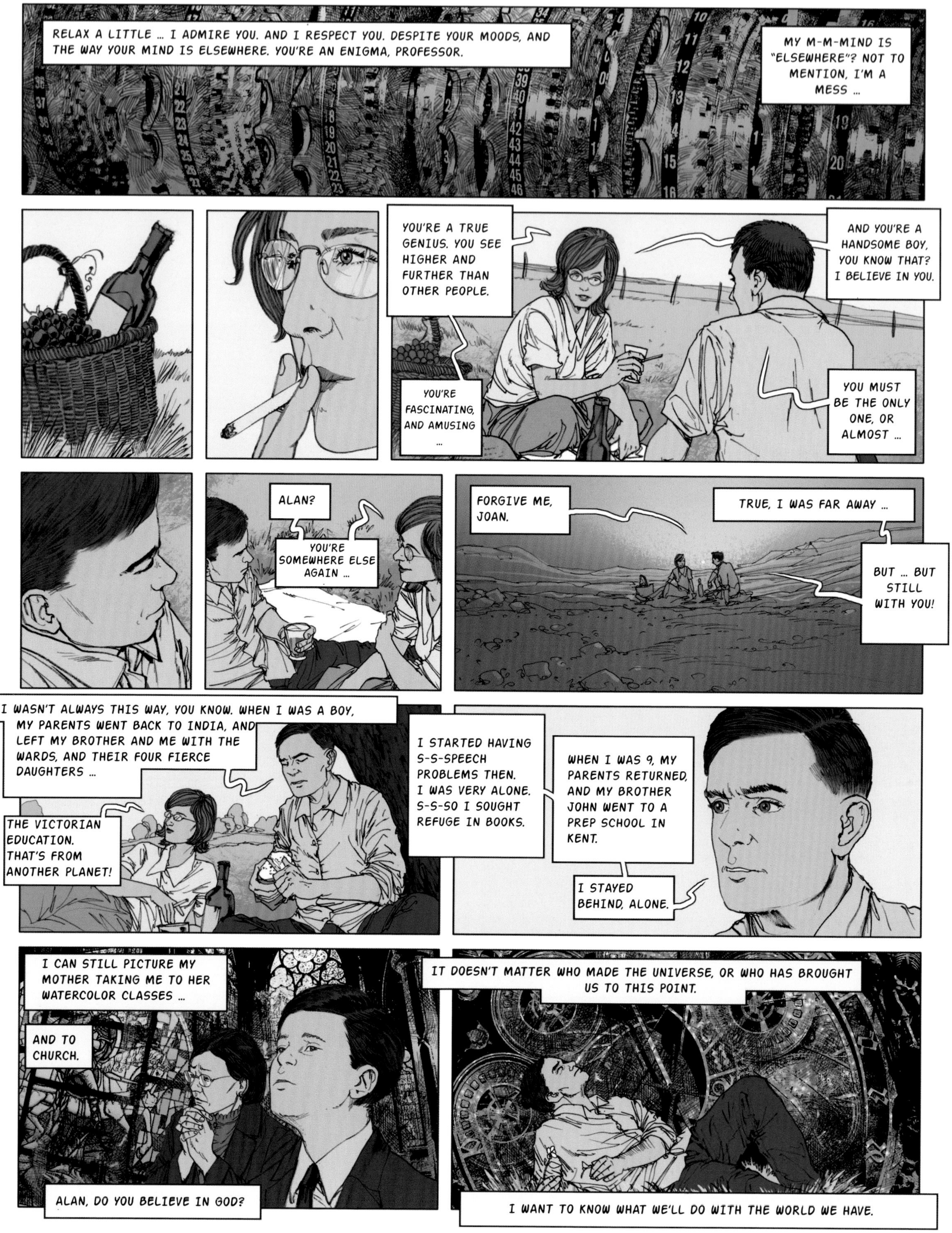
RELAX A LITTLE ... I ADMIRE YOU. AND I RESPECT YOU. DESPITE YOUR MOODS, AND THE WAY YOUR MIND IS ELSEWHERE. YOU'RE AN ENIGMA, PROFESSOR.
MY M-M-MIND IS "ELSEWHERE"? NOT TO MENTION, I'M A MESS ...
YOU'RE A TRUE GENIUS. YOU SEE HIGHER AND FURTHER THAN OTHER PEOPLE.
YOU'RE FASCINATING, AND AMUSING ...
AND YOU'RE A HANDSOME BOY, YOU KNOW THAT? I BELIEVE IN YOU.
YOU MUST BE THE ONLY ONE, OR ALMOST ...
ALAN?
YOU'RE SOMEWHERE ELSE AGAIN ...
FORGIVE ME, JOAN.
TRUE, I WAS FAR AWAY ...
BUT ... BUT STILL WITH YOU!
I WASN'T ALWAYS THIS WAY, YOU KNOW. WHEN I WAS A BOY,
MY PARENTS WENT BACK TO INDIA, AND LEFT MY BROTHER AND ME WITH THE WARDS, AND THEIR FOUR FIERCE DAUGHTERS ...
THE VICTORIAN EDUCATION. THAT'S FROM ANOTHER PLANET!
I STARTED HAVING S-S-SPEECH PROBLEMS THEN. I WAS VERY ALONE. S-S-SO I SOUGHT REFUGE IN BOOKS.
WHEN I WAS 9, MY PARENTS RETURNED, AND MY BROTHER JOHN WENT TO A PREP SCHOOL IN KENT.
I STAYED BEHIND, ALONE.
I CAN STILL PICTURE MY MOTHER TAKING ME TO HER WATERCOLOR CLASSES ...
AND TO CHURCH.
ALAN, DO YOU BELIEVE IN GOD?
IT DOESN'T MATTER WHO MADE THE UNIVERSE, OR WHO HAS BROUGHT US TO THIS POINT.
I WANT TO KNOW WHAT WE'LL DO WITH THE WORLD WE HAVE.

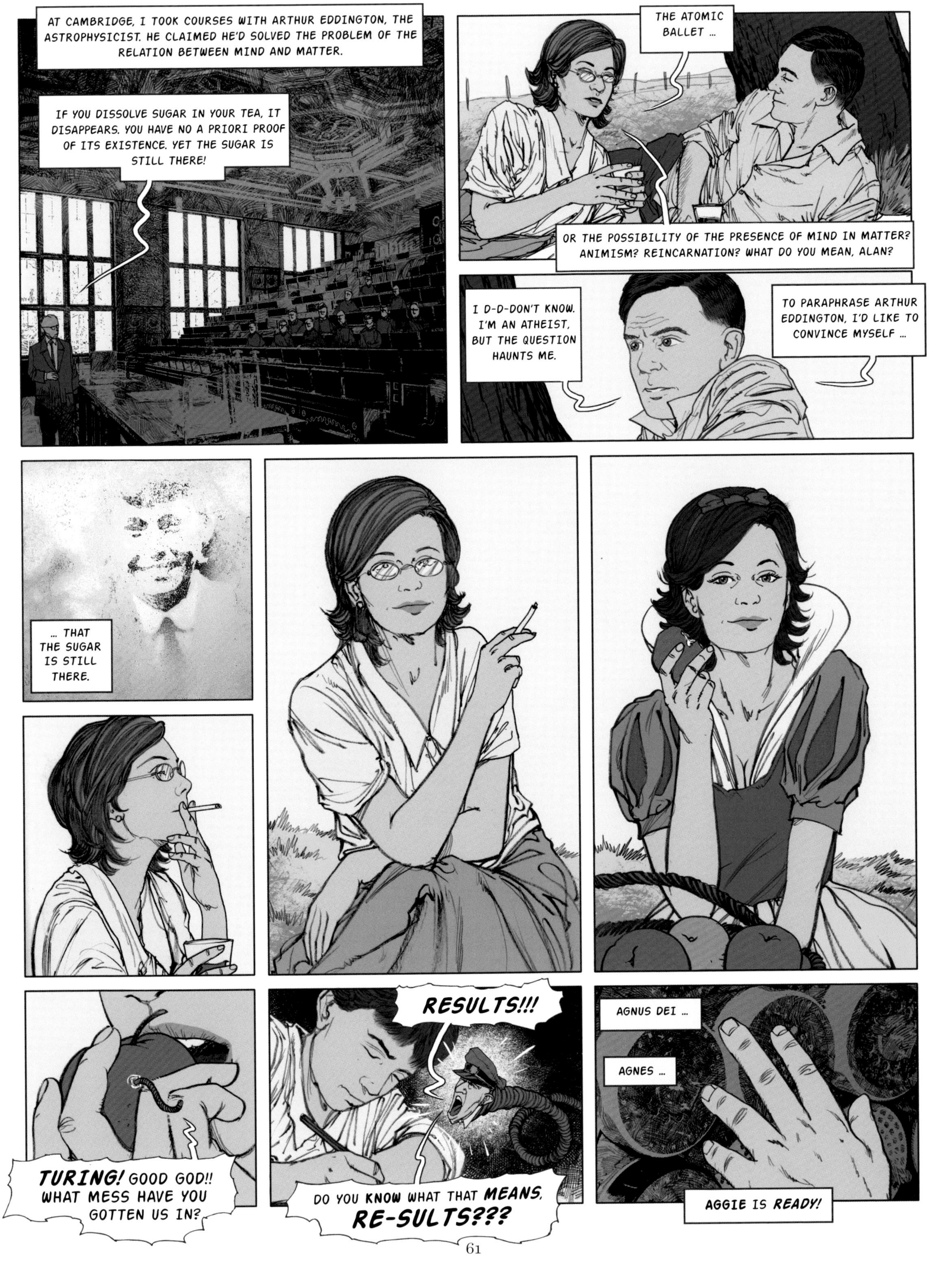
AT CAMBRIDGE, I TOOK COURSES WITH ARTHUR EDDINGTON, THE ASTROPHYSICIST. HE CLAIMED HE'D SOLVED THE PROBLEM OF THE RELATION BETWEEN MIND AND MATTER.
IF YOU DISSOLVE SUGAR IN YOUR TEA, IT DISAPPEARS. YOU HAVE NO A PRIORI PROOF OF ITS EXISTENCE. YET THE SUGAR IS STILL THERE!
THE ATOMIC BALLET ...
OR THE POSSIBILITY OF THE PRESENCE OF MIND IN MATTER? ANIMISM? REINCARNATION? WHAT DO YOU MEAN, ALAN?
I D-D-DON'T KNOW. I'M AN ATHEIST, BUT THE QUESTION HAUNTS ME.
TO PARAPHRASE ARTHUR EDDINGTON, I'D LIKE TO CONVINCE MYSELF ...
... THAT THE SUGAR IS STILL THERE.
TURING! GOOD GOD!! WHAT MESS HAVE YOU GOTTEN US IN?
RESULTS!!!
DO YOU KNOW WHAT THAT MEANS, RE-SULTS???
AGNUS DEI ...
AGNES ...
AGGIE IS READY!

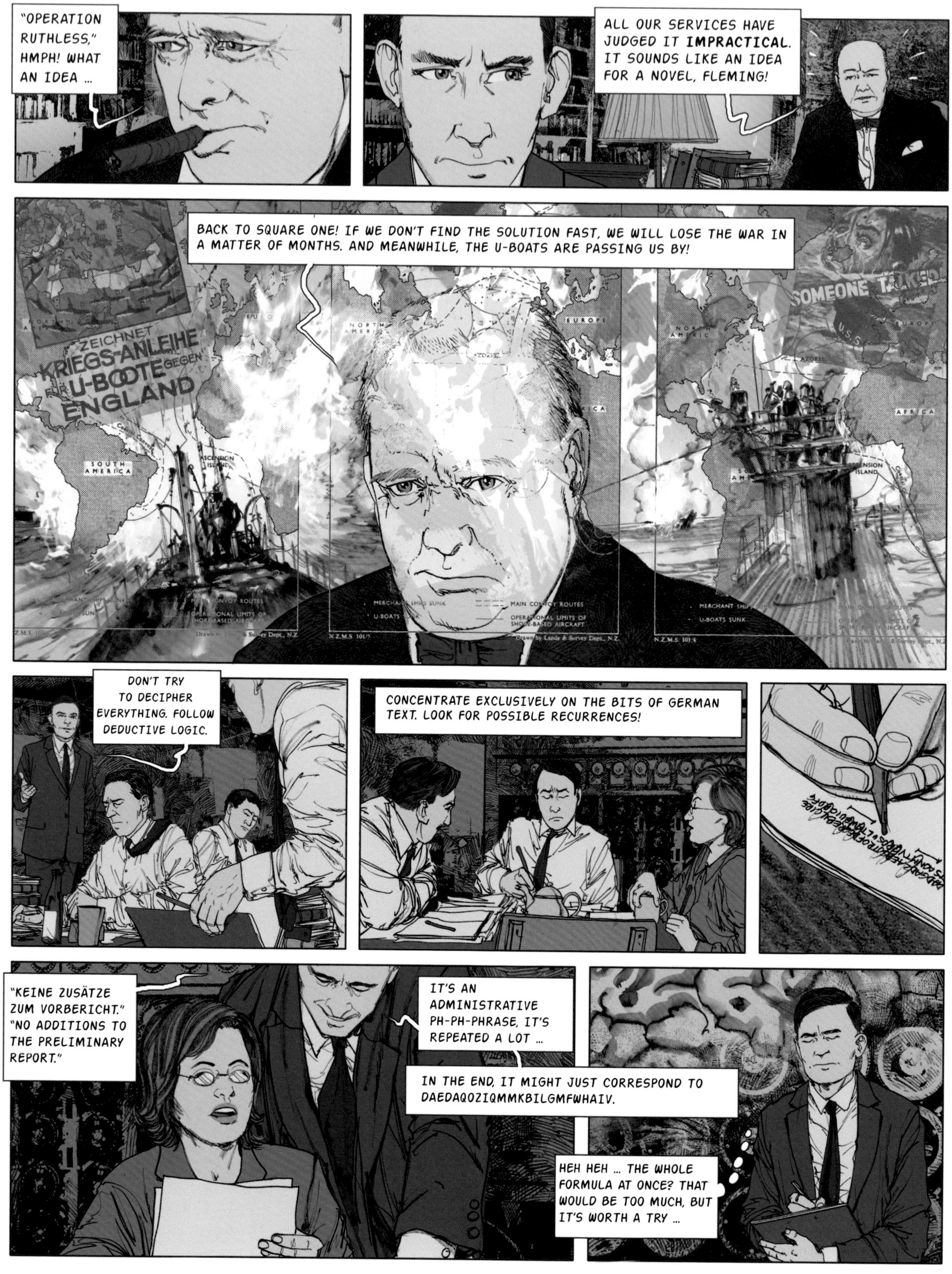
"OPERATION RUTHLESS," HMPH! WHAT AN IDEA ...
ALL OUR SERVICES HAVE JUDGED IT **IMPRACTICAL**. IT SOUNDS LIKE AN IDEA FOR A NOVEL, FLEMING!
BACK TO SQUARE ONE! IF WE DON'T FIND THE SOLUTION FAST, WE WILL LOSE THE WAR IN A MATTER OF MONTHS. AND MEANWHILE, THE U-BOATS ARE PASSING US BY!
ZEICHNET KRIEGS-ANLEIHE GEGEN ENGLAND FÜR U-BOOTE
SOMEONE TALKED!
NORTH AMERICA
EUROPE
AFRICA
SOUTH AMERICA
ASCENSION ISLAND
MERCHANT SHIPS SUNK
U-BOATS SUNK
MAIN CONVOY ROUTES
OPERATIONAL LIMITS OF SHORE-BASED AIRCRAFT
N.Z.M.S. 101/7
Drawn by Lands & Survey Dept., N.Z.
DON'T TRY TO DECIPHER EVERYTHING. FOLLOW DEDUCTIVE LOGIC.
CONCENTRATE EXCLUSIVELY ON THE BITS OF GERMAN TEXT. LOOK FOR POSSIBLE RECURRENCES!
"KEINE ZUSÄTZE ZUM VORBERICHT." "NO ADDITIONS TO THE PRELIMINARY REPORT."
IT'S AN ADMINISTRATIVE PH-PH-PHRASE, IT'S REPEATED A LOT ...
IN THE END, IT MIGHT JUST CORRESPOND TO DAEDAQOZIQMMKBILGMFWHAIV.
HEH HEH ... THE WHOLE FORMULA AT ONCE? THAT WOULD BE TOO MUCH, BUT IT'S WORTH A TRY ...

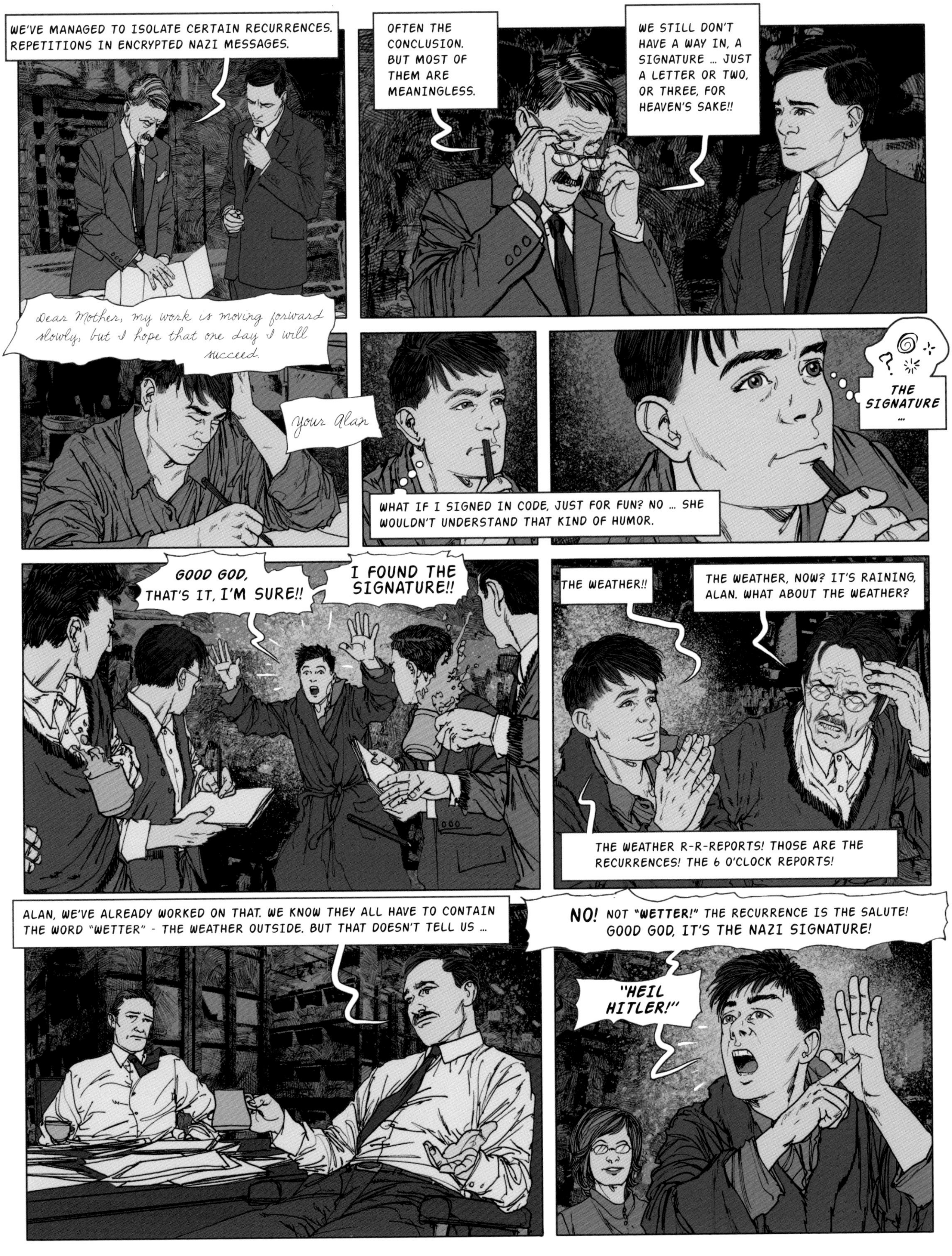
WE'VE MANAGED TO ISOLATE CERTAIN RECURRENCES. REPETITIONS IN ENCRYPTED NAZI MESSAGES.
OFTEN THE CONCLUSION. BUT MOST OF THEM ARE MEANINGLESS.
WE STILL DON'T HAVE A WAY IN, A SIGNATURE ... JUST A LETTER OR TWO, OR THREE, FOR HEAVEN'S SAKE!!
Dear Mother, my work is moving forward slowly, but I hope that one day I will succeed.
Your Alan
WHAT IF I SIGNED IN CODE, JUST FOR FUN? NO ... SHE WOULDN'T UNDERSTAND THAT KIND OF HUMOR.
THE SIGNATURE ...
GOOD GOD, THAT'S IT, I'M SURE!!
I FOUND THE SIGNATURE!!
THE WEATHER!!
THE WEATHER, NOW? IT'S RAINING, ALAN. WHAT ABOUT THE WEATHER?
THE WEATHER R-R-REPORTS! THOSE ARE THE RECURRENCES! THE 6 O'CLOCK REPORTS!
ALAN, WE'VE ALREADY WORKED ON THAT. WE KNOW THEY ALL HAVE TO CONTAIN THE WORD "WETTER" - THE WEATHER OUTSIDE. BUT THAT DOESN'T TELL US ...
NO! NOT "WETTER!" THE RECURRENCE IS THE SALUTE! GOOD GOD, IT'S THE NAZI SIGNATURE!
"HEIL HITLER!"

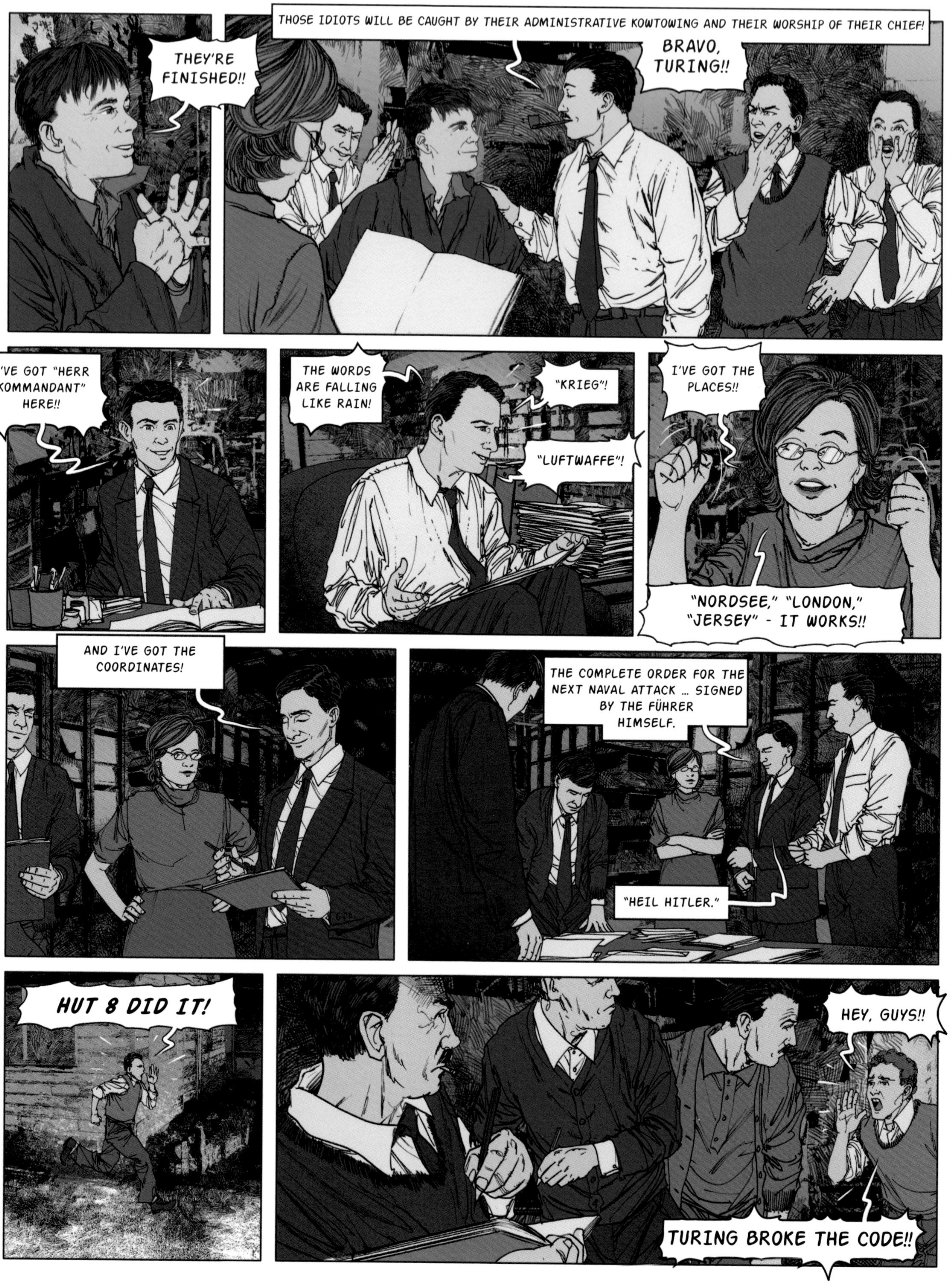
THEY'RE FINISHED!!
THOSE IDIOTS WILL BE CAUGHT BY THEIR ADMINISTRATIVE KOWTOWING AND THEIR WORSHIP OF THEIR CHIEF!
BRAVO, TURING!!
I'VE GOT "HERR KOMMANDANT" HERE!!
THE WORDS ARE FALLING LIKE RAIN!
"KRIEG"!
"LUFTWAFFE"!
I'VE GOT THE PLACES!!
"NORDSEE," "LONDON," "JERSEY" - IT WORKS!!
AND I'VE GOT THE COORDINATES!
THE COMPLETE ORDER FOR THE NEXT NAVAL ATTACK ... SIGNED BY THE FÜHRER HIMSELF.
"HEIL HITLER."
HUT 8 DID IT!
HEY, GUYS!!
TURING BROKE THE CODE!!

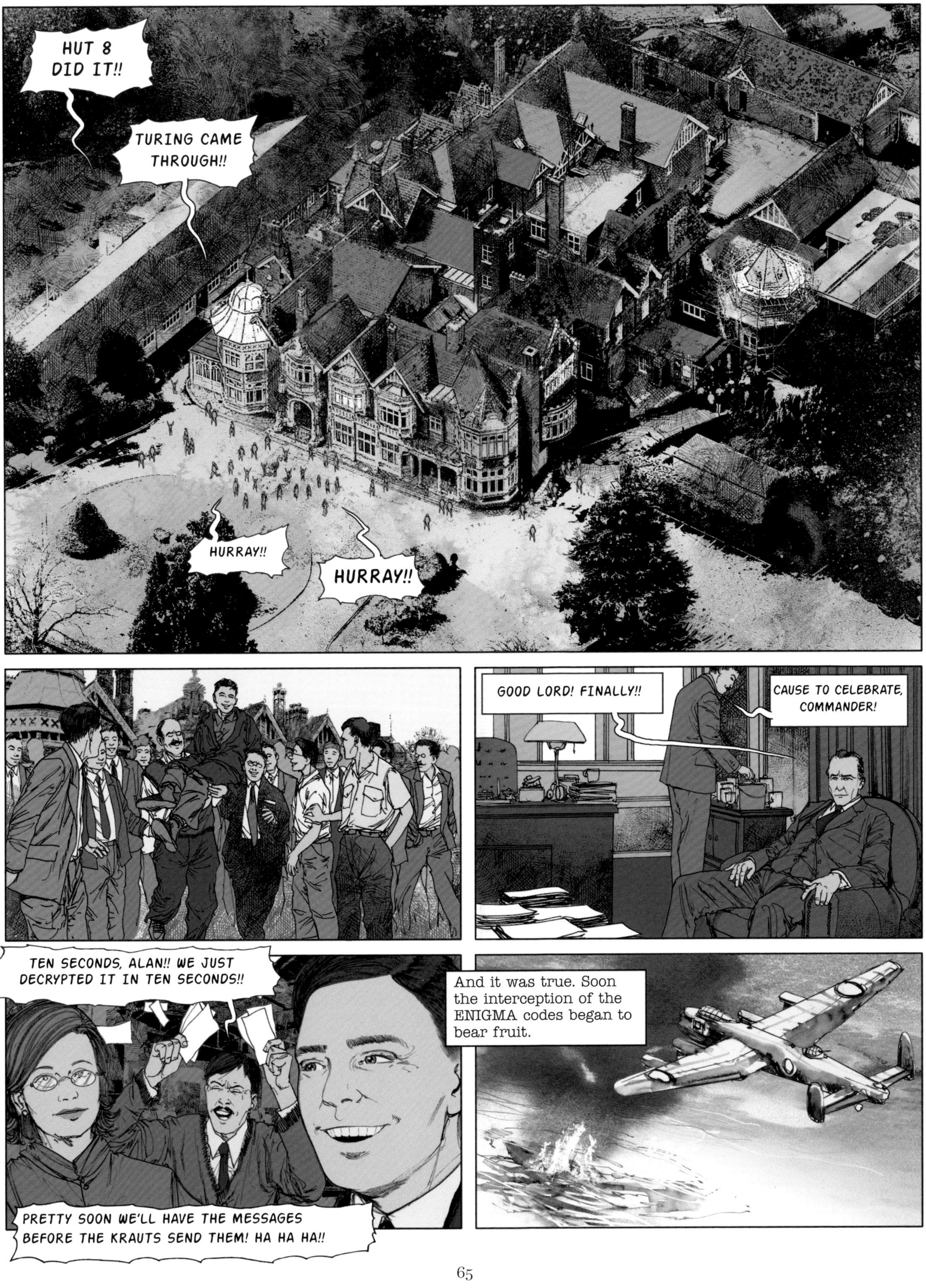
HUT 8 DID IT!!
TURING CAME THROUGH!!
HURRAY!!
HURRAY!!
GOOD LORD! FINALLY!!
CAUSE TO CELEBRATE, COMMANDER!
TEN SECONDS, ALAN!! WE JUST DECRYPTED IT IN TEN SECONDS!!
PRETTY SOON WE'LL HAVE THE MESSAGES BEFORE THE KRAUTS SEND THEM! HA HA HA!!
And it was true. Soon the interception of the ENIGMA codes began to bear fruit.

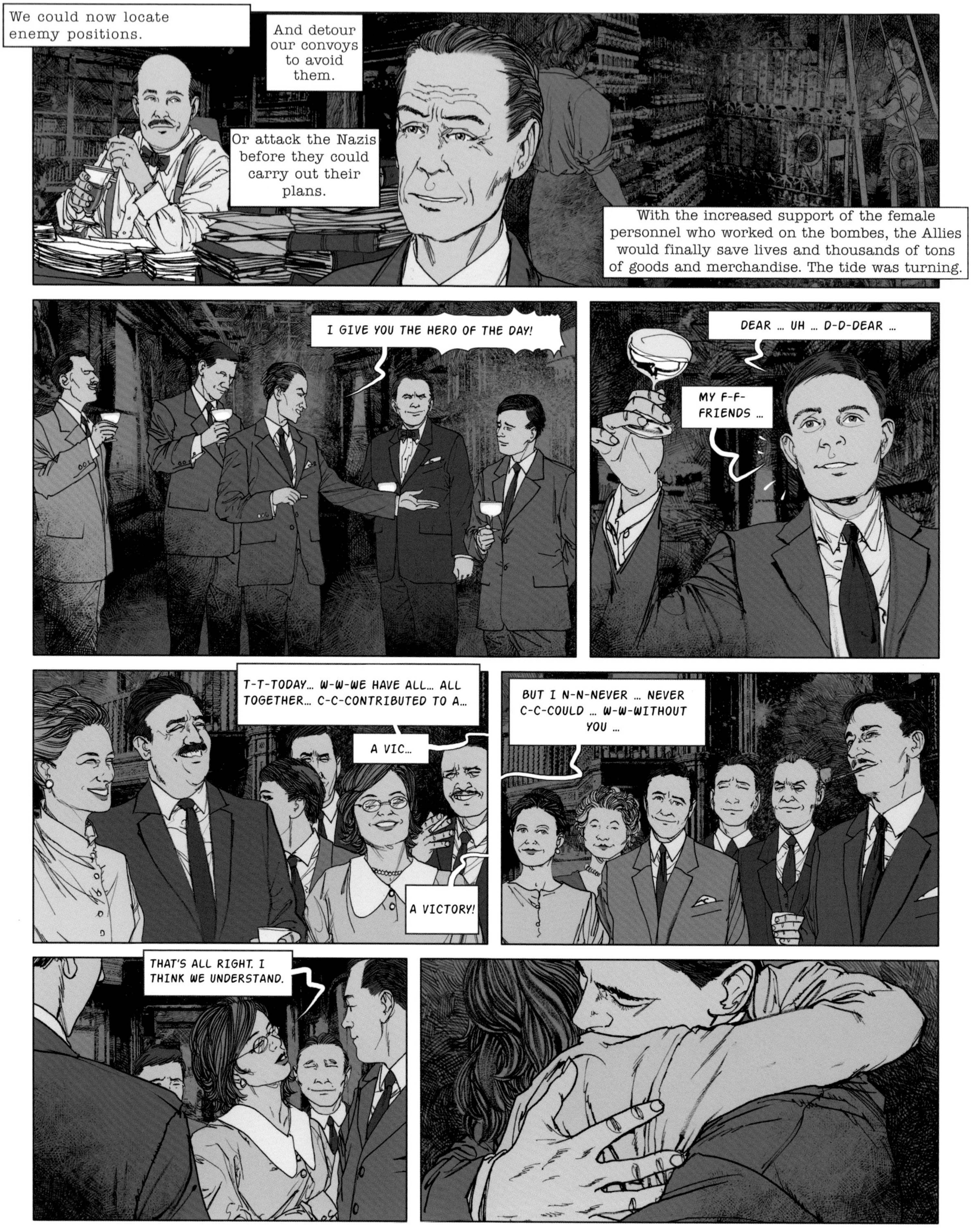
We could now locate enemy positions.
And detour our convoys to avoid them.
Or attack the Nazis before they could carry out their plans.
With the increased support of the female personnel who worked on the bombes, the Allies would finally save lives and thousands of tons of goods and merchandise. The tide was turning.
I GIVE YOU THE HERO OF THE DAY!
DEAR ... UH ... D-D-DEAR ...
MY F-F-FRIENDS ...
T-T-TODAY... W-W-WE HAVE ALL... ALL TOGETHER... C-C-CONTRIBUTED TO A...
A VIC...
A VICTORY!
BUT I N-N-NEVER ... NEVER C-C-COULD ... W-W-WITHOUT YOU ...
THAT'S ALL RIGHT. I THINK WE UNDERSTAND.

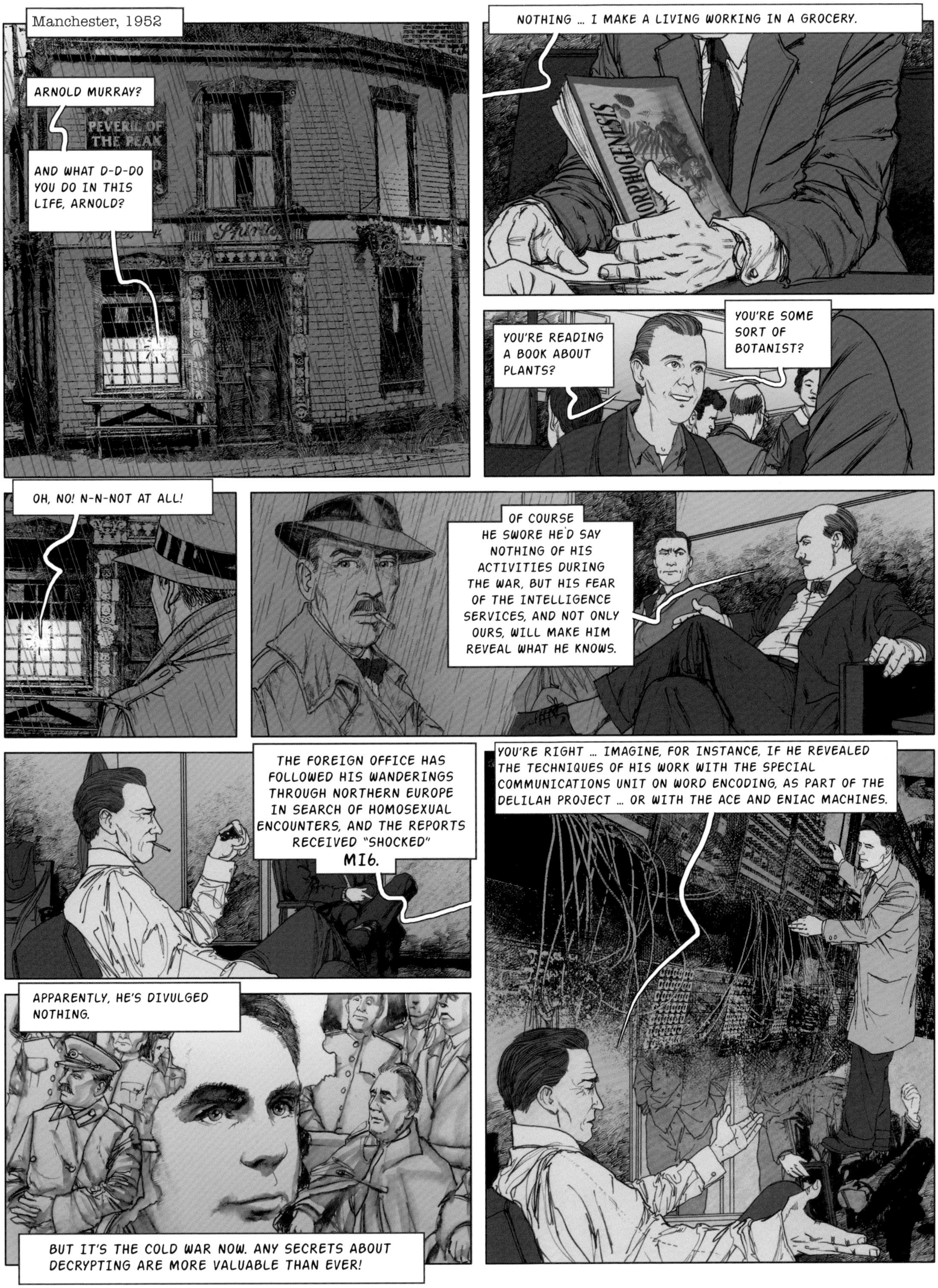
Manchester, 1952
ARNOLD MURRAY?
AND WHAT D-D-DO YOU DO IN THIS LIFE, ARNOLD?
NOTHING ... I MAKE A LIVING WORKING IN A GROCERY.
YOU'RE READING A BOOK ABOUT PLANTS?
YOU'RE SOME SORT OF BOTANIST?
OH, NO! N-N-NOT AT ALL!
OF COURSE HE SWORE HE'D SAY NOTHING OF HIS ACTIVITIES DURING THE WAR, BUT HIS FEAR OF THE INTELLIGENCE SERVICES, AND NOT ONLY OURS, WILL MAKE HIM REVEAL WHAT HE KNOWS.
THE FOREIGN OFFICE HAS FOLLOWED HIS WANDERINGS THROUGH NORTHERN EUROPE IN SEARCH OF HOMOSEXUAL ENCOUNTERS, AND THE REPORTS RECEIVED "SHOCKED" MI6.
YOU'RE RIGHT ... IMAGINE, FOR INSTANCE, IF HE REVEALED THE TECHNIQUES OF HIS WORK WITH THE SPECIAL COMMUNICATIONS UNIT ON WORD ENCODING, AS PART OF THE DELILAH PROJECT ... OR WITH THE ACE AND ENIAC MACHINES.
APPARENTLY, HE'S DIVULGED NOTHING.
BUT IT'S THE COLD WAR NOW. ANY SECRETS ABOUT DECRYPTING ARE MORE VALUABLE THAN EVER!

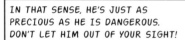

IN THAT SENSE, HE'S JUST AS PRECIOUS AS HE IS DANGEROUS. DON'T LET HIM OUT OF YOUR SIGHT!

I'M RATHER G-G-GIFTED WHEN IT COMES TO MATH, YOU KNOW ...

I'VE JUST BEEN N-N-NAMED TO THE ROYAL SOCIETY! YES, YOUNG MAN ...

I HELPED THE C-C-COUNTRY A LOT DURING THE WAR.

DURING THE WAR?! THAT'S REALLY SOMETHING!

WHAT DID YOU DO? KILL A LOT OF NAZIS? NOT WITH PANSIES, I FIGURE ...

THAT'S A GOOD ONE! NOT FAR FROM THE TRUTH. WITH PANSIES ...

ANYWAY, I C-C-CAN'T TALK ABOUT IT ...

SO LET'S TALK ABOUT THE PRESENT AND THE FUTURE!

SINCE I WAS A BOY, I'VE BEEN F-F-FASCINATED BY MORPHOGENESIS.

THE GROWTH OF ORGANISMS, Y-Y-YOU SEE?

WANT ANOTHER D-D-DRINK?

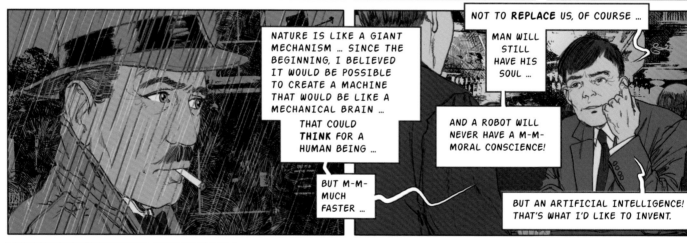

NATURE IS LIKE A GIANT MECHANISM ... SINCE THE BEGINNING, I BELIEVED IT WOULD BE POSSIBLE TO CREATE A MACHINE THAT WOULD BE LIKE A MECHANICAL BRAIN ...

THAT COULD **THINK** FOR A HUMAN BEING ...

BUT M-M-MUCH FASTER ...

NOT TO **REPLACE** US, OF COURSE ...

MAN WILL STILL HAVE HIS SOUL ...

AND A ROBOT WILL NEVER HAVE A M-M-MORAL CONSCIENCE!

BUT AN ARTIFICIAL INTELLIGENCE! THAT'S WHAT I'D LIKE TO INVENT.

WANT ... TO GO FOR A WALK?

BUT SERIOUSLY ... WHAT DID YOU DO DURING THE WAR?

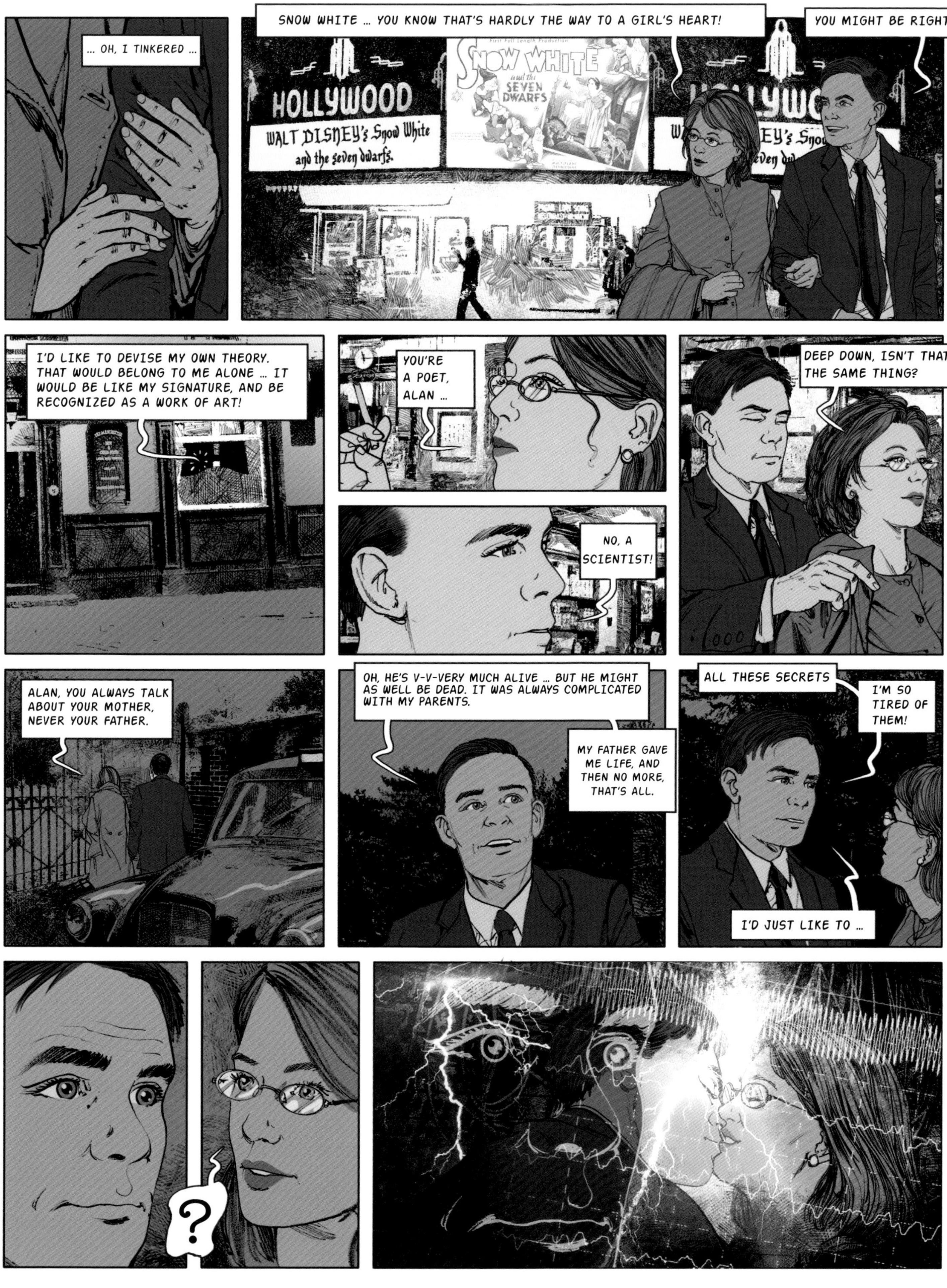
... OH, I TINKERED ...
SNOW WHITE ... YOU KNOW THAT'S HARDLY THE WAY TO A GIRL'S HEART!
YOU MIGHT BE RIGHT!
HOLLYWOOD
WALT DISNEY's Snow White and the seven dwarfs.
SNOW WHITE and the SEVEN DWARFS
I'D LIKE TO DEVISE MY OWN THEORY. THAT WOULD BELONG TO ME ALONE ... IT WOULD BE LIKE MY SIGNATURE, AND BE RECOGNIZED AS A WORK OF ART!
YOU'RE A POET, ALAN ...
NO, A SCIENTIST!
DEEP DOWN, ISN'T THAT THE SAME THING?
ALAN, YOU ALWAYS TALK ABOUT YOUR MOTHER, NEVER YOUR FATHER.
OH, HE'S V-V-VERY MUCH ALIVE ... BUT HE MIGHT AS WELL BE DEAD. IT WAS ALWAYS COMPLICATED WITH MY PARENTS.
MY FATHER GAVE ME LIFE, AND THEN NO MORE, THAT'S ALL.
ALL THESE SECRETS
I'M SO TIRED OF THEM!
I'D JUST LIKE TO ...
?

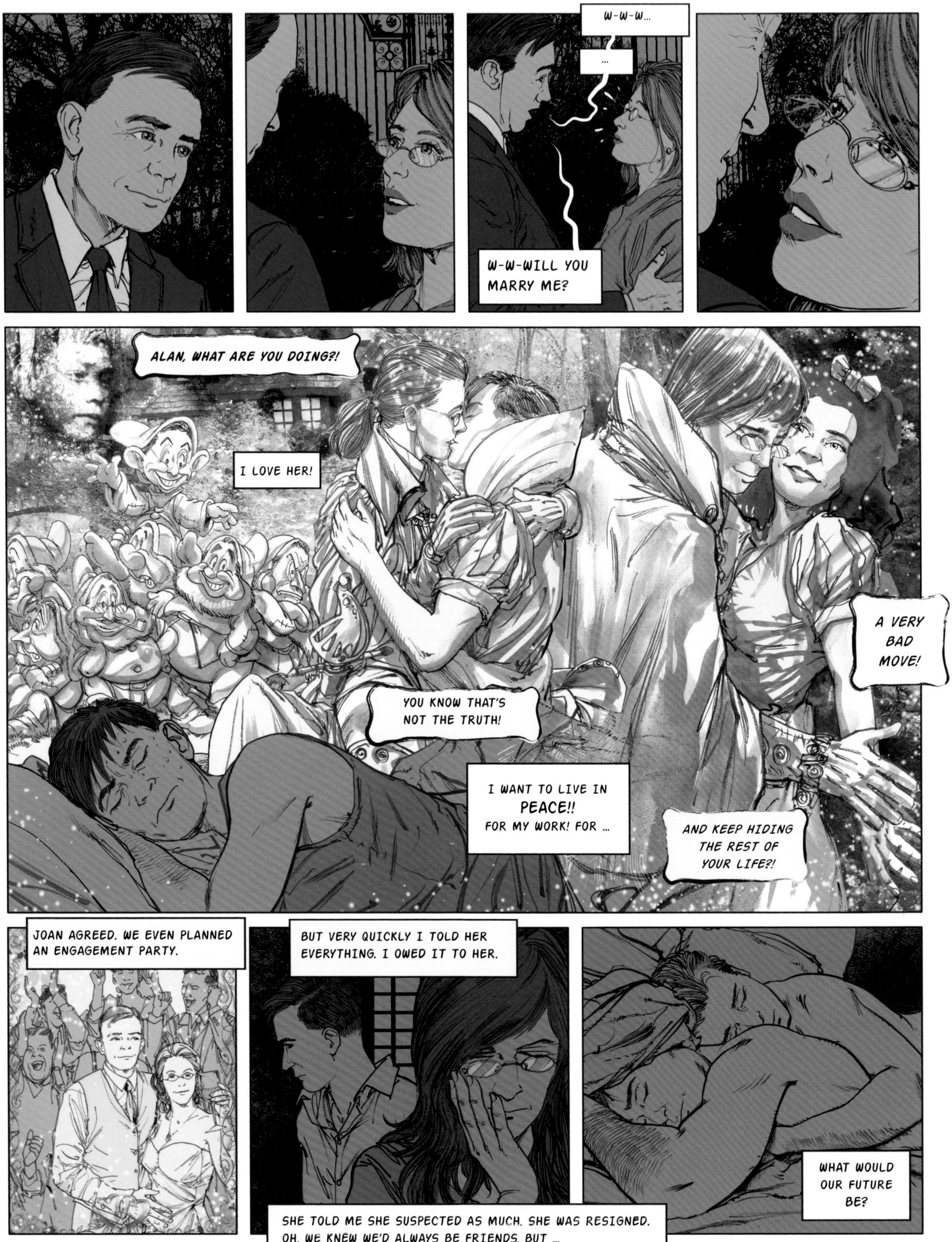
W-W-W…
…
W-W-WILL YOU MARRY ME?
ALAN, WHAT ARE YOU DOING?!
I LOVE HER!
YOU KNOW THAT'S NOT THE TRUTH!
I WANT TO LIVE IN PEACE!! FOR MY WORK! FOR …
A VERY BAD MOVE!
AND KEEP HIDING THE REST OF YOUR LIFE?!
JOAN AGREED. WE EVEN PLANNED AN ENGAGEMENT PARTY.
BUT VERY QUICKLY I TOLD HER EVERYTHING. I OWED IT TO HER.
SHE TOLD ME SHE SUSPECTED AS MUCH. SHE WAS RESIGNED. OH, WE KNEW WE'D ALWAYS BE FRIENDS, BUT …
WHAT WOULD OUR FUTURE BE?

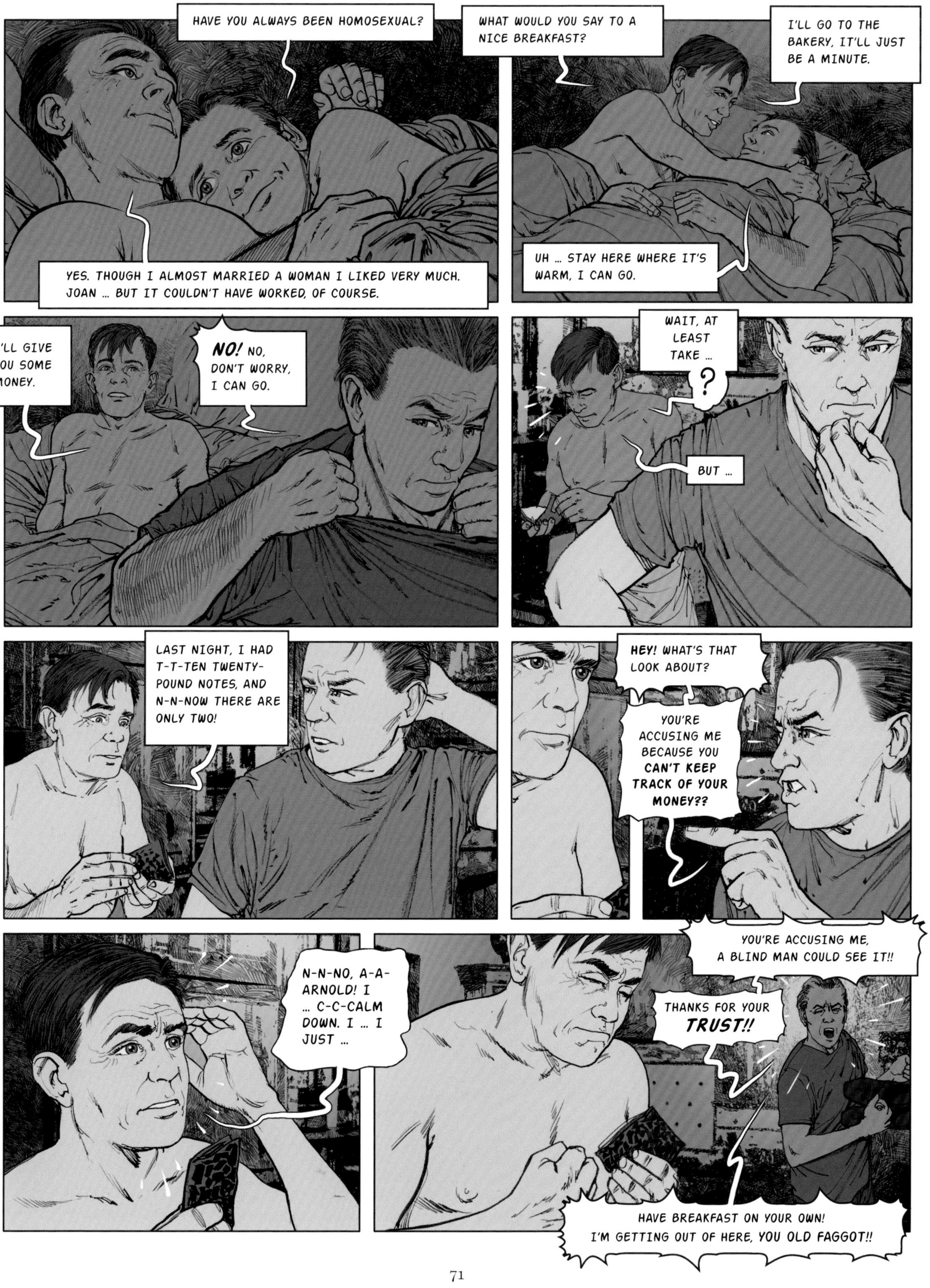
HAVE YOU ALWAYS BEEN HOMOSEXUAL?
YES. THOUGH I ALMOST MARRIED A WOMAN I LIKED VERY MUCH. JOAN ... BUT IT COULDN'T HAVE WORKED, OF COURSE.
WHAT WOULD YOU SAY TO A NICE BREAKFAST?
I'LL GO TO THE BAKERY, IT'LL JUST BE A MINUTE.
UH ... STAY HERE WHERE IT'S WARM, I CAN GO.
I'LL GIVE YOU SOME MONEY.
NO! NO, DON'T WORRY, I CAN GO.
WAIT, AT LEAST TAKE ...
?
BUT ...
LAST NIGHT, I HAD T-T-TEN TWENTY-POUND NOTES, AND N-N-NOW THERE ARE ONLY TWO!
HEY! WHAT'S THAT LOOK ABOUT?
YOU'RE ACCUSING ME BECAUSE YOU CAN'T KEEP TRACK OF YOUR MONEY??
N-N-NO, A-A-ARNOLD! I ... C-C-CALM DOWN. I ... I JUST ...
YOU'RE ACCUSING ME, A BLIND MAN COULD SEE IT!!
THANKS FOR YOUR TRUST!!
HAVE BREAKFAST ON YOUR OWN! I'M GETTING OUT OF HERE, YOU OLD FAGGOT!!

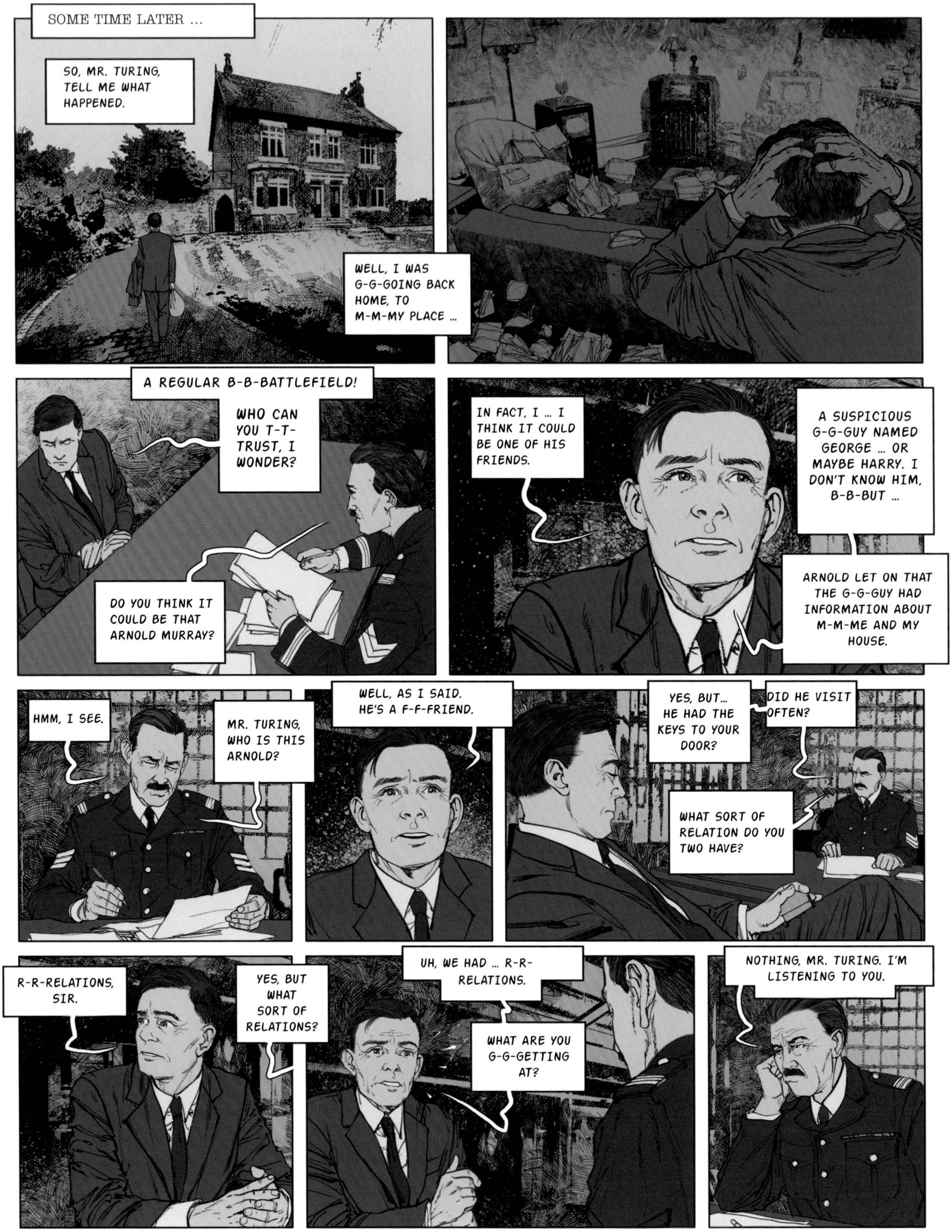
SOME TIME LATER ...
SO, MR. TURING, TELL ME WHAT HAPPENED.
WELL, I WAS G-G-GOING BACK HOME, TO M-M-MY PLACE ...
A REGULAR B-B-BATTLEFIELD!
WHO CAN YOU T-T-TRUST, I WONDER?
DO YOU THINK IT COULD BE THAT ARNOLD MURRAY?
IN FACT, I ... I THINK IT COULD BE ONE OF HIS FRIENDS.
A SUSPICIOUS G-G-GUY NAMED GEORGE ... OR MAYBE HARRY. I DON'T KNOW HIM, B-B-BUT ...
ARNOLD LET ON THAT THE G-G-GUY HAD INFORMATION ABOUT M-M-ME AND MY HOUSE.
HMM, I SEE.
MR. TURING, WHO IS THIS ARNOLD?
WELL, AS I SAID. HE'S A F-F-FRIEND.
YES, BUT... HE HAD THE KEYS TO YOUR DOOR?
DID HE VISIT OFTEN?
WHAT SORT OF RELATION DO YOU TWO HAVE?
R-R-RELATIONS, SIR.
YES, BUT WHAT SORT OF RELATIONS?
UH, WE HAD ... R-R-RELATIONS.
WHAT ARE YOU G-G-GETTING AT?
NOTHING, MR. TURING. I'M LISTENING TO YOU.

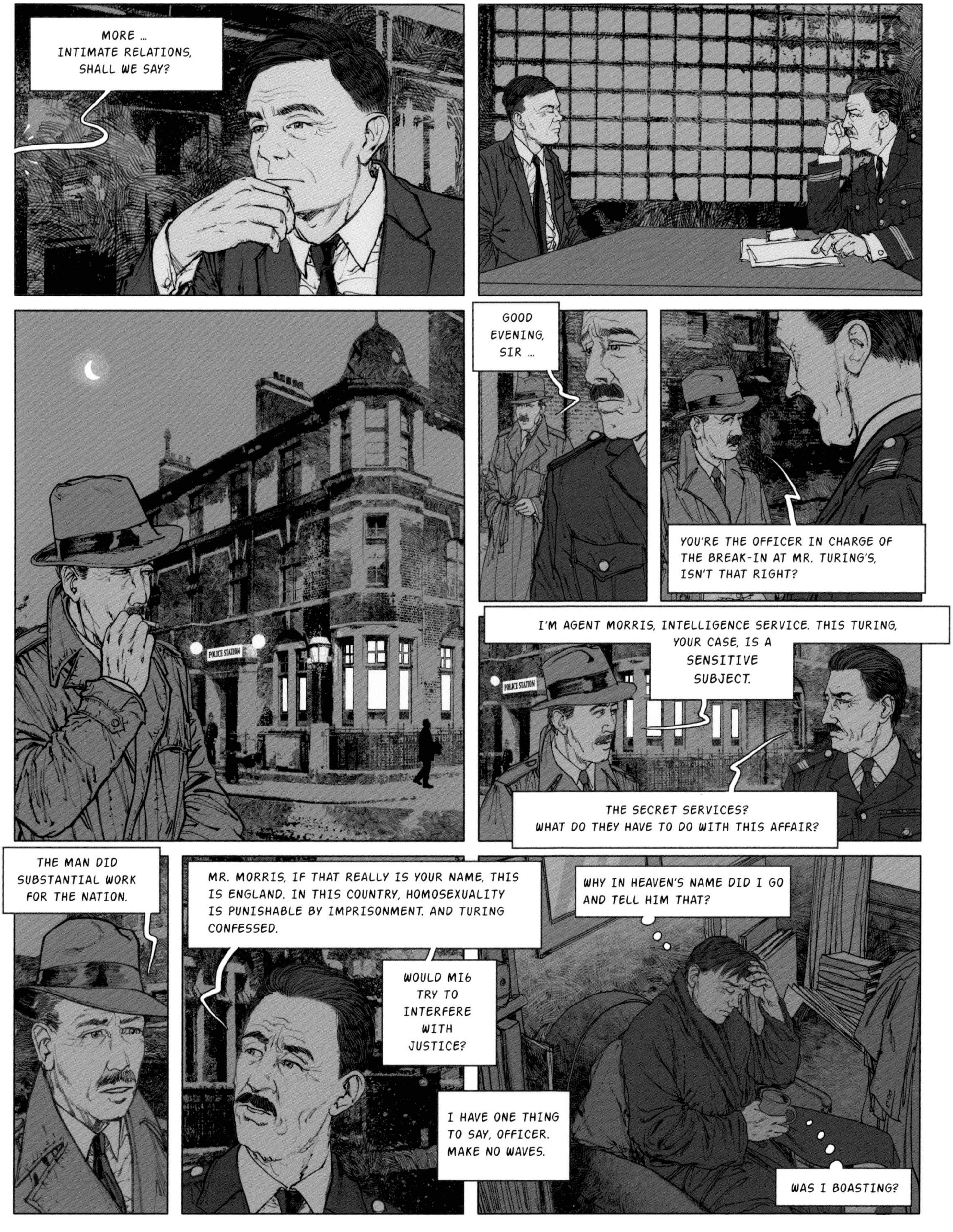
MORE ... INTIMATE RELATIONS, SHALL WE SAY?
GOOD EVENING, SIR ...
YOU'RE THE OFFICER IN CHARGE OF THE BREAK-IN AT MR. TURING'S, ISN'T THAT RIGHT?
POLICE STATION
I'M AGENT MORRIS, INTELLIGENCE SERVICE. THIS TURING, YOUR CASE, IS A SENSITIVE SUBJECT.
POLICE STATION
THE SECRET SERVICES? WHAT DO THEY HAVE TO DO WITH THIS AFFAIR?
THE MAN DID SUBSTANTIAL WORK FOR THE NATION.
MR. MORRIS, IF THAT REALLY IS YOUR NAME, THIS IS ENGLAND. IN THIS COUNTRY, HOMOSEXUALITY IS PUNISHABLE BY IMPRISONMENT. AND TURING CONFESSED.
WOULD MI6 TRY TO INTERFERE WITH JUSTICE?
I HAVE ONE THING TO SAY, OFFICER. MAKE NO WAVES.
WHY IN HEAVEN'S NAME DID I GO AND TELL HIM THAT?
WAS I BOASTING?

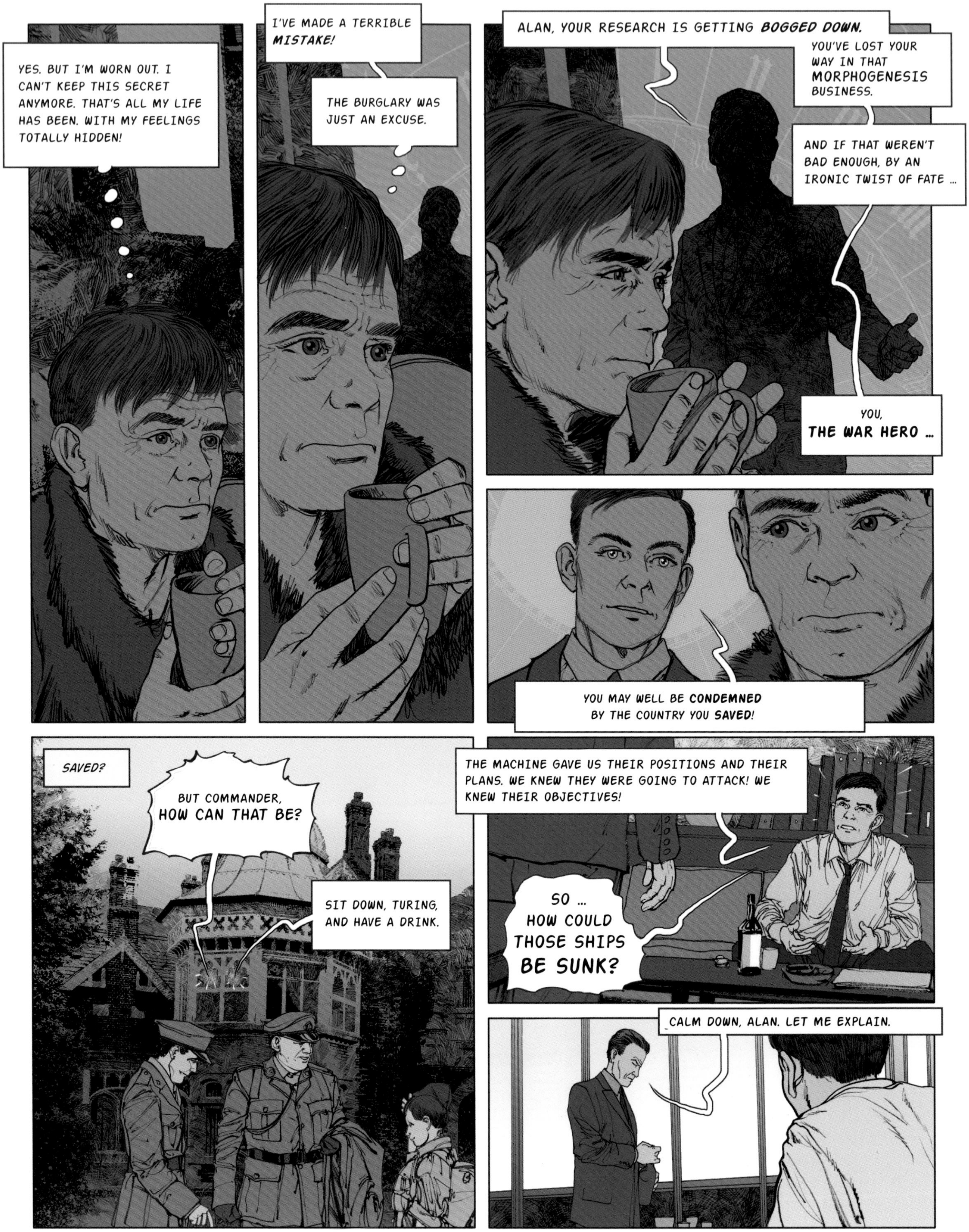
YES. BUT I'M WORN OUT. I CAN'T KEEP THIS SECRET ANYMORE. THAT'S ALL MY LIFE HAS BEEN. WITH MY FEELINGS TOTALLY HIDDEN!
I'VE MADE A TERRIBLE *MISTAKE!*
THE BURGLARY WAS JUST AN EXCUSE.
ALAN, YOUR RESEARCH IS GETTING ***BOGGED DOWN.***
YOU'VE LOST YOUR WAY IN THAT MORPHOGENESIS BUSINESS.
AND IF THAT WEREN'T BAD ENOUGH, BY AN IRONIC TWIST OF FATE ...
YOU, **THE WAR HERO ...**
YOU MAY WELL BE **CONDEMNED** BY THE COUNTRY YOU **SAVED!**
SAVED?
BUT COMMANDER, **HOW CAN THAT BE?**
SIT DOWN, TURING, AND HAVE A DRINK.
THE MACHINE GAVE US THEIR POSITIONS AND THEIR PLANS. WE KNEW THEY WERE GOING TO ATTACK! WE KNEW THEIR OBJECTIVES!
SO ... HOW COULD THOSE SHIPS BE SUNK?
CALM DOWN, ALAN. LET ME EXPLAIN.

THE DECISION CAME FROM THE TOP. I KNOW IT'S TERRIBLE. BUT IT'S A NECESSARY EVIL.

IF WE SYSTEMATICALLY FOIL EVERY ENEMY ATTACK, THE NAZIS WILL KNOW WE HAVE BROKEN THE ENIGMA CODE ...

AND THAT WILL BE THE END.

OUR STRATEGY WILL BE SUNK!

WE HAVE TO LET OUR SOLDIERS D-D-DIE SO THE GERMANS W-W-W ...

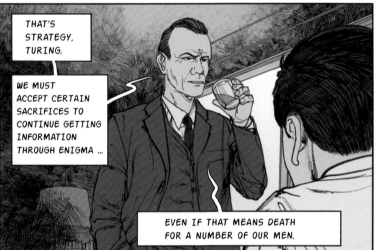

THAT'S STRATEGY, TURING.

WE MUST ACCEPT CERTAIN SACRIFICES TO CONTINUE GETTING INFORMATION THROUGH ENIGMA ...

EVEN IF THAT MEANS DEATH FOR A NUMBER OF OUR MEN.

December 7, 1941. Japanese aircraft destroy the American base at PEARL HARBOR. War breaks out in the Pacific.

FRIENDS, HOW MANY LIVES C-C-CAN WE SAVE WITHOUT THE ENEMY DISCOVERING WE HAVE DECRYPTED THEIR MESSAGES?

ESTABLISH THE COEFFICIENTS! CALCULATE IN REAL TIME!

ANOTHER IMPOSSIBLE PROBLEM TO RESOLVE - JUST MY STYLE. TO WORK!

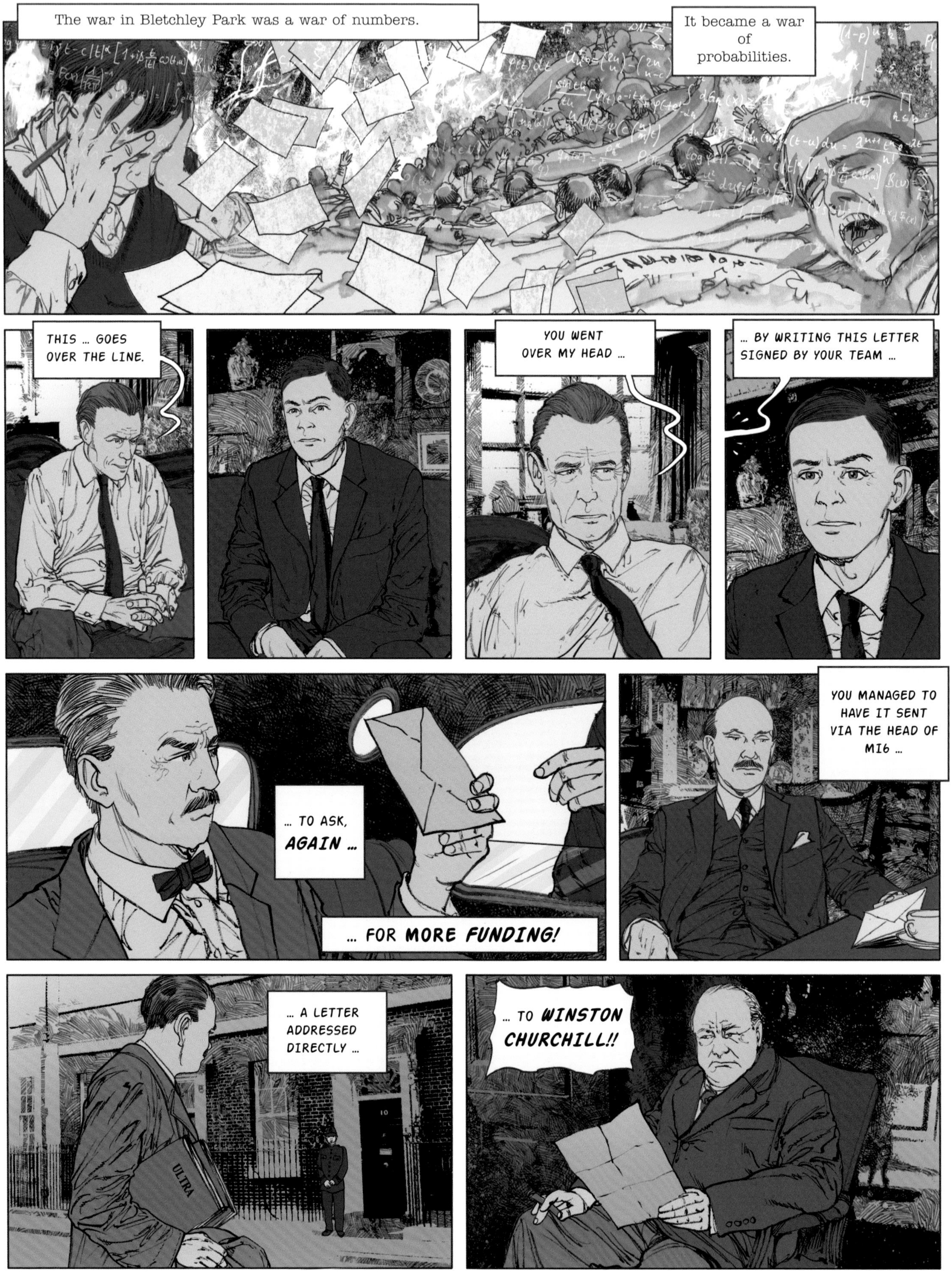
The war in Bletchley Park was a war of numbers.
It became a war of probabilities.
THIS ... GOES OVER THE LINE.
YOU WENT OVER MY HEAD ...
... BY WRITING THIS LETTER SIGNED BY YOUR TEAM ...
... TO ASK, AGAIN ...
... FOR MORE FUNDING!
YOU MANAGED TO HAVE IT SENT VIA THE HEAD OF MI6 ...
... A LETTER ADDRESSED DIRECTLY ...
10
ULTRA
... TO WINSTON CHURCHILL!!

AND IN THE PROCESS, YOU HAVE THE GALL TO PRAISE "THE ENERGY AND FORESIGHT" OF MY ASSISTANT, TRAVIS.

COMMANDER ... WE'VE HAD THE LUFTWAFFE C-C-CODES FOR SOME TIME NOW.

BUT WE M-M-MUST NOT SLACK OFF ON OUR CRYPTANALYSIS OF THEIR NAVY'S ENIGMA.

IT CONTINUES TO CAUSE US BIG PROBLEMS. WE NEED MORE FINANCING AND COOPERATION BETWEEN THE ALLIES.

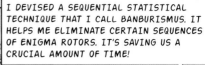

I DEVISED A SEQUENTIAL STATISTICAL TECHNIQUE THAT I CALL BANBURISMUS. IT HELPS ME ELIMINATE CERTAIN SEQUENCES OF ENIGMA ROTORS. IT'S SAVING US A CRUCIAL AMOUNT OF TIME!

WE MUST FIGHT ON ALL FRONTS!!

THE NAZI ENCRYPTERS, ESPECIALLY THE SUBMARINERS, APPLY ALL THE SECURITY PROCEDURES. WE CAN ONLY DECRYPT MESSAGES WHEN THOSE PROCEDURES ARE NOT IN PLACE, OR THANKS TO BIGRAM TABLES CAPTURED BY THE ALLIES.

THAT'S ENOUGH!!

I JUST KNOW YOU'RE DOING YOUR BEST ...

BUT I DON'T LIKE YOUR METHODS. I SHOULD DISMISS YOU ...

I UNDERSTAND NOTHING OF YOUR HOCUS-POCUS!

... BUT CHURCHILL REACTED IMMEDIATELY!

YOU'LL HAVE YOUR FUNDS.

BECAUSE ORDERS ARE ORDERS.

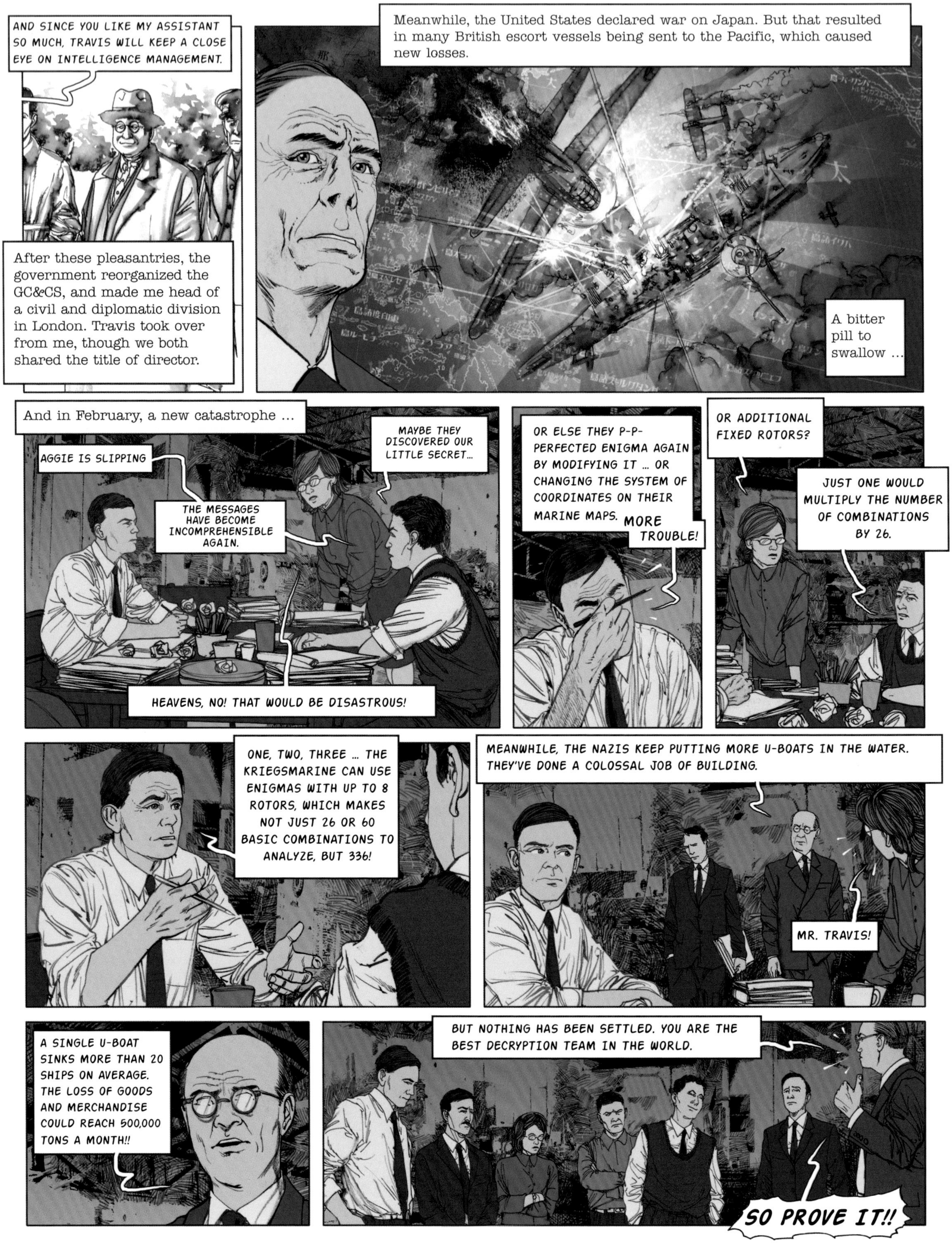
AND SINCE YOU LIKE MY ASSISTANT SO MUCH, TRAVIS WILL KEEP A CLOSE EYE ON INTELLIGENCE MANAGEMENT.
After these pleasantries, the government reorganized the GC&CS, and made me head of a civil and diplomatic division in London. Travis took over from me, though we both shared the title of director.
Meanwhile, the United States declared war on Japan. But that resulted in many British escort vessels being sent to the Pacific, which caused new losses.
A bitter pill to swallow …
And in February, a new catastrophe …
AGGIE IS SLIPPING
THE MESSAGES HAVE BECOME INCOMPREHENSIBLE AGAIN.
MAYBE THEY DISCOVERED OUR LITTLE SECRET…
HEAVENS, NO! THAT WOULD BE DISASTROUS!
OR ELSE THEY P-P-PERFECTED ENIGMA AGAIN BY MODIFYING IT … OR CHANGING THE SYSTEM OF COORDINATES ON THEIR MARINE MAPS.
MORE TROUBLE!
OR ADDITIONAL FIXED ROTORS?
JUST ONE WOULD MULTIPLY THE NUMBER OF COMBINATIONS BY 26.
ONE, TWO, THREE … THE KRIEGSMARINE CAN USE ENIGMAS WITH UP TO 8 ROTORS, WHICH MAKES NOT JUST 26 OR 60 BASIC COMBINATIONS TO ANALYZE, BUT 336!
MEANWHILE, THE NAZIS KEEP PUTTING MORE U-BOATS IN THE WATER. THEY'VE DONE A COLOSSAL JOB OF BUILDING.
MR. TRAVIS!
A SINGLE U-BOAT SINKS MORE THAN 20 SHIPS ON AVERAGE. THE LOSS OF GOODS AND MERCHANDISE COULD REACH 500,000 TONS A MONTH!!
BUT NOTHING HAS BEEN SETTLED. YOU ARE THE BEST DECRYPTION TEAM IN THE WORLD.
SO PROVE IT!!

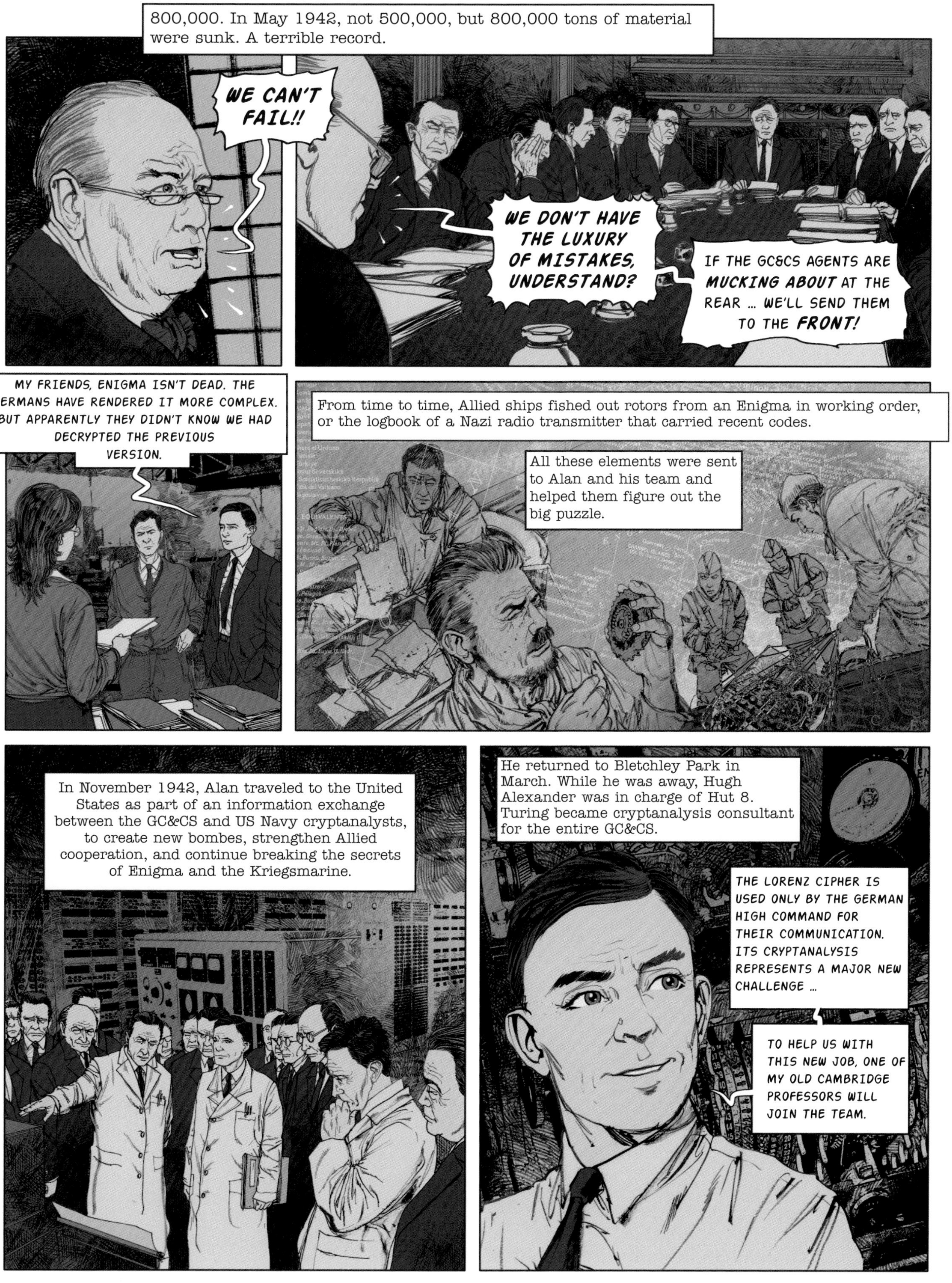
800,000. In May 1942, not 500,000, but 800,000 tons of material were sunk. A terrible record.
WE CAN'T FAIL!!
WE DON'T HAVE THE LUXURY OF MISTAKES, UNDERSTAND?
IF THE GC&CS AGENTS ARE MUCKING ABOUT AT THE REAR ... WE'LL SEND THEM TO THE FRONT!
MY FRIENDS, ENIGMA ISN'T DEAD. THE GERMANS HAVE RENDERED IT MORE COMPLEX. BUT APPARENTLY THEY DIDN'T KNOW WE HAD DECRYPTED THE PREVIOUS VERSION.
From time to time, Allied ships fished out rotors from an Enigma in working order, or the logbook of a Nazi radio transmitter that carried recent codes.
All these elements were sent to Alan and his team and helped them figure out the big puzzle.
In November 1942, Alan traveled to the United States as part of an information exchange between the GC&CS and US Navy cryptanalysts, to create new bombes, strengthen Allied cooperation, and continue breaking the secrets of Enigma and the Kriegsmarine.
He returned to Bletchley Park in March. While he was away, Hugh Alexander was in charge of Hut 8. Turing became cryptanalysis consultant for the entire GC&CS.
THE LORENZ CIPHER IS USED ONLY BY THE GERMAN HIGH COMMAND FOR THEIR COMMUNICATION. ITS CRYPTANALYSIS REPRESENTS A MAJOR NEW CHALLENGE ...
TO HELP US WITH THIS NEW JOB, ONE OF MY OLD CAMBRIDGE PROFESSORS WILL JOIN THE TEAM.

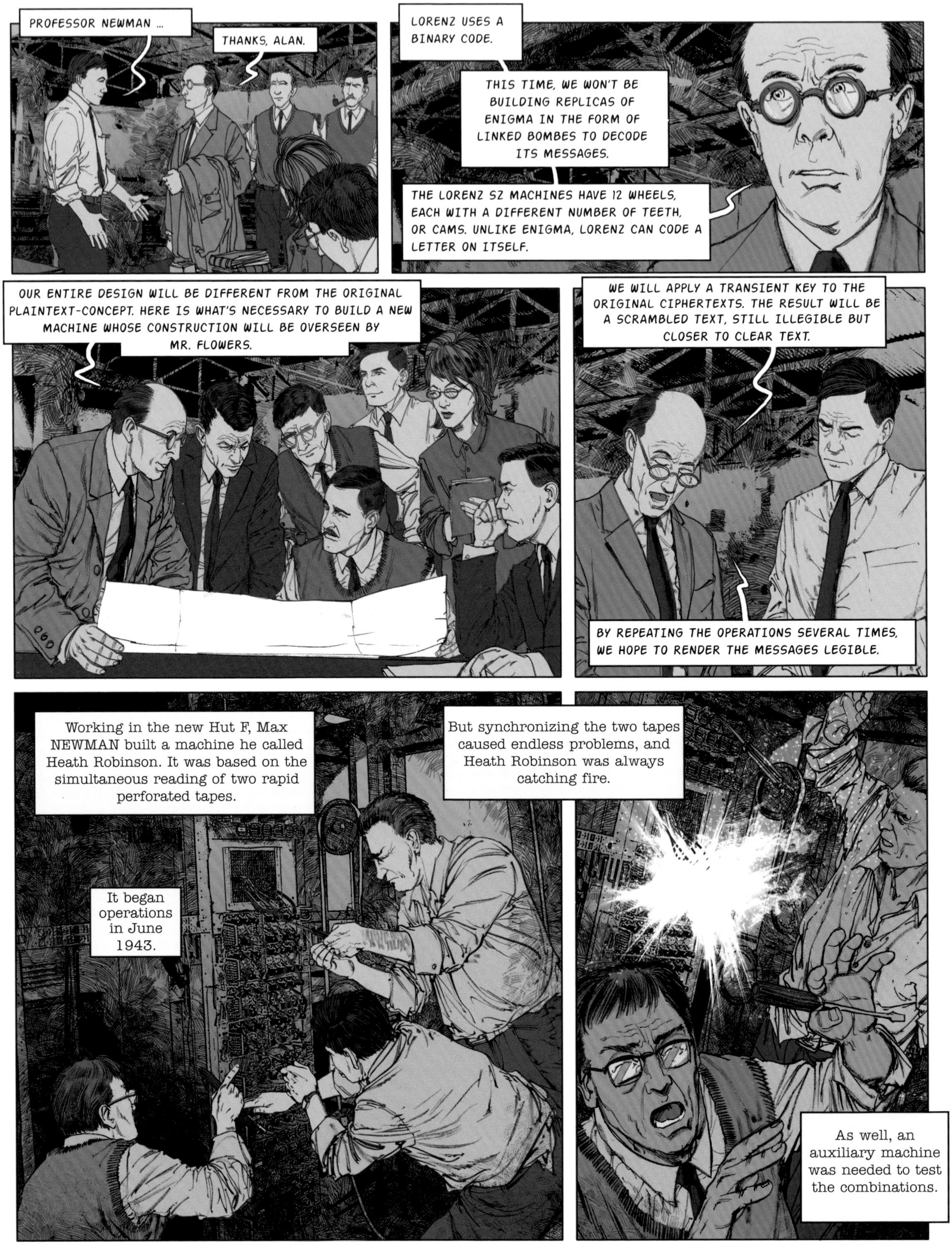
PROFESSOR NEWMAN ...
THANKS, ALAN.
LORENZ USES A BINARY CODE.
THIS TIME, WE WON'T BE BUILDING REPLICAS OF ENIGMA IN THE FORM OF LINKED BOMBES TO DECODE ITS MESSAGES.
THE LORENZ SZ MACHINES HAVE 12 WHEELS, EACH WITH A DIFFERENT NUMBER OF TEETH, OR CAMS. UNLIKE ENIGMA, LORENZ CAN CODE A LETTER ON ITSELF.
OUR ENTIRE DESIGN WILL BE DIFFERENT FROM THE ORIGINAL PLAINTEXT-CONCEPT. HERE IS WHAT'S NECESSARY TO BUILD A NEW MACHINE WHOSE CONSTRUCTION WILL BE OVERSEEN BY MR. FLOWERS.
WE WILL APPLY A TRANSIENT KEY TO THE ORIGINAL CIPHERTEXTS. THE RESULT WILL BE A SCRAMBLED TEXT, STILL ILLEGIBLE BUT CLOSER TO CLEAR TEXT.
BY REPEATING THE OPERATIONS SEVERAL TIMES, WE HOPE TO RENDER THE MESSAGES LEGIBLE.
Working in the new Hut F, Max NEWMAN built a machine he called Heath Robinson. It was based on the simultaneous reading of two rapid perforated tapes.
It began operations in June 1943.
But synchronizing the two tapes caused endless problems, and Heath Robinson was always catching fire.
As well, an auxiliary machine was needed to test the combinations.

Tommy FLOWERS suggested replacing the tapes as a medium for the patterns with an electronic memory.

Designed using Turing's ideas, in eleven months Colossus was built in Dollis Hill by a team under Flowers' direction. It went into operation in Bletchley Park in December 1943.

The first version of the machine had 1,500 vacuum tubes.

All it had to do was learn to think.

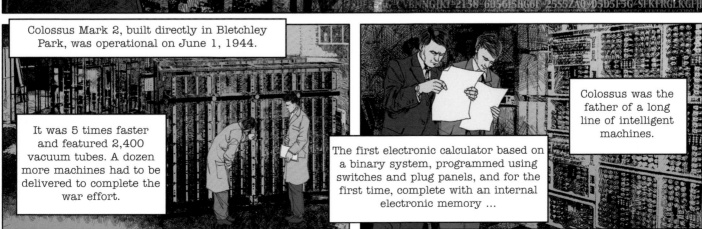

Colossus Mark 2, built directly in Bletchley Park, was operational on June 1, 1944.

It was 5 times faster and featured 2,400 vacuum tubes. A dozen more machines had to be delivered to complete the war effort.

The first electronic calculator based on a binary system, programmed using switches and plug panels, and for the first time, complete with an internal electronic memory ...

Colossus was the father of a long line of intelligent machines.

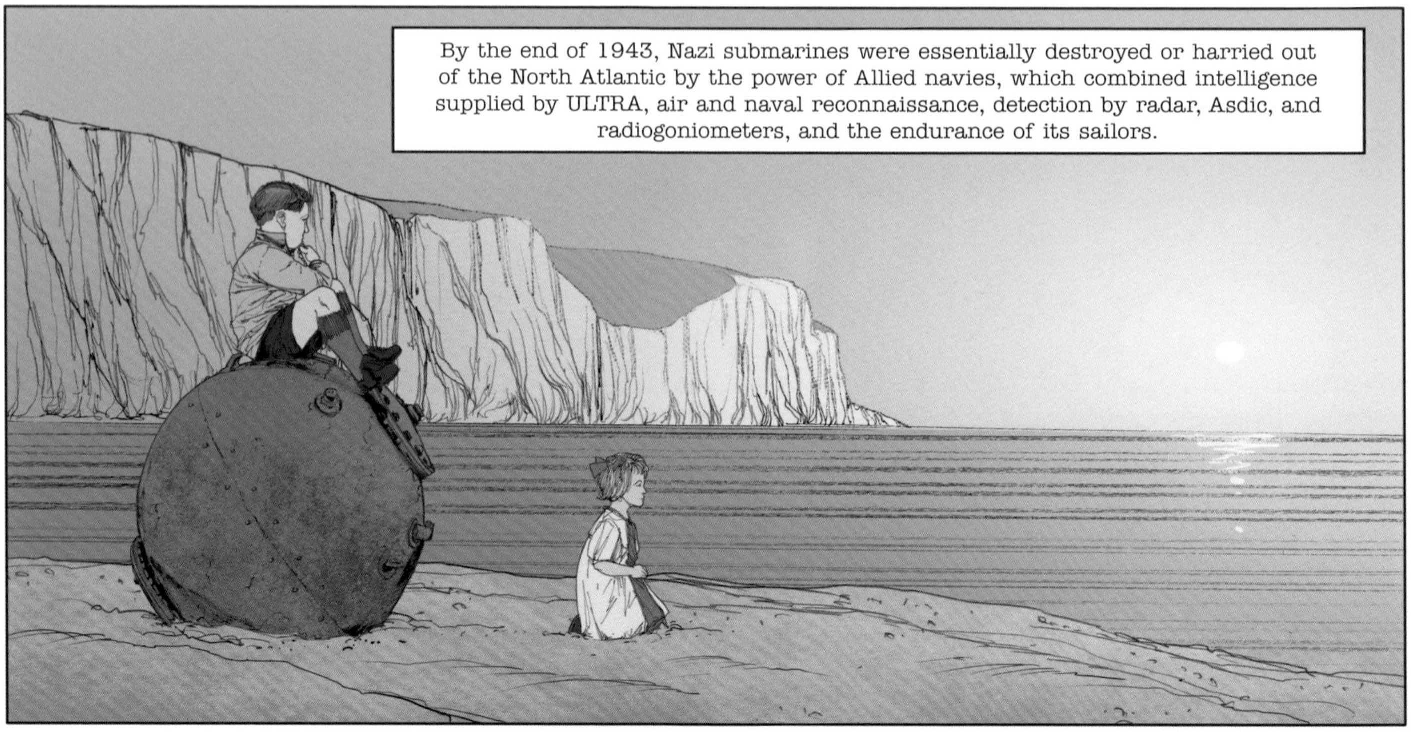
By the end of 1943, Nazi submarines were essentially destroyed or harried out of the North Atlantic by the power of Allied navies, which combined intelligence supplied by ULTRA, air and naval reconnaissance, detection by radar, Asdic, and radiogoniometers, and the endurance of its sailors.

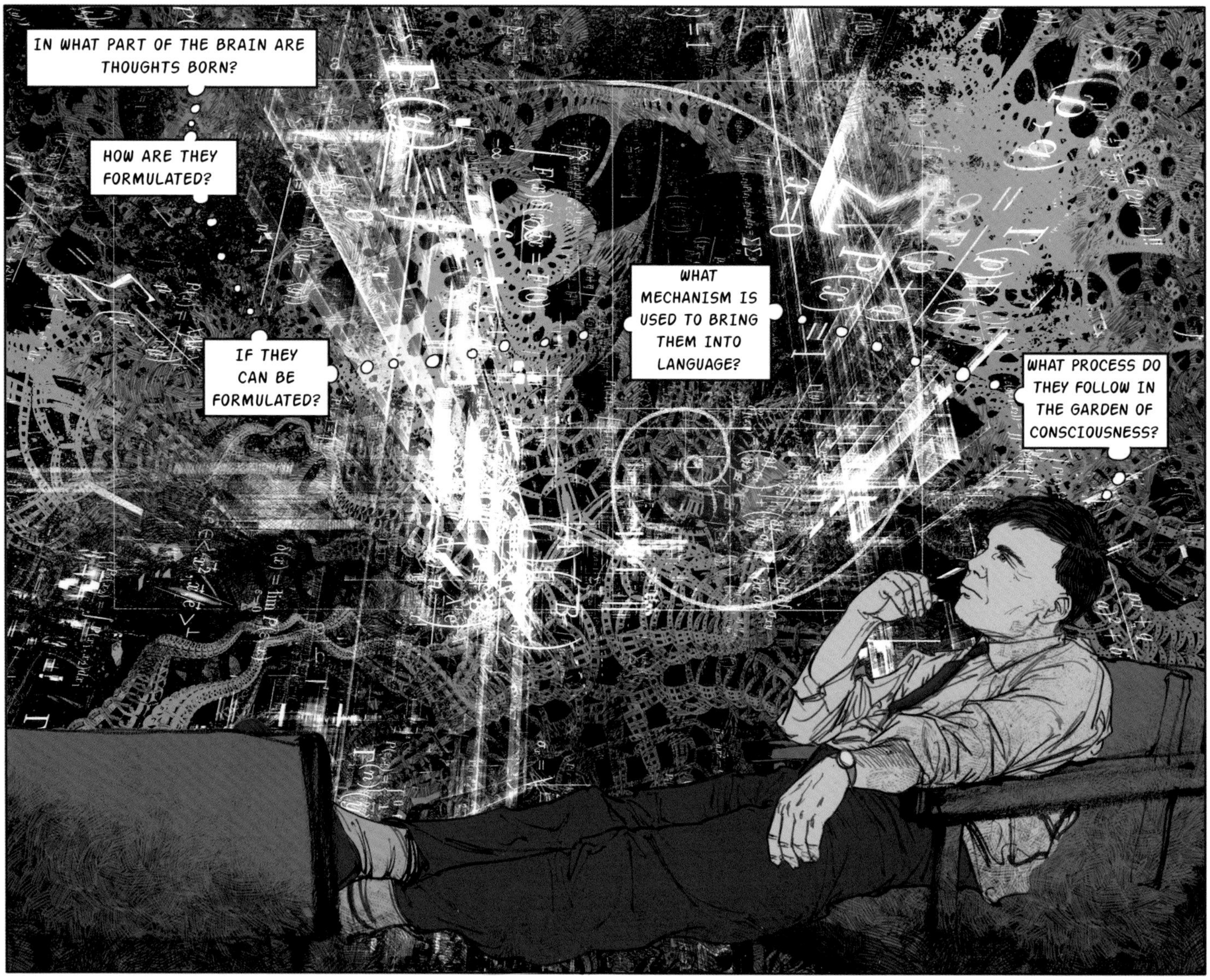
IN WHAT PART OF THE BRAIN ARE THOUGHTS BORN?
HOW ARE THEY FORMULATED?
IF THEY CAN BE FORMULATED?
WHAT MECHANISM IS USED TO BRING THEM INTO LANGUAGE?
WHAT PROCESS DO THEY FOLLOW IN THE GARDEN OF CONSCIOUSNESS?

ARE YOU REALLY LEAVING US?

YES. I N-N-NEED TO CONTINUE MY RESEARCH. GO FURTHER WITH MY THINKING M-M-MACHINE.

LOOK INTO THE CONDITIONS OF THE EVOLUTION OF LIFE AND HOW W-W-WORDS ARE BORN.

I UNDERSTAND ... TURING, YOU HAVE FULFILLED YOUR MISSION, AND MORE.

DESPITE OUR DIFFERENCES ...

I THANK YOU, TRULY.

SO, IN THAT CASE ...

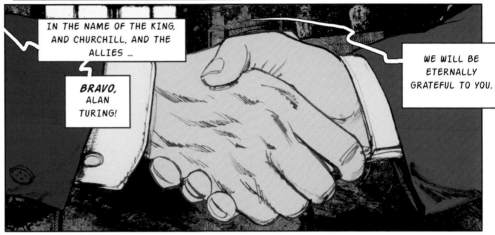

IN THE NAME OF THE KING, AND CHURCHILL, AND THE ALLIES ...

BRAVO, ALAN TURING!

WE WILL BE ETERNALLY GRATEFUL TO YOU.

YOU'LL CONTINUE WATCHING HIM, RIGHT?

YOU'LL BE HIS GUARDIAN ANGEL.

HIS ANGEL, OR HIS DEMON. OR NEITHER ONE NOR THE OTHER.

I DON'T BELIEVE HE NEEDS ANYONE.

NO DOUBT YOU'RE RIGHT. THE MAN HAS NO OTHER ANGEL OR DEMON THAN HIMSELF.

BUT KEEP AN EYE ON HIM ALL THE SAME.

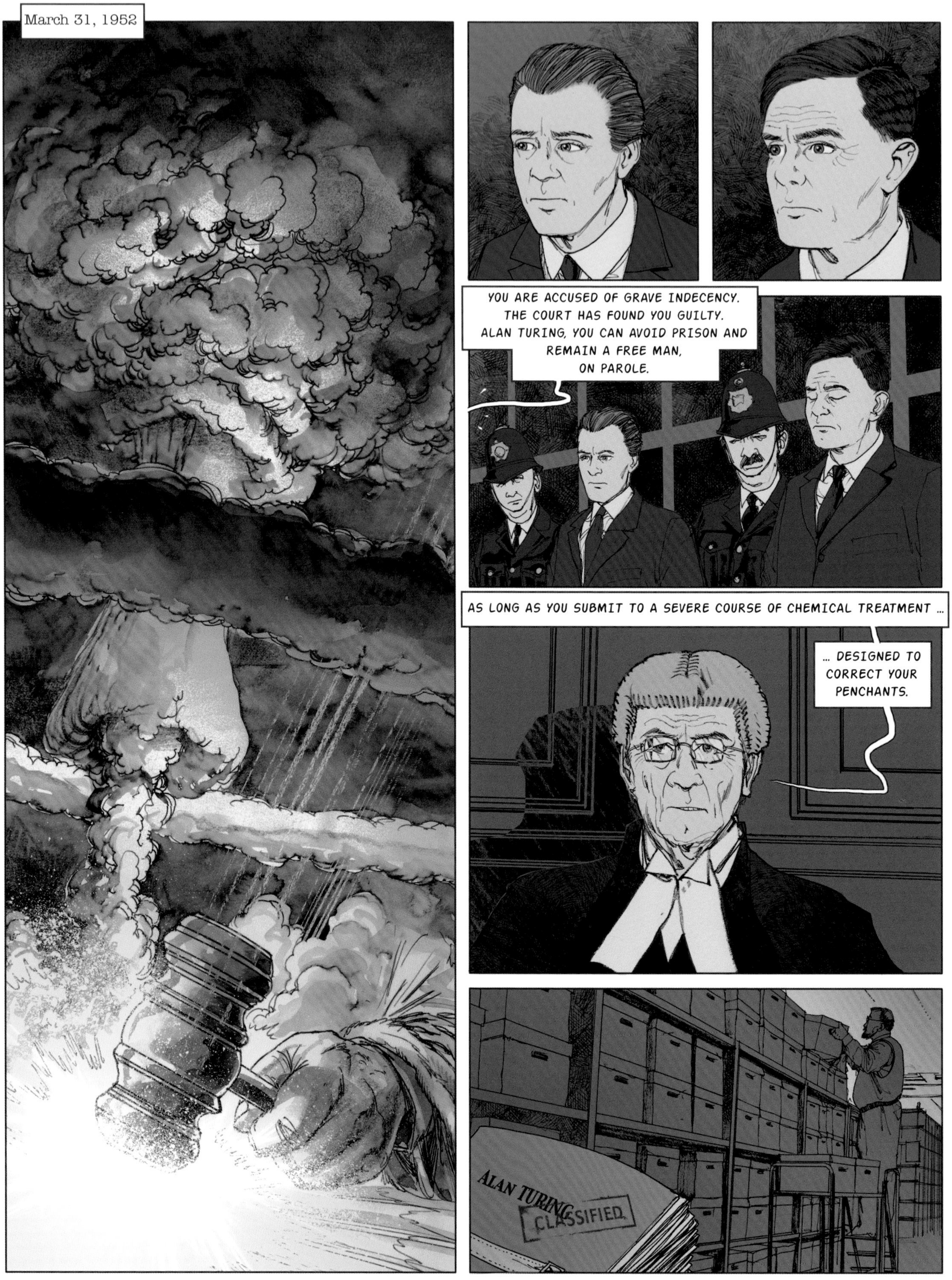
March 31, 1952
YOU ARE ACCUSED OF GRAVE INDECENCY. THE COURT HAS FOUND YOU GUILTY. ALAN TURING, YOU CAN AVOID PRISON AND REMAIN A FREE MAN, ON PAROLE.
AS LONG AS YOU SUBMIT TO A SEVERE COURSE OF CHEMICAL TREATMENT ...
... DESIGNED TO CORRECT YOUR PENCHANTS.
ALAN TURING
CLASSIFIED

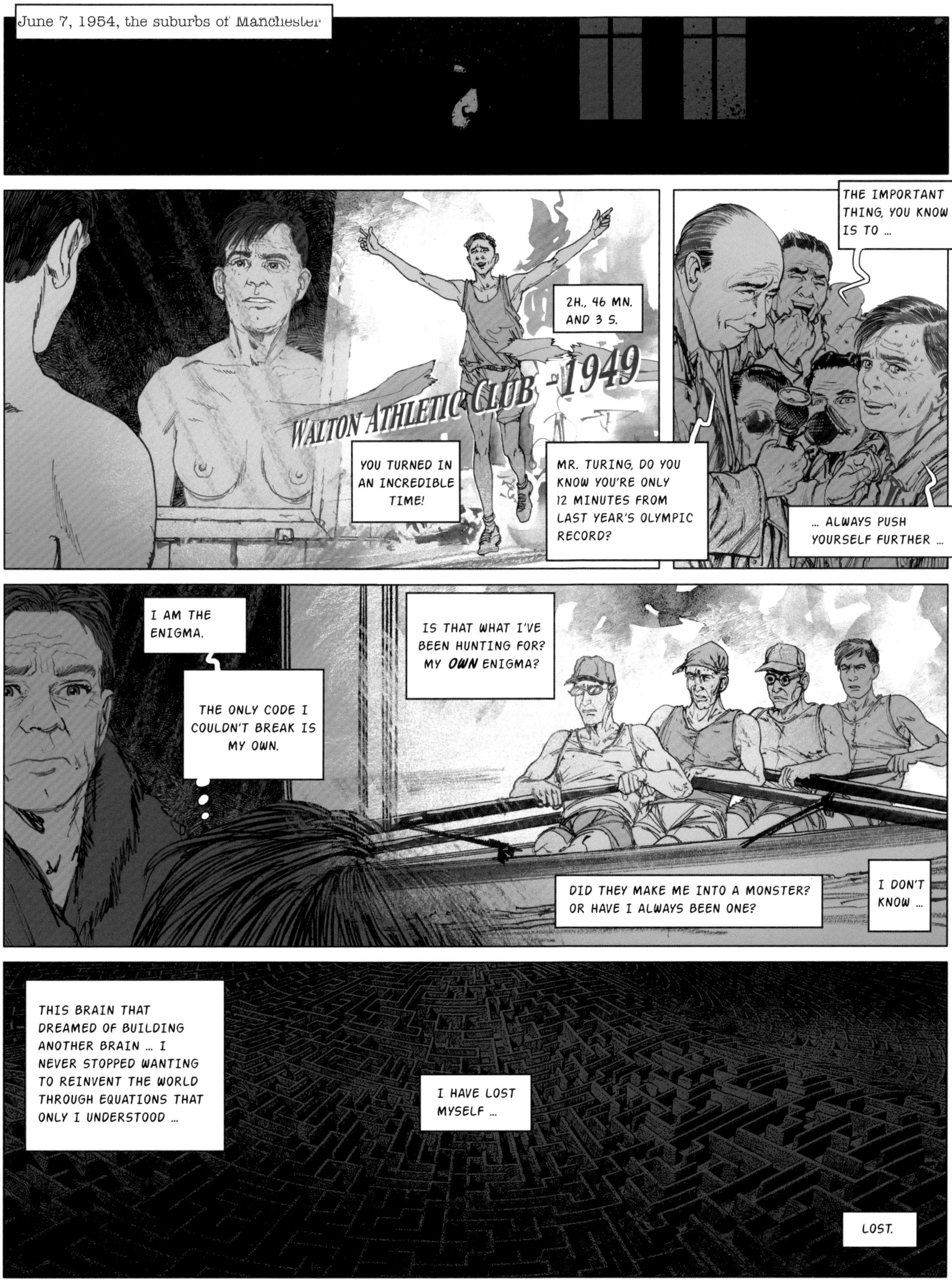
June 7, 1954, the suburbs of Manchester
WALTON ATHLETIC CLUB -1949
YOU TURNED IN AN INCREDIBLE TIME!
2H., 46 MN. AND 3 S.
MR. TURING, DO YOU KNOW YOU'RE ONLY 12 MINUTES FROM LAST YEAR'S OLYMPIC RECORD?
THE IMPORTANT THING, YOU KNOW ... IS TO ...
... ALWAYS PUSH YOURSELF FURTHER ...
I AM THE ENIGMA.
THE ONLY CODE I COULDN'T BREAK IS MY OWN.
IS THAT WHAT I'VE BEEN HUNTING FOR? MY *OWN* ENIGMA?
DID THEY MAKE ME INTO A MONSTER? OR HAVE I ALWAYS BEEN ONE?
I DON'T KNOW ...
THIS BRAIN THAT DREAMED OF BUILDING ANOTHER BRAIN ... I NEVER STOPPED WANTING TO REINVENT THE WORLD THROUGH EQUATIONS THAT ONLY I UNDERSTOOD ...
I HAVE LOST MYSELF ...
LOST.

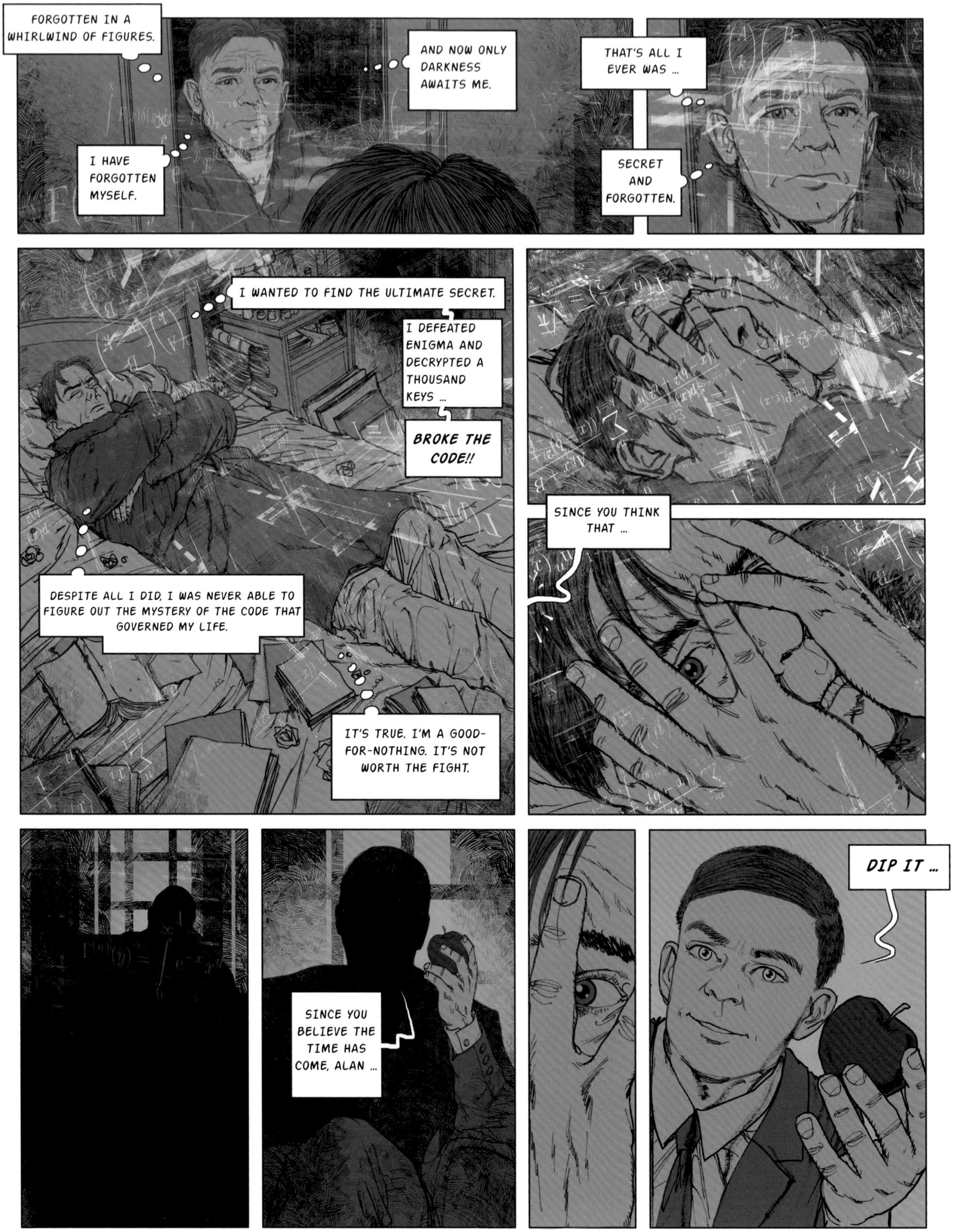
FORGOTTEN IN A WHIRLWIND OF FIGURES.
AND NOW ONLY DARKNESS AWAITS ME.
I HAVE FORGOTTEN MYSELF.
THAT'S ALL I EVER WAS ...
SECRET AND FORGOTTEN.
I WANTED TO FIND THE ULTIMATE SECRET.
I DEFEATED ENIGMA AND DECRYPTED A THOUSAND KEYS ...
BROKE THE CODE!!
DESPITE ALL I DID, I WAS NEVER ABLE TO FIGURE OUT THE MYSTERY OF THE CODE THAT GOVERNED MY LIFE.
IT'S TRUE. I'M A GOOD-FOR-NOTHING. IT'S NOT WORTH THE FIGHT.
SINCE YOU THINK THAT ...
SINCE YOU BELIEVE THE TIME HAS COME, ALAN ...
DIP IT ...

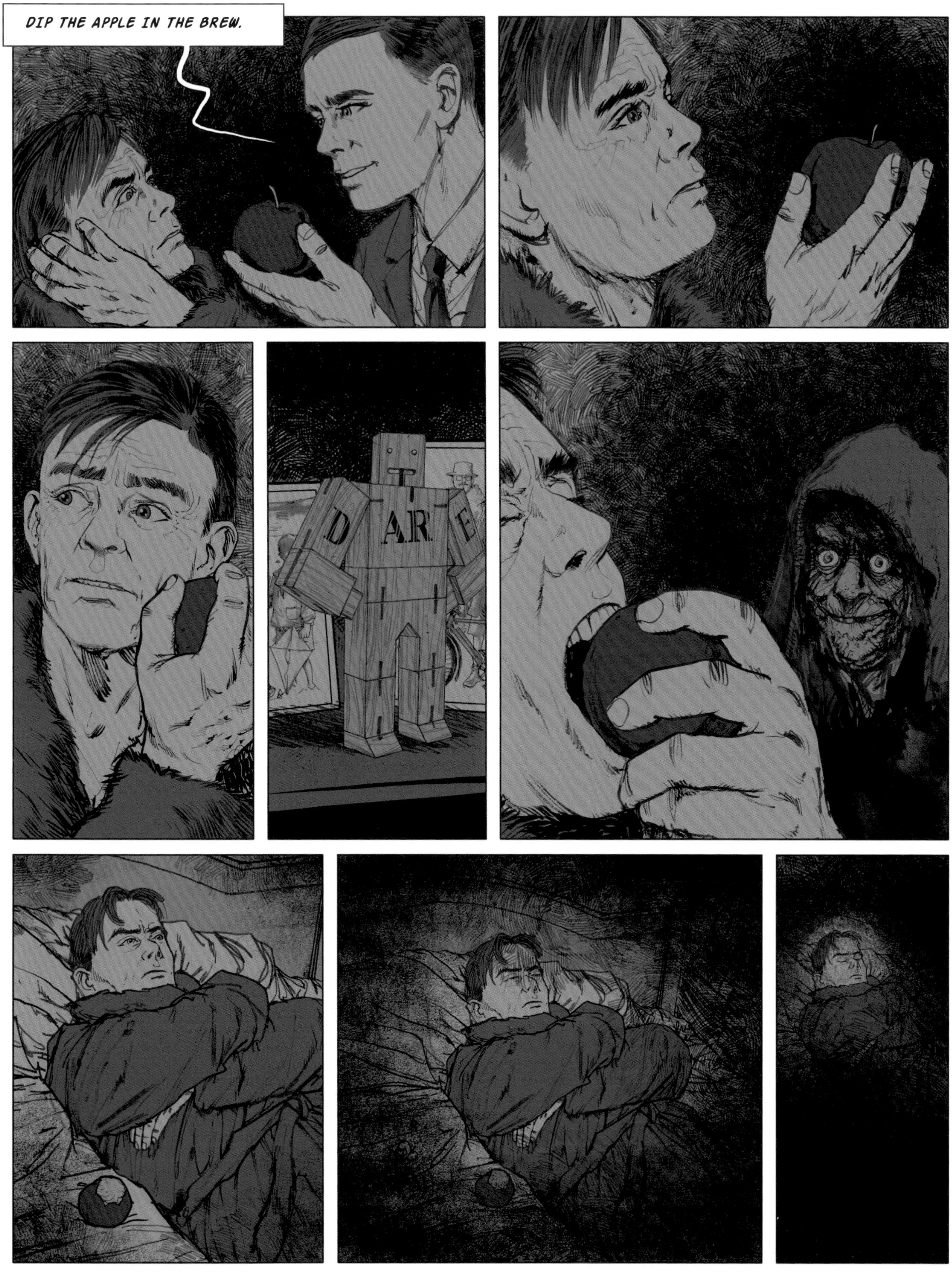
DIP THE APPLE IN THE BREW.

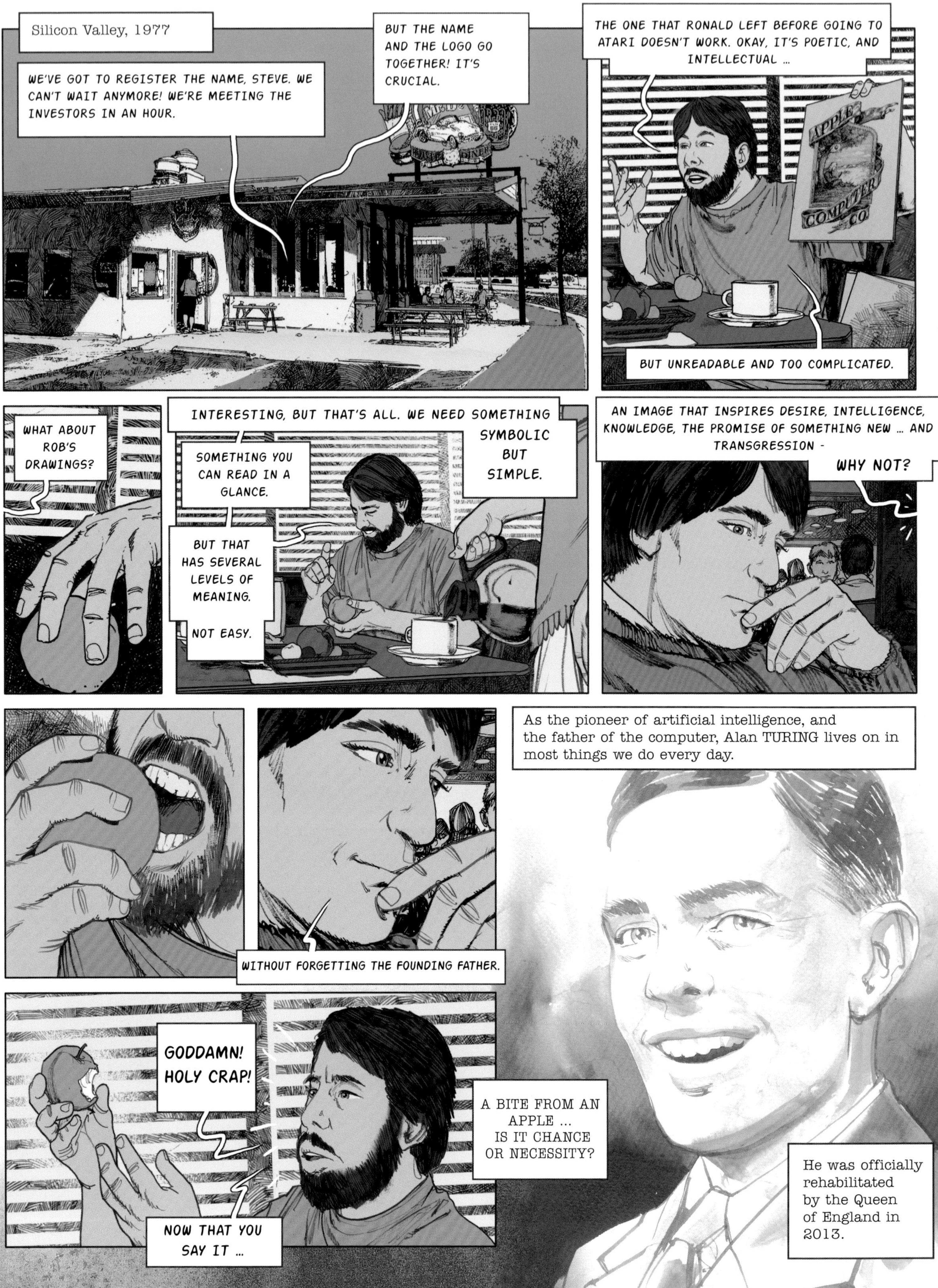
Silicon Valley, 1977
WE'VE GOT TO REGISTER THE NAME, STEVE. WE CAN'T WAIT ANYMORE! WE'RE MEETING THE INVESTORS IN AN HOUR.
BUT THE NAME AND THE LOGO GO TOGETHER! IT'S CRUCIAL.
THE ONE THAT RONALD LEFT BEFORE GOING TO ATARI DOESN'T WORK. OKAY, IT'S POETIC, AND INTELLECTUAL …
APPLE COMPUTER CO
BUT UNREADABLE AND TOO COMPLICATED.
WHAT ABOUT ROB'S DRAWINGS?
INTERESTING, BUT THAT'S ALL. WE NEED SOMETHING
SYMBOLIC BUT SIMPLE.
SOMETHING YOU CAN READ IN A GLANCE.
BUT THAT HAS SEVERAL LEVELS OF MEANING.
NOT EASY.
AN IMAGE THAT INSPIRES DESIRE, INTELLIGENCE, KNOWLEDGE, THE PROMISE OF SOMETHING NEW … AND TRANSGRESSION -
WHY NOT?
As the pioneer of artificial intelligence, and the father of the computer, Alan TURING lives on in most things we do every day.
WITHOUT FORGETTING THE FOUNDING FATHER.
GODDAMN! HOLY CRAP!
A BITE FROM AN APPLE … IS IT CHANCE OR NECESSITY?
NOW THAT YOU SAY IT …
He was officially rehabilitated by the Queen of England in 2013.

SOURCES

THE AUTHORS DREW INSPIRATION AND INFORMATION FROM THE FOLLOWING FILMS, ARTICLES, AND BOOKS:

•*Alan Turing ou l'enigme de l'intelligence,* Andrew Hodges, Payot, 1988. (Original English-language edition: *Alan Turing: The Enigma of Intelligence*, HarperCollins, 1985.)

•*La Pomme d'Alan Turing / un genie sacrifié,* Philippe Langenieux-Villard, éd. Héloïse d'Ormesson, 2013, specially for certain biographical anecdotes, elements of cryptanalysis, and citations inspired by thoughts, letters, or writings from Alan Turing's journal reproduced in this book.

•*Alan Turing, l'homme qui a croqué la pomme,* Laurent Lemire, Fayard, 2012, particularly for the insight into the problems of David Hilbert.

•*Alan M. Turing: Centenary Edition,* Sara Turing, University of Cambridge, 2014.

•*The Imitation Game*, a film by Morten Tyldum, 2014.

•*Breaking the Code*, a film by Herbert Wise, WGBH Boston Video, 1997.

•"Alan Turing et le décryptage des codes secrets nazis," article in *CNRS / le Journal*, https://lejournal.cnrs.fr/articles/alan-turing-et-le-decryptage-des-codes-secrets-nazis.

•"Turing à l'assaut d'Enigma," article in *Interstices / Explorez les sciences du numérique,* http://interstices.info/jcms/int_70884/turing-a-lassaut-denigma.

•"Alan Turing et la naissance de la cryptographie moderne," by Anne Canteaut and Christopher Castro, *Inriality,* 14/06/2012, http://www.inria.fr/actualite/actualities-inria/alan-turing-et-la-naissance-de-la-cryptographie-moderne.

•"Alan Turing, une vie de secrets" by Vincent Fleury, Laboratoire GMCM Université de Rennes 1.

THE BOMBE, so named for the noise it produced. This device used by British cryptologists helped to decipher German communications produced by Enigma.

THE CRYPTOGRAPHY WAR

WRITING ITSELF IS A CODE. BY GIVING SYMBOLS THE VALUE OF A SOUND OR THE MEANING OF A WORD, HUMAN SOCIETIES HAVE MADE GREAT STRIDES, SINCE THE INVENTION OF WRITING LETS THEM SET DOWN, CONSERVE, AND TRANSMIT INFORMATION THEY CHOOSE TO PROCESS, FREEING THEM FROM FALLIBLE INDIVIDUAL MEMORY AND TRANSITORY SPEECH. THIS IS SOMETHING THE GREAT ARCHEO-LOGISTS KNOW. THEY DEVELOPED THEIR TALENTS AS CRYPTANALYSTS TO READ THE INSCRIPTIONS HANDED DOWN FROM ANCIENT TIMES.

BRUNO FULIGNI is a writer, historian, government consultant, and university professor, and the author of twenty books.

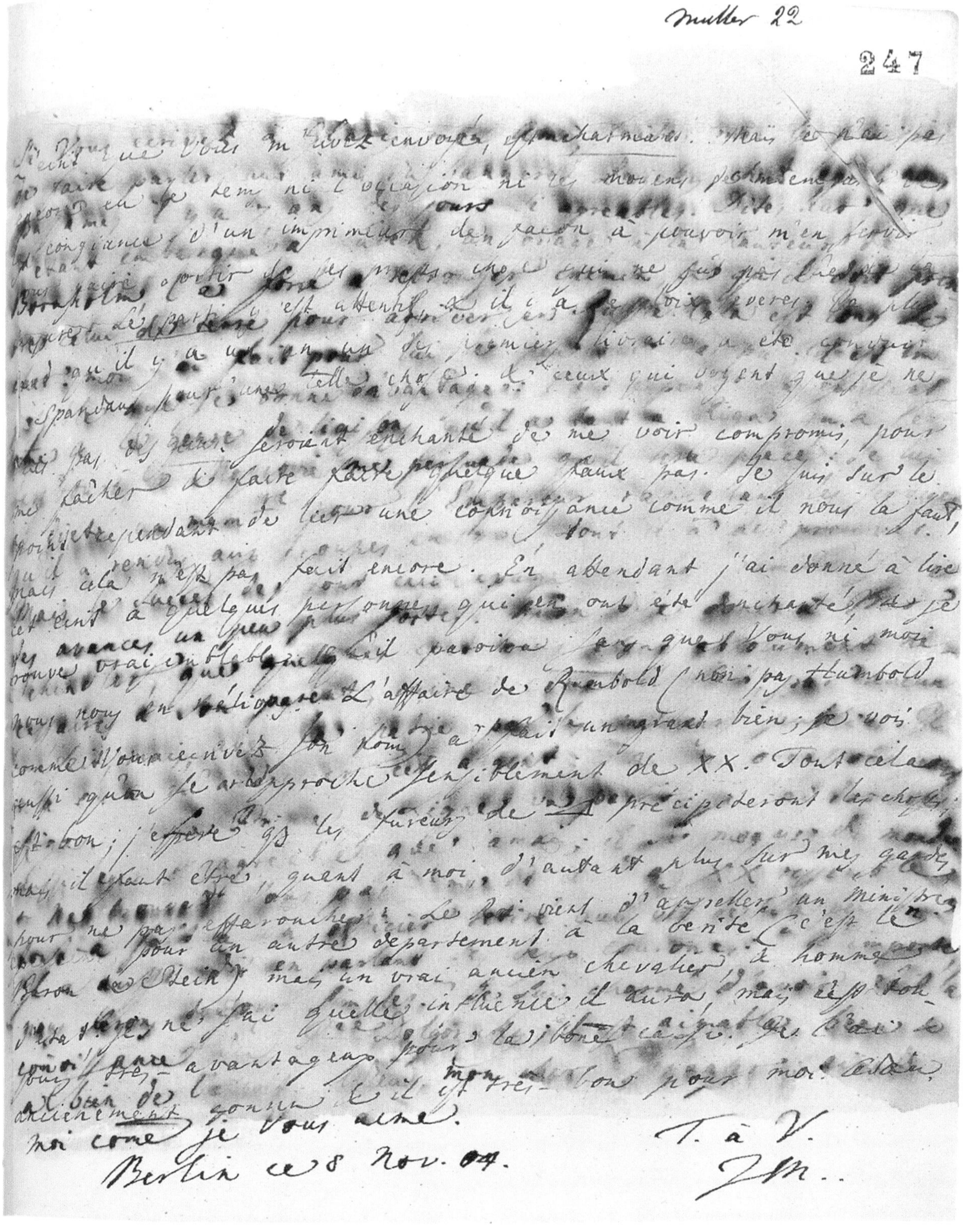
muller 22

247

Berlin ce 8 Nov. 04.

T. à V.

A LETTER FROM JEAN DE MÜLLER TO THE COUNT OF ENTREVUES, NOVEMBER 8, 1804. Between the lines of an ordinary text (in black), we see the text written in invisible ink (in blue) that appears when subjected to a chemical solution..

STEGANOGRAPHY

Stolen from the gods, according to more than one mythology, the strategic power of writing soon ceased to be the exclusive property of princes, wise men and scribes. As the use of writing spread, countries could not allow their sensitive information to be seen by all. Such information had to be hidden or enciphered; sometimes both techniques were used for greater security. The names of these two ways of concealing written messages have Greek roots: steganography and cryptography.

Steganography, or hidden writing, seems to be the *ne plus ultra* of clever procedures. Herodotus tells us of one of the oldest processes known: a slave would have his head shaved, a confidential message would be written on his bald skull, and the writer would wait until the slave's hair grew back to send him and his message to the receiver ... who would shave the slave's head again to read the information. A little time-consuming, this method is just one of the many ways of concealing a message on the human body, or in the clothing of the messenger. The seams of a cloak, the position of the buttons, and the inside of a belt or a hollow heel were all used to carry messages without awakening suspicions.

What's clever about steganography is that a hidden message doesn't need a human messenger, but can be carried within a text or document readable by the human eye. That's the principle behind using invisible inks, where messages can be read once they have been revealed. An even more clever technique, the use of semagrams involves a message or a figure inserted inside another figure. Within the drawing of a casual painter or the sketch of a butterfly quickly executed by a harmless entomologist, with little fear of detection, a person can communicate the layout of a harbor or a castle. A modern variation of this process, watermarking, is often employed by terrorists; sent as an e-mail attachment, a sunny vacation photo can conceal plans for an attack.

CRYPTOGRAPHY

An experienced specialist could foil these plans and obtain access to information that someone wanted to hide. It's better, then, to make the message unreadable for others, and to do that it has to be scrambled. That's the object of cryptography, or enciphered writing.

Whereas steganography depends on inventiveness and clever application, cryptography is based on the human mind's ability to build pure systems. Like the ancient writers

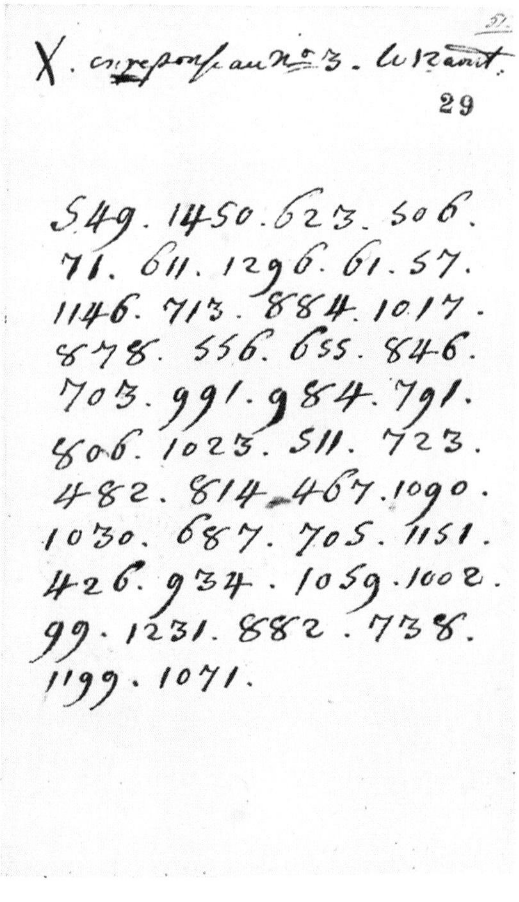
29

549. 1450. 623. 506.
71. 611. 1296. 61. 57.
1146. 713. 884. 1017.
878. 556. 655. 846.
703. 991. 984. 791.
806. 1023. 511. 723.
482. 814. 467. 1090.
1030. 687. 705. 1151.
426. 934. 1059. 1002.
99. 1231. 882. 738.
1199. 1071.

AN ENCIPHERED LETTER written by the French politician Mirabeau, April 12, 1787.

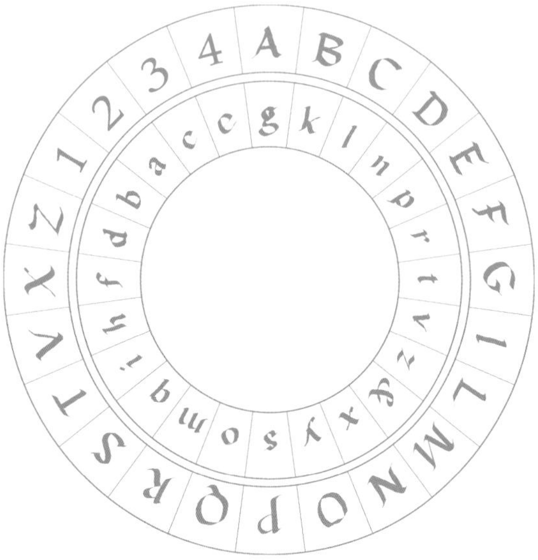
A B C D E F G I L M N O P Q R S T V X Z 1 2 3 4

ALBERTI'S CIPHER DISK. On this model dating back to 1466, two disks turning on the same axis form a manual machine for enciphering and deciphering.

of the Kabala, cryptographers try to convert letters into figures, words into numbers. The most complex propositions take on the form of streams that at first appear incomprehensible; they have to be deciphered by the receiver, generally without contact with the sender.

In *The Gallic Wars*, Julius Caesar describes how, when it was time to exchange messages carried by riders on horses, he used a simple code that replaced each letter by a character three spots further on in the alphabet. This method is called "substitution," which means that each element (a letter or a word) that composes the clear text—the content of the message—is substituted for another element in adherence to an unchanging rule. Such a code is fragile because of its unchanging, mechanical aspect. Unintelligible at first, the coded message nevertheless has the same structure as the "clear" text, and all anyone has to do is find the rule of substitution to move easily from one to the other. That's where the sworn enemy of the cryptographer steps in: the cryptanalyst.

It's simple to decipher a message when you know the code and have the patience to retranscribe, but still, the art of code-breaking demands intelligence and skill; a little intuition helps as well. Facing a thread of figures and letters whose meaning is opaque, the cryptanalyst is like a detective at the scene of the crime. He or she will search for clues to get on the right track, and the smallest detail can lead to validating a very fruitful hypothesis. Let's take the example of a message that an uninventive secret agent would have written using the old "Caesar's code." In a long message, the letter "h" would recur on more occasions than others, since it is three spots further on than "e," a letter used more often. A cryptanalyst worth his or her salt would spot this, uncover the rule of enciphering that was used, and thus have access to the unmasked message. For every language, intelligence services use tables that indicate the average frequency of every letter; this tool makes simple substitution a precarious business.

ENCRYPTION

To hide their schemes, cryptographers work in two main areas: transposition and encryption.

In the first case, communication is not conducted by the substitution of letters by other letters, or words by other words, but by their order or alignment. A classic transposition method uses receptables; in a bar, the alignment of bottles could provide information through the succession of different color liquids or the level in the bottles. The most poetic transposition is without a doubt the "talking music" mentioned in the *Contr'espion*, a work that came out during the Terror of the French Revolution in 1793: it transformed a text into sheet music. An analogous technique was taught to the budding young spies of Hitler's Germany.

The transposition methods are complex for the person doing the enciphering, and the risk of making an encryption mistake is high.

M. de Voltaire

a la haye ce premier aoust 1743

Monseigneur

Le Roy de Prusse fait negocier secretement un emprunt de 400 mille florins a Amsterdam

pour cent. Je conclus que son tresor n'est pas aussi considerable

veut emprunter a petit interest

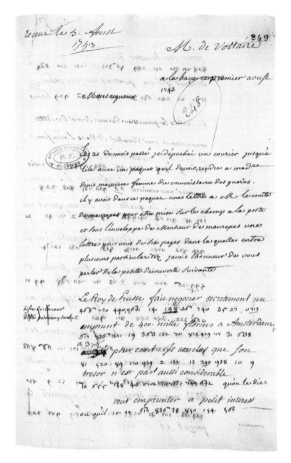

A LETTER FROM VOLTAIRE TO THE STATESMAN AMELOT DE CHAILLOU, AUGUST 1, 1743. A passage about the King of Prussia is enciphered and the plaintext added after the letter was received.

These methods are used only for short periods of time and for short messages. When they need to embark on longer conversations, and more substantial exchanges, cryptographers prefer to use substitution codes, which can be made more secure by different means of encryption. There are ways of increasing the difficulty by making the rules of encryption more complex. Instead of being one-dimensional, subtlety and boxes within boxes are employed, which operate on several levels. Vowels and consonants can be treated differently, the alphabet can be reordered in random fashion, or from back to front, shared key words can be manipulated at will ... Through precaution and mathematical refinement, highly hermetic systems can be constructed. There is the example of the "Grand Chiffre" (Great Cipher), Louis XIV's encryption system developed by the Rossignol brothers. This code from the 1700s wasn't broken until 1893 by a certain Captain Bazeries.

The more elaborate the encryption, the more the opposing cryptanalyst will have trouble finding the key that will open the message. To make matters more complex, armies and intelligence services often use several different codes at the same time—not to mention the fact that easy-to-break codes are always handy when you want to transmit erroneous information to the enemy ...

THE ENIGMA REVOLUTION

In the chess game of human conflict, the arrival of electricity was a major turning point. As long as calculations and tables had to be done by hand, the battle between cryptographer and cryptanalyst remained a strictly human endeavor. It was a battle of intelligence, but of time as well, since both designing a code and cracking it were extremely time-consuming.

Mathematicians proved long ago that possible numeric combinations are infinite, and skilled engineers, to help cryptanalysts or to facilitate encryption and decryption operations, have developed various mechanical apparatuses to aid in transcription.

Arthur Scherbius, a German inventor, revolutionized everything when he began to turn out the first Enigma prototypes. His coding machine was designed for commercial correspondence, since industrial espionage was rampant, and large manufacturing and financial enterprises wanted to protect themselves. But soon the German army was using the machine. In 1926, German coded communications became unreadable to other European countries such as France, England, and Poland.

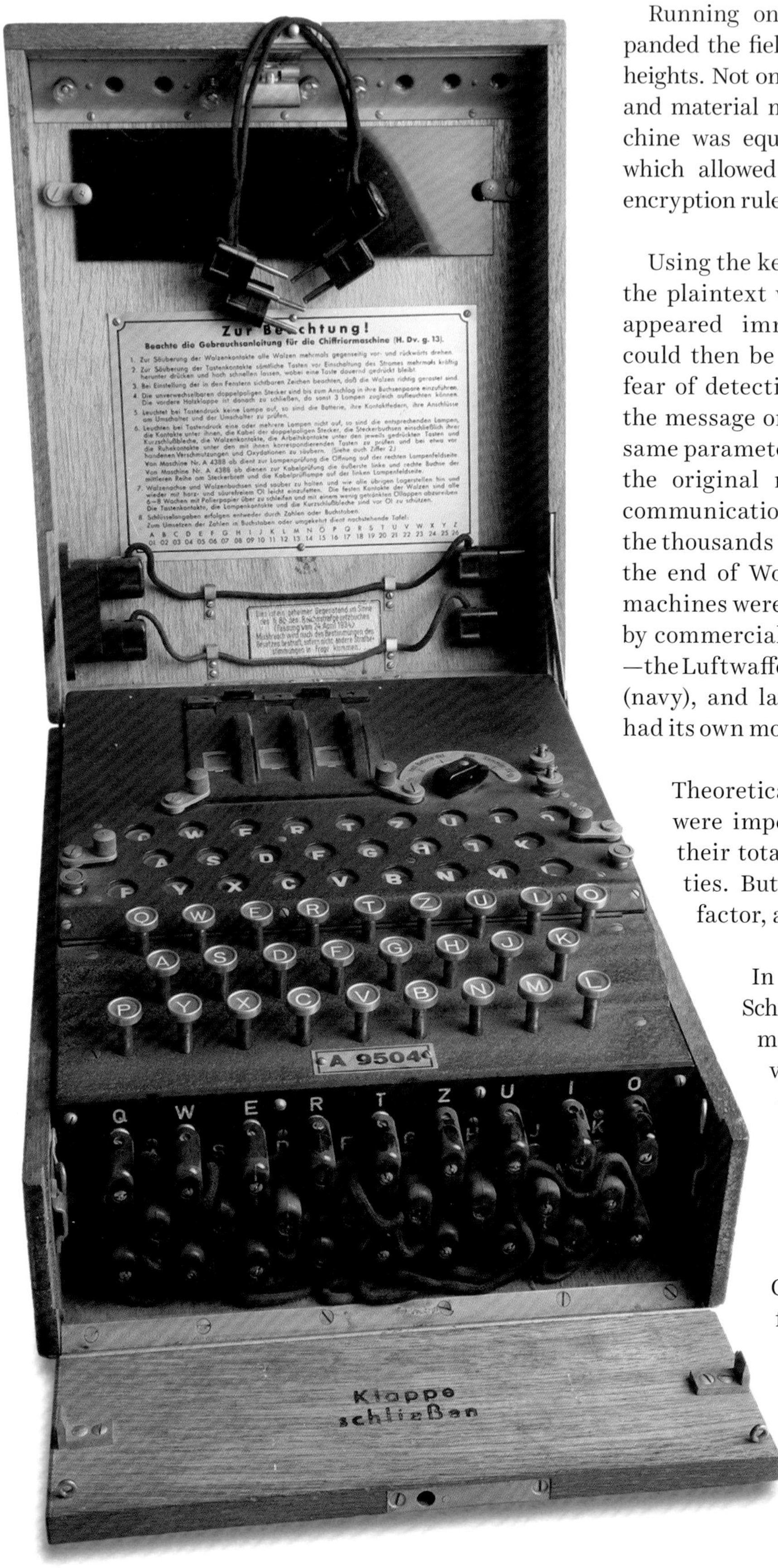
A 9504
Klappe
schließen

Running on electric power, Enigma expanded the field of encryption to unforeseen heights. Not only was it not subject to fatigue and material mistakes, this new coding machine was equipped with scrambler rotors, which allowed the operator to modify the encryption rule in the middle of the process.

Using the keyboard, the operator entered the plaintext whose encrypted translation appeared immediately. The cryptogram could then be sent to the receiver without fear of detection. The receiver would type the message on another Enigma set for the same parameters, which would reconstitute the original message. Ideal for military communications, Enigma was ordered by the thousands for the German army up until the end of World War II. Of course these machines were different from the ones used by commercial enterprises, and each army—the Luftwaffe (air force), the Kriegsmarine (navy), and later Rommel's Afrikakorps—had its own model with its own conventions.

Theoretically, the encoded messages were impenetrable. The Germans put their total trust in Enigma's capabilities. But there is always the human factor, and it was neglected.

In this case, General Rudolf Schmidt, who directed Germany's military communication services, committed a terrible error thanks to his generous sense of family values. He recruited his brother Hans-Thilo, who was going through a personal and financial crisis, to work at the Chiffrierstelle, the cipher office of Germany's Ministry of War, the very heart of encrypted communications.

THE ELECTROMECHANICAL ENCRYPTION MACHINE known as Enigma. This model, kept by the French secret services, works perfectly well today.

ENIGMA IN THE FIELD. A portable machine with a wooden case complete with handle, thousands of copies were produced to equip the German armies.

A VARIATION OF ENIGMA. Numerous models of the enciphering machine exist. This one features a supplementary reading console.

A soldier in the Great War, Hans-Thilo Schmidt was unable to remain in the army after the end of hostilities. He tried his hand at business, and the resulting bankruptcy of his company only increased his resentment. His brother Rudolf, a general and the head of a prestigious service, provoked bitter jealousy, especially since Hans-Thilo owed him his only means of livelihood, a small salary as an encryption clerk. The French were able to play on his wounded ego. In 1931, at the Grand Hôtel de Verviers in Belgium, amid an atmosphere of complete discretion, an exchange took place that turned out to be crucial for the outcome of World War II. For the price of 10,000 marks, Hans-Thilo Schmidt allowed photos to be taken of two German-language technical manuals that made Enigma's functioning understandable.

France, on the side of the victors in 1918, had neglected Germany at the time, and considered the USSR a greater danger. The Poles, France's ally, were exchanging secret information with the French, and so Poland soon obtained a copy of the documents sold by "Asche," a.k.a. Hans-Thilo Schmidt. For the Poles, who claimed a large part of the territory lost by Germany after the latter's defeat in 1918, it was essential that they break the German codes. Their cipher service spared no effort; Marian Rejewski had a replica of Enigma built. It was not sufficient to decode messages, but it did help the service understand the principle and the functioning behind Enigma's encryption processes, an indispensable first step. In 1939, the Poles, now threatened directly by Germany and soon to be invaded, passed on the results of their work to their French and British allies, and that information quickly arrived in Bletchley Park.

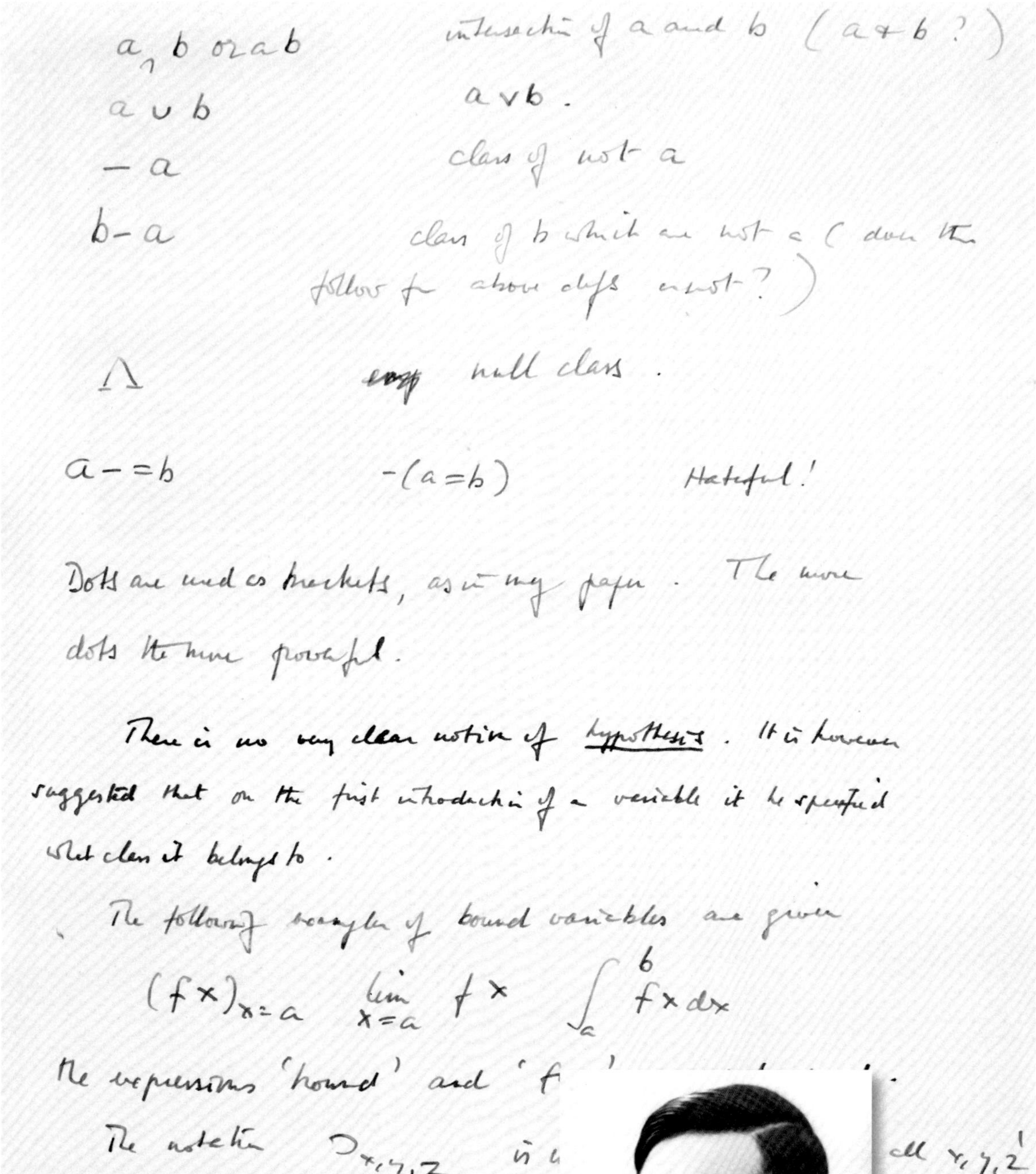

a, b or ab intersection of a and b $(a + b\,?)$

$a \cup b$ $a \vee b$.

$-a$ class of not a

$b - a$ class of b which are not a (does this follow from above defs or not?)

$\wedge$ null class.

$a -= b$ $-(a = b)$ Hateful!

Dots are used as brackets, as in my paper. The more dots the more powerful.

There is no very clear notion of *hypothesis*. It is however suggested that on the first introduction of a variable it be specified what class it belongs to.

The following examples of bound variables are given

$$(fx)_{x=a} \quad \lim_{x=a} fx \quad \int_a^b fx\,dx$$

The expressions 'bound' and 'f...'

The notation $\supset_{x,y,z}$ is ... all x, y, z

There seem to be no quantifiers. $\supset$, ... main implication.

A MANUSCRIPT PAGE from one of Alan Turing's notebooks. Dated 1942, this precious 56-page book was sold at auction in New York in April 2015.

ALAN TURING, the father of the computer, committed suicide at age 41 after being forced to undergo chemical castration for his homosexuality.

BRITISH ENGINEERS USING THE DEUCE COMPUTER in 1958, the first commercial computer built according to Alan Turing's design.

BLETCHLEY PARK. This manor in Buckinghamshire and the "huts" and "blocks" built on the grounds were home to teams of British cryptanalysts during World War II. Today it houses a computer museum.

The first computers owe nothing to the laws of the market or rational thought. They were military inventions, conceived in the greatest secrecy to defeat the Nazi madness, and they ushered humans into the digital era, which no system of thought had predicted or even desired. In a matter of a few decades, these machines from the shadowy world of espionage have taken over the world, transformed human work, and now compromise the very notion of private life. We should not be surprised that they are being used to control those who use them, and that the National Security Agency and its rivals have their eyes and ears everywhere. The new generation of secret agents must reacquaint themselves with archaic techniques to escape the giant sweep of intelligence gathering—that got its start in the struggle against totalitarianism ...

ALAN TURING reaching the finish line in 1946. The brilliant mathematician was also a top long-distance runner.

Eric Liberge has authored or co-authored over thirty graphic novels in his native France, including books on Versailles and World War II, as well as numerous books in the fantasy genre.

Arnaud Delalande is the author of nine novels as well as numerous graphic novels in France, including *Le Piège de Dante (Dante's Trap), translated into twenty languages.* His prizes include le Prix du Roman d'Evasion and le Prix Charles-Oulmont de la Fondation de France.

David Homel (translator) is a writer, journalist, filmmaker, and translator. His most recent novel is *The Fledgings* (Cormorant Books). He has translated many French-language books, and is a two-time Governor General's Literary Award winner. He lives in Montreal.